T0226196

Lecture Notes of the Institute for Computer Sciences, Social Informatics and Telecommunications Engineering 234

More information about this series at http://www.springer.com/series/8197

Lei Wang · Tie Qiu
Wenbing Zhao (Eds.)

Quality, Reliability, Security and Robustness in Heterogeneous Systems

13th International Conference, QShine 2017
Dalian, China, December 16–17, 2017
Proceedings

Editors
Lei Wang
School of Software
Dalian University of Technology
Dalian
China

Tie Qiu
School of Computer Science
and Technology
Tianjin University
Tianjin
China

Wenbing Zhao
Department of Electrical Engineering
and Computer Science
Cleveland State University
Cleveland, OH
USA

ISSN 1867-8211   ISSN 1867-822X (electronic)
Lecture Notes of the Institute for Computer Sciences, Social Informatics
and Telecommunications Engineering
ISBN 978-3-319-78077-1   ISBN 978-3-319-78078-8   (eBook)
https://doi.org/10.1007/978-3-319-78078-8

Library of Congress Control Number: 2018937376

Printed on acid-free paper

This Springer imprint is published by the registered company Springer International Publishing AG
part of Springer Nature
The registered company address is: Gewerbestrasse 11, 6330 Cham, Switzerland

Preface

We are delighted to introduce the proceedings of the 2017 European Alliance for Innovation (EAI) International Conference on Heterogeneous Networking for Quality, Reliability, Security and Robustness (Qshine). This conference brought together researchers and practitioners around the world who are working on heterogeneous networks.

The technical program of Qshine 2017 consisted of 25 papers in oral presentation sessions during the main conference tracks. The conference tracks were: Session 1 and 4, Mobile and Wireless Networks; Session 2 and 5, Quality and Reliability; Session 3, Wireless Networking Algorithms and Protocols; Session 6, Smart Applications. Aside from the high-quality technical paper presentations, the technical program also featured two keynote speeches. The two keynote speakers were Prof. Yan Zhang from the University of Oslo, Norway, and Prof. Song Guo from the Department of Computing, the Hong Kong Polytechnic University, SAR China.

Coordination with the steering chairs, Zhongxuan Luo, Lei Wang, Tie Qiu, Baochao Chen, Chen Ling, Jialin Liu, and Jian Fang, was essential for the success of the conference. We sincerely appreciate their constant support and guidance. It was also a great pleasure to work with such an excellent Organizing Committee and we thank them for their hard work in organizing and supporting the conference. In particular, we thank the Technical Program Committee, led by Prof. Lei Wang, Wenbing Zhao, and Tie Qiu, who completed the peer-review process of technical papers and compiled a high-quality technical program. We are also grateful to all the conference managers, chairs, and all the authors who submitted their papers to Qshine 2017.

We believe that Qshine provides a good platform for all researchers to discuss the latest developments in science and technology. We expect that future Qshine conferences will also be as successful and stimulating, as indicated by the contributions presented in this volume.

February 2018

Lei Wang
Tie Qiu
Wenbing Zhao

Conference Organization

Steering Committee

Imrich Chlamtac	Create-Net, Italy/EAI
Sherman Xuemin Shen	Electrical and Computer Engineering, University of Waterloo, Canada
Xi Zhang	Electrical and Computer Engineering, Texas A&M University, USA
Der-Jiunn Deng	National Changhua University of Education, Taiwan
Jong-Hyouk Lee	Sangmyung University, South Korea

Organizing Committee

General Chair

Zhongxuan Luo	Dalian University of Technology, China

Technical Program Committee Chairs

Lei Wang	Dalian University of Technology, China
Wenbing Zhao	Cleveland State University, USA
Tie Qiu	Tianjin University, China

Web Chair

Chen Chen	Xidian University, China

Publicity and Social Media Chairs

Chen Ling	Dalian University of Technology, China
Songtao Lu	Iowa State University, USA
Qianzhen Sun	Dalian University of Technology, China

Workshops Chairs

Panlong Yang	University of Science and Technology of China, China
Zhangbing Zhou	China University of Geosciences, China

Publications Chairs

Guangjie Han	Hohai University, China
Bin Wu	Tianjing University, China
Zhaolong Ning	Dalian University of Technology, China

Panels Chairs

Yang Peng   University of Washington, USA
Chunsheng Zhu   University of British Columbia, Canada

Local Chairs

Naigao Jin   Dalian University of Technology, China
Zhenquan Qin   Dalian University of Technology, China

Sponsorship and Exhibits Chair

Mithun Mukherjee   Guangdong Provincial Key Lab of Petrochemical
                              Equipment Fault Diagnosis, GUPT, China

Conference Manager

Lenka Bilska   EAI

Technical Program Committee

Lei Wang   Dalian University of Technology, China
Wenbing Zhao   Cleveland State University, USA
Tie Qiu   Tianjin University, China
Chen Chen   Xidian University, China
Chen Ling   Dalian University of Technology, China
Songtao Lu   Iowa State University, USA
Qianzhen Sun   Dalian University of Technology, China
Panlong Yang   University of Science and Technology of China
Zhangbing Zhou   China University of Geosciences, China
Guangjie Han   Hohai University, China
Zhaolong Ning   Dalian University of Technology, China
Chunsheng Zhu   University of British Columbia, Canada
Naigao Jin   Dalian University of Technology, China
Zhenquan Qin   Dalian University of Technology, China
Ming Zhu   Dalian University of Technology, China
Liang Sun   Dalian University of Technology, China
Jian Fang   Dalian University of Technology, China
Jialin Liu   Dalian University of Technology, China
Wei Chen   China University of Mining and Technology, China
Lei Shu   Guangdong University of Petrochemical Technology
Bin Wu   Tianjin University, China

Contents

Wireless Networking Algorithms and Protocols

Smart Applications

Mobile and Wireless Networks

Coordinate-Free Boundary Nodes Identification by Angle Comparison in Wireless Sensor Networks

Linna Wei$^{(\boxtimes)}$, Xiaoxiao Song, and Xiao Zheng

School of Computer Science and Technology, Anhui University of Technology,
Maanshan 243032, Anhui, China
linnawahut@gmail.com, xxiaosong_ahut@sina.com, Xzheng@ahut.edu.cn

Abstract. Identifying the boundary nodes of a wireless sensor network (WSN) is one of the prerequisites for healing coverage holes, which belongs to the main problems of QoS in a network. Most of the existing solutions for this problem rely on the usage of coordinates or a relatively even distribution of sensors on the underlying network. However, as equipping localization devices on sensors usually means considerably higher cost, coordinates are often unavailable in low-budget networks. And it is often hard to guarantee the distribution of nodes. Therefore, identifying the boundary nodes without coordinates still faces difficulties. In this paper, we propose a distributed algorithm to solve this problem. In our method, a checking node first finds out all the potential triangles that with vertices from the 1-hop neighbors of the node. Then, the sensor keeps triangles containing it by calculating angles. At last, triangles with gap edges are identified by angle comparison to avoid wrong identification of a boundary node which has a U shaped ring locates beside. Illustrated simulation results show the performance effectiveness of our method, especially in networks with random and uneven sensor deployment.

Keywords: Boundary node identification · Coordinate-free method
Angle comparison · Coverage problem · Wireless sensor networks

1 Introduction

The nodes in a WSN are responsible for sensing the events appear in the Region of Interest (ROI), collecting data, and transmitting them to background for data analyzing. Therefore, a WSN should have a sufficient number of nodes[1] to fully cover the entire ROI. Otherwise, events appear in places where sensors are missing would be omitted and further affects the results of data analysis.

The work is supported by the National Natural Science Foundation of China under Grant No. 61502010 and No. 61402009 and Natural Science Foundation of Anhui Province under Grant No. 1608085QF146.

[1] We interchangeably use the words 'node' and 'sensor' in this paper.

© ICST Institute for Computer Sciences, Social Informatics and Telecommunications Engineering 2018
L. Wang et al. (Eds.): QShine 2017, LNICST 234, pp. 3–12, 2018.
https://doi.org/10.1007/978-3-319-78078-8_1

Sometimes, this situation may lead to fatal consequences. Such as a missing detection of moving troops on a battlefield or a neglect of the leakage of toxic gases [1].

Accordingly, it is essential that a WSN fully cover the ROI in the entire lifetime. However, nodes in it are often vulnerable. They are easily to be moved away from original positions by animals, destroyed by harsh environments, shut down by limited energy supply, or simply been settled outside of the ROI due to random deployment. If there are no extra sensors to replace the failed (or disappeared) ones, blank areas would arise and weaken the QoS of the network. Researchers usually refer those areas as 'coverage holes'. In order to fully cover the ROI (again), one often need to use redundant nodes to 'heal' the coverage holes, which means that moving additional sensors to cover the blank area in the ROI [2]. In order to perform this work, the network needs to know where the holes are. One method of finding them is to first identify the boundary nodes and then distinguish the border of the holes and the frontier of the network, without help from coordinates. In this paper, we propose a distributed algorithm using techniques of point in triangle test and angle comparison to solve the problem in networks where sensors are randomly deployed and coexist a number of small scattered coverage holes.

2   Related Work

The method of boundary node detection can be categorized into three main ways. The first one are the geometrical approaches. In these algorithms, all the nodes know their coordinates [3]. Thus, Voronoi Diagrams or Delaunay Triangles or anchor nodes can be used to help locating the boundary sensors [4]. Although, the calculations are easy, the mechanism requires extra cost for the usage of localization equipments. The second methods are statistical ones. They often assume that the distribution of nodes in networks follow certain statistical functions and have threshold values. The calculations in them are straightforward but they rely on the uniform distribution of nodes in networks and often require high density [5]. The topological methods are the third kind of solutions. They do not need coordinates of sensors and often only need connectivity information between nodes [6,7]. Due to limited information, most of them do not perform well in sparse networks, especially when executed distributively.

Beghdad et al. [8] suggested a distributed algorithm BDCIS that using 1-hop neighbors of a sensor. It requires less communication than most of the existing works and avoids false detection of boundary nodes with the existence of some U-shaped rings in the network. However, the critical cardinal value used in it may not fit for randomly deployed sensor networks with small holes. Dhanapala et al. [9] presented a distributed algorithm (we refer to it as VCSTPM) that uses geometric relationship for boundary detection. It uses hop distances from nodes to anchors to build a virtual coordinate system. Based on the system, the algorithm finds out triangles and performs Point in Triangle (PIT) test by calculating areas of them. But, when a U-shaped ring locates beside a checking sensor, this algorithm may misidentify a boundary node as an inner sensor.

3   The Neighborhood of a Sensor

We assume that each sensor node has an unique ID and they cannot move after deployment. Through communication, each sensor v obtains its one-hop-neighbor set N_v^1. A sensor v can obtain the value of an angle formed by it with other two nodes in N_v^1. And two connected sensors u and v can obtain the distance between them by evaluating the RSSI value, assuming there are no obstacles stand on the plain network. The communication radius of a sensor is no greater than twice the length of its sensing radius. We first define the terms of 'inner sensors' and 'boundary nodes' used in this paper. From the definition of inner nodes, we know that if a node v is an inner nodes it should be surrounded by a 'ring' formed by a number of other sensors.

Definition 1 (Inner Sensors). *Given a node v and the circumference c_v of its sensing area A_v, if c_v is fully covered by other sensors in the same network, v is an inner sensor.*

Definition 2 (Boundary Nodes). *Given a sensor v in a network, if v is not an inner sensor, v is a boundary node.*

3.1   Rings in the Neighborhood

Definition 3 (k-Hop Neighbor). *If node u is connected with node v and u is k-hop away from v, then u is a k-hop neighbor of v. The set N_v^k contains all the k-hop neighbors of v.*

Proposition 1. *Given a node v, if v is an inner node, it is surrounded by a ring R_v formed by the nodes in N_v^1.*

Proof. Assuming there is a ring R_v' surrounds a node v, one node $u' \in N_v^2$ is in R_v'. We remove u' from R_v', the remainder of it becomes a gap ring R_v^g. Two end points u_1 and u_2 of R_v^g together with node v and sensor u' construct a quadrilateral $Q_{u'}$. There is a gap between node v and sensor u', which means a coverage hole in the ROI of $Q_{u'}$. If else, node v and sensor u' should be directly connected and $u' \in N_v^1$. When the quadrilateral $Q_{u'}$ contains a hole, a part of circumference c_v is not covered by any sensor. This violates the definition of inner nodes. The same result also applies in a ring R_v'' which contains any node $u'' \in N_v^k, k > 2$.   □

From the above proposition, we know that one method to distinguish the inner nodes from the boundary sensors is to find out if there is a ring in N_v^1. However, there are some difficulties. The first one is we cannot affirm the number of nodes on the ring around sensor v (length of the ring). The second comes from the fact that it is hard to confirm if the ring we found out is surround sensor v (position of the ring), without coordinates. Trying to solve the first problem, we may examine that if all the nodes in N_v^1 can build a ring by finding out a Hamiltonian circle in a graph HNG_v^1. The graph is constructed by all the nodes in N_v^1 and the connections between sensors. However, searching for a Hamiltonian circle in a graph is an NP problem, it is not promising to provide a solution under limited resources when $|N_v^1|$ is large in a dense network. Therefore, we put our focus on the second problem. If we first discover a ring R and then check out if R is surrounds v or locates beside v, it is difficult. But, if we only focus on searching a ring R surrounds v, it is relatively much easier.

3.2   Triangles in the Neighborhood

Theorem 1. *Given a node v, if v is an inner node, there is a triangle T_v formed by the nodes on ring R_v surrounds v.*

Proof. From Proposition 1, we obtain a ring R_v surrounds v. There are at least three nodes on R_v, otherwise no ring can be formed. We randomly pick out three sensors u_1, u_2, and u_3 on R_v to construct a triangle T_{test}. We enumerate all the potential triangles by finding out all combinations of the vertices on R_v. For each test triangle, we do Point in Triangle (PIT) test to check if it contains v. If none of them fits, the area of R_v does not cover v, R_v locates beside v.   □

Corollary 1. *Given a node v and a set $S_v = N_v^1 - \bigcup R_v$, if v is an inner node, either the elements in S_v forms no triangle or none of the triangles contains v.*

Proof. Assuming there exists a triangle T' built by nodes in S_v contains v, nodes on the three vertices of T' form a ring R_v^*. As $R_v^* \subseteq \bigcup R_v$, any sensor u' on the vertex of T' is not in S_v.   □

From the above we know, if we obtain a triangle T_{test} built by nodes on N_v^1 that contains v, we may identify v as an inner node. The uncertainty comes from the possibility that there may exist an 'U' shaped ring locates beside the checking node. Two ends of the U-ring with another points on it may form a triangle that containing v.

3.3   Difference Between Triangles

Definition 4 (Gap Edge). *Given a U-shape ring R_v^U constructed by the nodes in N_v^1 of sensor v, the connection between two ends $p_{R_v^U}$ and $q_{R_v^U}$ of R_v^U provides an edge e_{pq} that filling the gap of the U-ring. Such edge e_{pq} is a gap edge.*

A triangle T_{test} built with a gap edge e_g may mislead an algorithm that identifying inner nodes by searching triangles containing a checking sensor. Thus, we need to remove these triangles (Fig. 1).

Lemma 1. *Given a boundary sensor v, a triangle T_v containing v is formed by the nodes on a U-ring R_v locates beside the node. Gap edge E_v on T_v divides area around v into two parts A_v^1 and A_v^2. Nodes u_1, u_2, and u_3 are the three vertices on T_v. Among them, u_1 and u_2 are the end points of E_v. The shortest path between u_1 and u_2 is on the same side of the area that containing T_v.*

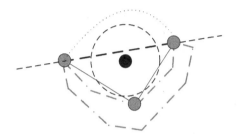

Fig. 1. An 'U' shaped ring locates beside the checking node (colored black). Three nodes on the U-ring (colored gray) build a triangle that containing the checking sensor. There is also a gap edge (black dotted line) built by two end nodes on the U-ring. The edge divides area around the checking sensor into two parts. There should be no shortest path between the end points of the gap edge on the opposite side of the U-ring.

Proof. We assume area A_v^1 contains T_v. If the shortest path $P_{u_2}^{u_1}$ between u_1 and u_2 is in area A_v^2, there exists at least one node p_v on the path. Then, the two edges other than E_v on T_v form a ring R_v', together with the path $P_{u_2}^{u_1}$. The area of R_v' includes the area of T_v. Since T_v contains v, the ring R_v' contains v. Node v is an inner sensor. $\qquad\square$

Theorem 2. *Given a boundary sensor v, a triangle T_v containing v is formed by the nodes on a U-ring R_v located beside the node. Edge e_v on T_v is the gap edge. Nodes u_1, u_2, and u_3 are the three vertices on T_v. And the former two nodes are end points of e_v. Angle $\angle u_2 u_1 u_3$ is a side angle of T_v. Randomly pick a node u_r on the shortest path $P_{u_2}^{u_1}$ between u_1 and u_2. The value of angle $\angle u_r u_1 u_3$ is no greater than the value of $\angle u_2 u_1 u_3$.*

Proof. The two end points on E_v divide the U-ring R_v into two parts R_v^1 and R_v^2. Since R_v is U-ring, the length of R_v^1 and R_v^2 is hardly to be equal. We assume R_v^1 is the longer one. If u_3 is on R_v^1 and $P_{u_2}^{u_1}$ is on R_v^2, it is easy to verify the result. The same situation holds when u_3 is on R_v^2 and $P_{u_2}^{u_1}$ is on R_v^2. $\qquad\square$

According to the above analysis, we propose our distributed coordinate-free boundary nodes identification algorithm based on point in triangle test and angle comparison.

4   Boundary Nodes Identification

Our distributed algorithm contains three parts. It first finds out all the potential triangles constructed by the 1-hop neighbors of a checking sensor. Then, it executes PIT for each triangle to test if it contains the node. At last, the triangles containing gap edges are removed by angle comparison.

In the algorithm, each sensor is initially set as an inner node. A node v collects the 1-hop neighbors of it by communication with directly connected neighbors. In this process, if $|N_v^1| < 3$, no ring can be built by nodes in the 1-hop neighborhood of v, thus v can be directly set as a boundary node. After the execution of this algorithm, each node v obtains a list of triangles, the vertices on them are the nodes in N_v^1.

4.1 Point in Triangles Test

Next, we do PIT test for each item in L_T to examine if it contains the checking sensor.

Algorithm 1. Point in triangle test by angles
_____

1: Input: node v, triangle T, angle $\phi = 0$.
2: Output: true or false.
3: Initially, output = false;
4: **for** each edge e in T: **do**
5:     Get the two end points p and q on e.
6:     Obtain value of the angle $\angle pvq$.
7:     $\phi = \phi + \angle pvq$.
8: **end for**
9: **if** $\phi = 2\pi$ **then**
10:     output = true.
11: **end if**

Since sensor v can obtain the value of an angle formed by it with other two nodes in N_v^1 and a triangle T in L_T is built by the nodes in N_v^1, for any two nodes p and q on T, we can obtain value of angle $\angle pvq$. We add up the value of the angles in T. If T contains v, the result should be 2π. Otherwise, T does not contain v. This is ensured by axiomatic geometry.

Each triangle T that contains node v is added into a list L_T^c. Then, we remove the items in L_T^c that containing gap edges (Fig. 2).

4.2 Remove the Triangle that with a Gap Edge

In the last step, we remove all the invalid triangles in L_T^c. We use a Test of Triangle Validity (TTV) algorithm to check the validity of each triangle in L_T^c. After running TTV, if $|L_T^c| > 0$, which means there exists at least one valid triangle, the checking sensor is an inner node. Otherwise, it is a boundary node.

Definition 5 (Valid Edge). *Given an edge e, if e is not a gap edge, e is a valid edge.*

Definition 6 (Valid Triangle). *Given a triangle T, if all the edges in T are valid edges, T is a valid triangle.*

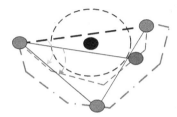 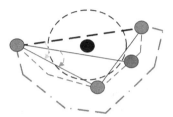

(a) The third vertex on the triangle containing the gap edge is on the longer segment of the divided U-ring.

(b) The third vertex on the triangle containing the gap edge is on the shorter segment of the divided U-ring.

Fig. 2. Angle comparison in triangles with gap edge. The blue dot is the sensor selected randomly on the shortest path between two nodes on the end of a gap edge. (Color figure online)

Algorithm 2. Test of triangle validity

1: Input: node v, triangle T.
2: Output: valid or invalid.
3: Initially, the validity V_T of T is $V_T = valid$.
4: **for** each edge e in T: **do**
5:   Set the initial validity V_e of e, $V_e = valid$.
6:   Get the two end points p and q on e.
7:   Get the third vertex w on T.
8:   Calculate value of the angle $\angle qpw$ by the Cosine Theorem.
9:   Find the shortest path P_q^p between node p and q within the set N_v^1.
10:   Pick a random node u on path P_q^p.
11:   Calculate value of the angle $\angle upw$ by the Cosine Theorem.
12:   **if** $\angle upw \leq \angle qpw$ **then**
13:     $V_e = invalid$.
14:   **end if**
15:   $V_T = V_T \wedge V_e$.
16: **end for**

In step 8 and 9 of TTV, we use the Cosine Theorem to calculate the value of an angle and this requires values of distance between two nodes. Given node p and q, if they are directly connected, by evaluating the RSSI value between them, d_{p-q} can be obtained. If node p and q are not directly connected, we can calculate d_{p-q}, as $p \in N_v^1$ and $q \in N_v^1$. We first obtain the distance d_{p-v} between node p and v. Then, we get the distance d_{q-v} between node q and v. At last, with the help of angle $\angle pvq$, we calculate the distance d_{p-q}.

4.3   Discussion

Performance Evaluation. Each sensor v in our distributed algorithm sends out and receives $O(n)$ messages, $n = |N_v^1|$. The computational complexity of it for each sensor v contains three parts. The first one comes from enumerating triangles in N_v^1, it is $O(n^3), n = |N_v^1|$. The second part is PIT, it contributes $O(n), n = |L_T|$. The main contribution of computational complexity in TTV comes from the search of a shortest path between two nodes. Depends on the breadth first algorithm used on the graph HNG_v^1 constructed by all the nodes in N_v^1 and the connections between sensors, the complexity of TTV can be up to $O(mn^2), m = |L_T^c|$, n is the number of vertices in HNG_v^1.

Algorithm Improvement. We do not need to visit all the triangles in L_T^c. If L_T^c contains at least one valid triangle, the checking sensor is an inner node. Thus, the algorithm only needs to visit the triangles in L_T^c one after another, if it meets a valid triangle, it stops.

Due to the lack of coordinates, it is hard to locate triangles containing the gap edges precisely by TTV, especially in a network with random sensor deployment. And interferences may be brought in TTV by the accuracy problem in floating point calculation. In order to refine the result, if a sensor is set as an inner node after running TTV and it has at least two 1-hop neighbors as boundary nodes, it checks the number of connected components of a graph built by its boundary neighbors. If the graph has more than one connected components, then the checking sensor should be a boundary node.

5   Simulations

We first build a 5 * 10 small ROI and randomly deploy 48 nodes in it. The network fully covers the ROI. Figure 3(a) shows that due to random position of sensors our algorithm without refinement has a little difficulty on fully distinguish the boundary nodes. After refinement, the defects can be compensated.

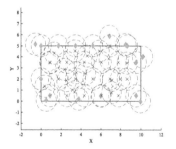
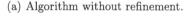

(a) Algorithm without refinement.

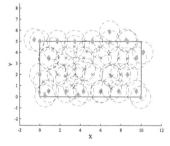

(b) Algorithm with refinement.

Fig. 3. Boundary nodes identification on a small random network. Red diamonds show the boundary nodes.

In order to further test the performance of our algorithm, we build a 40 * 30 ROI containing 848 randomly deployed nodes. Among these sensors, 524 of them

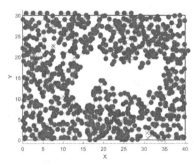

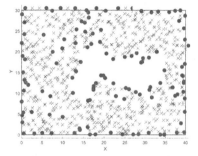

(a) BDCIS performance. Boundary nodes are overly picked out.

(b) VCSTPM performance. Inner nodes are overly identified.

Fig. 4. Boundary nodes identification on a random network. (Color figure online)

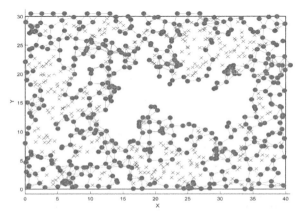

Fig. 5. Our algorithm performance. Most of the boundary nodes and inner ones are correctly distinguished. (Color figure online)

are boundary nodes. In this network, there is an irregular shaped coverage hole at the center, together with several small holes randomly scattered in it. In the simulation results, the red dots are the boundary nodes and the light blue crosses are the inner ones. Our algorithm correctly identified 450 boundary sensors and 304 inner nodes (Fig. 5). The correctness rate is 85.8% for the boundary nodes and 93.8% for the inner ones. The boundaries of most of the small holes are also correctly depicted. However, we see from Fig. 4 that BDCIS overly picked out too many boundary nodes (Fig. 4(a)) and VCSTPM overly identified too many inner sensors (Fig. 4(b)). Though both of them show their efficiency in distinguishing the boundary of the center hole and the frontier of the entire network, they can hardly recognize the random small holes. Due to lack of space, other simulation results are omitted in this part.

6 Conclusions

In this paper we studied the problem of identifying boundary nodes without coordinates in a distributed fashion. We analyzed the feature of an inner sensor and proved that each inner node has a triangle containing it. We extracted the difference between triangles containing inner nodes and the ones containing boundary nodes next to U-rings. According to these analyses, we presented a three-step algorithm to identifying the boundary sensors. The effectiveness of it has been verified by simulation results. Our future work will be focus on improving this algorithm, reducing the usage of angles, and studying problems in three dimensional environments.

References

1. Shu, L., Mukherjee, M., Wu, X.: Toxic gas boundary area detection in large-scale petrochemical plants with industrial wireless sensor networks. IEEE Commun. Mag. **54**, 22–28 (2016)
2. Senouci, M., Mellouk, A., Assnoune, K.: Localized movement-assisted sensor deployment algorithm for hole detection and healing. IEEE Trans. Parallel Distrib. Syst. **25**, 1267–1277 (2014). ISSN: 1045-9219
3. Fang, F., Gao, J., Guibas, L.: Locating and bypassing holes in sensor networks. Mobile Netw. Appl. **11**, 187–200 (2006)
4. Li, W., Zhang, W., Sneddon, I.N.: Coverage hole and boundary nodes detection in wireless sensor networks. J. Netw. Comput. Appl. **48**, 35–43 (2015)
5. Fekete, S.P., Kaufmann, M., Krooller, A., Lehmann, K.: A new approach for boundary recognition in geometric sensor networks. In: Proceedings of the 17th Canadian Conference on Computational Geometry, pp. 82–85 (2005)
6. Kroller, A., Fekete, S.P., Pfistere, D., Fischer, S.: Deterministic boundary recognition and topology extraction. In: Proceedings of the Seventeenth Annual ACM-SIAM Symposium on Discrete Algorithm, SODA 2006, Miami, pp. 1000–1009 (2006)
7. Wang, Y., Gao, J., Mitchell, J.: Boundary recognition in sensor networks by topological methods. In: Proceedings of the 12th Annual International Conference on Mobile Computing and Networking, MobiCom 2006, Los Angeles, pp. 122–133 (2006)
8. Beghdad, R., Lamraoui, A.: Boundary and holes recognition in wireless sensor Networks. J. Innov. Digit. Ecosyst. **3**(1), 1–14 (2016)
9. Dhanapala, D., Jayasumana, A., Mehta, S.: On boundary detection of 2D and 3D wireless sensor networks. In: 2011 IEEE Global Telecommunications Conference - GLOBECOM 2011, Houston, pp. 1–5 (2011)

Community Preserving Sign Prediction
for Weak Ties of Complex Networks

Kangya He[1] , Donghai Guan[1,2], and Weiwei Yuan[1,2(✉)]

[1] College of Computer Science and Technology,
Nanjing University of Aeronautics and Astronautics, Nanjing, China
kangyahe@gmail.com, {dhguan,yuanweiwei}@nuaa.edu.cn
[2] Collaborative Innovation Center of Novel Software Technology and Industrialization,
Nanjing, China

Abstract. The weak ties are crucial bridges between the tightly coupled node groups in complex networks. Despite of their importance, no existing work has focused on the sign prediction of weak ties. A community preserving sign prediction model is therefore proposed to predict the sign of the weak ties. Nodes are firstly divided into different communities. The weak ties are then detected via the connections of the divided communities. SVM classifier is finally trained and used to predict the sign of weak ties. Experiments held on the real world dataset verify the high prediction performances of our proposed method for weak ties of complex networks.

Keywords: Sign prediction · Weak tie · Link prediction · Signed network

1 Introduction

One basic topology of the complex network is its small-worldness [1], i.e., nodes of the complex network could connect to each other within limited number hops of propagations. However, nodes usually have closed relationship with very limited number of other nodes. Nodes of the complex network cannot be widely connected to most nodes without the existence of weak ties. Weak ties are the links which connect different groups of users who have strong relationships. And the links connect nodes inside the groups in which users have strong relationships are called strong ties. The weak tie is not merely a trivial acquaintance tie between nodes, but rather a crucial bridge between the two densely knitted clumps of close friends [2].

Despite of the importance of weak ties, to the best of our knowledge, no existing work has focused on the sign prediction problem of weak ties in complex networks. Existing works of sign prediction predicts the signs of link in the complex network. A positive sign means the source node of the link trusts or likes the target node of the link. A negative sign means the source node of the link distrusts or dislikes the target node of the link. A common sign prediction method is to extract a set of attributes related to the links, train a classifier to learn the attributes and the related signs, and then predict the sign of the target link with given attributes according to the trained sign classifier. However, the target link of the sign prediction does not differentiate the weak ties and

© ICST Institute for Computer Sciences, Social Informatics and Telecommunications Engineering 2018
L. Wang et al. (Eds.): QShine 2017, LNICST 234, pp. 13–22, 2018.
https://doi.org/10.1007/978-3-319-78078-8_2

the strong ties. Since the weak tie is curial for the connection of complex networks, this work focuses on the sign prediction of weak ties.

To predict the sign of the weak ties in complex networks, a community preserving sign prediction model is proposed in this work. Nodes are firstly divided into different communities. This is achieved by learning the weight of nodes, the belonging degree of nodes and the modularity of the complex network. The weak ties are then detected via the connections of the divided communities. To predict the sign of the detected weak ties, five attributes are extracted for each weak tie, including the Jaccard similarity, the negative outdegree ratio of the source node, the negative indegree ratio of the target node, the positive link ratio between communities, and the negative link ratio between communities. SVM classifier is finally trained and used to predict the sign of weak ties based on the extracted attributes. Experiments held on real world application dataset show that the proposed method has high sign prediction accuracy and high negative sign prediction F1-score for weak ties of complex networks.

The following of this paper is organized as follows: Sect. 2 introduces the related works, Sect. 3 gives the proposed method, Sect. 4 presents the experimental results and Sect. 5 concludes this paper and points out the future directions.

2 Related Works

The related works of sign prediction can mainly be divided into two categories. One uses the triad information of nodes in signed networks [3]. The other calculates the similarities between node and trains machine learning algorithms to predict the signs. The latter category of related works is more related to this work. Some of the most popular node similiarity measurements are summarized as follows:

A. CN

CN [4] measures the similarity of users by the number of their common neighbors. The more common neighbors two nodes have, the more similar they are. Suppose node v_i and node v_j are two nodes of graph G, the CN similarity of v_i and v_j is:

$$S^{CN} = \left| N_1^G(v_i) \cap N_1^G(v_j) \right| \tag{1}$$

where $N_1^G(v_i)$ is the neighbors of v_i in G, $N_1^G(v_j)$ is the neighbors of v_j in G, and $|\bullet|$ means the number of $\bullet$.

B. RA

RA [5] is based on the idea of resource allocation. As mentioned in [6], the resource of each node is regarded as a unit; each node allocates its resource evenly to its neighbors, and the resource between each pair of nodes are transferred via their common neighbors. The similarity of two nodes are defined as the resource one node can get from the other node.

For node v_i and node v_j of graph G, their RA similarity is calculated as:

$$S^{RA} = \sum_{z \in N_1^G(v_i) \cap N_1^G(v_j)} \frac{1}{d(z)} \tag{2}$$

where $N_1^G(v_i)$ and $N_1^G(v_j)$ are the neighbors of v_i and v_j in G respectively, $d(z)$ is degree of the selected common neighbor.

The difference of CN and RA is that: CA does not differentiate the common neighbors, i.e., each common neighbor is supposed to have the same contribution to the similarity calculation; while RA differentiates common neighbors by their degrees. i.e., the higher degree a common neighbor has, the less important of this selected common neighbor is. This is because the higher degree a common neighbor has, the less resource it can allocate to the target node. RA sets the importance of the common neighbor linearly relate to the reciprocal of the common neighbor's degree.

C. AA

AA [7] is similar as RA: they both differentiates common neighbors by their degrees. The difference is that AA uses the logarithm of degrees to differentiate the contribution of common neighbors to user similarity, while RA directly uses the degrees to differentiate the contribution of common neighbors to user similarity. In some networks, the degrees of nodes tend to be very high, if the user similarity calculation uses the reciprocal of degrees directly, some similarity tends to be very small. AA therefore improves RA by enlarging the value of similarity. For node v_i and node v_j of G, their AA similarity is calculated as:

$$S^{AA} = \sum_{z \in N_1^G(v_i) \cap N_1^G(v_j)} \frac{1}{\log(d(z))} \tag{3}$$

3 The Proposed Sign Prediction Method for Weak Ties

The architecture of the proposed method is given in Fig. 1. The input is the graph representation of the complex network, and the outputs are the predicted signs for the weak ties. It consists of three modules. The details of these modules are given in the following subsections.

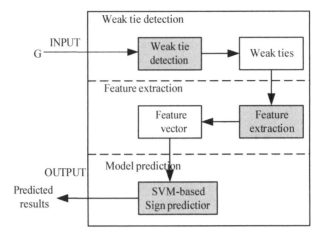

Fig. 1. The architecture of the proposed method

3.1   Weak Tie Detection

The weak tie detection module is based on the community detection method proposed by [8]. The algorithm is mainly based on the following attributes: A. The weight of nodes. It is described by the degree of the node in this work:

$$w(v) = \sum_{u \in \Gamma_{in}(v)} d_{in}(u) \tag{4}$$

where $\Gamma_{in(v)}$ is the set of nodes which have indegree in the network, and is the indegree of the node. B. The belonging degree of nodes. It represents the relationship between nodes and communities. If a node has high belonging degree with a community, this node will be categorized into this community:

$$B(i, C) = \frac{\sum\limits_{j \in C} \left(w_{ij} + w_{ji}\right)}{\sum\limits_{j \notin C} \left(w_{ij} + w_{ji}\right)} \tag{5}$$

where w_{ij} is the weight represents the connection from node i to node j: $w_{ij} = 1$ if there exists a directed edge from to, otherwise, $w_{ij} = 0$.

C. The modularity of the network. It is also known as the Q value. The bigger it is, the better performance of the community clustering:

$$Q = \frac{1}{m} \sum_{1 \leq i,j \leq n} \left[a_{ij} - \frac{k_i^{in} k_j^{out}}{m} \right] \delta\left(C_i, C_j\right) \tag{6}$$

where a_{ij} represents the existence of the edge pointing from node i to node j, $a_{ij} = 1$ if there exists a directed edge pointing from i to j, otherwise, $a_{ij} = 0$; m is the scale of E;

C_i and C_j represent the community of i and j respectively; $\delta(C_i, C_j)$ represents the consistency of C_i and C_j, $\delta(C_i, C_j) = 1$ if $C_i = C_j$, otherwise, $\delta(C_i, C_j) = 0$.

Using the above attributes, the algorithm given in Algorithm 1 is used to divide the communities of the complex network: the node with the largest weight, which is calculated by (4), is used as the initial community; the neighbors of the initial community are firstly involved in the community. For each neighbor of the updated community, calculating its belonging degree to this community, if it is bigger than 1, this neighbor is added to the community. This procedure is repeated until each node is involved in some community. The community division is then optimized by maximizing the modularity of the network, which is calculated by (6).

Algorithm 1 The algorithm of community division.

Input: $G = (V, E)$,V and E are the vertex set and edge set of the graph G

Parameters: $\Gamma(v)$ is the neighbor set of vertex v;W is the array of weight, n is the scale of V;V_0 is the nodes whose indegree is 0, tC are communities.

Output: the community set CS.

1: $V \leftarrow V - V_0$
2: $CS \leftarrow \Phi$
3: **while** $V \neq \Phi$ **do**
4:     $C \leftarrow \Phi$
5:     Get the vertex v_{max} with the largest weight $W(v)$ in V
6:     $C \leftarrow C \cup \{v_{max}\} \cup \Gamma(v_{max})$
7:     $V \leftarrow V - C$
8:     $tC \leftarrow \Phi$
9:     **for** $\forall v \in V$ **do**
10:        **if** $B(v, C) > 1$ **then**
11:            $tC \leftarrow tC \cup \{v\}$
12:        **end if**
13:     **end for**
14:     $C \leftarrow C \cup tC$
15:     $CS \leftarrow CS \cup \{C\}$
16: **end while**
17: **for** $\forall v_0 \in V_0$ **do**
18:     Get G_i which has the most links with v_0
19:     $C_i \leftarrow C_i \cup \{v_0\}$
20: **end for**
21: Caculate Q_1 of G with CS
22: $Q_2 \overset{\Delta}{=} Q_1 + 1$
23: **while** $Q_1 < Q_2$ **do**
24:     Traversal CS to find the largest Q_2 when merging C_i, C_j
25:     $t = C_i \cup C_j$
26:     $CS \leftarrow CS - \{C_i, C_j\}$
27:     $CS \leftarrow CS \cup \{t\}$
28: **end while**
29: **Return** CS

With the communities divided by the algorithm shown in Algorithm 1, the weak ties of the network are detected, as shown in Algorithm 2. For the signed directed network $G = (V, E)$, a positive signed network $G^+ = (V_1, E_1)$ and a negative signed network

$G^- = (V_2, E_2)$ are first extracted for the weak tie detection. G^+ is composed by all the positive edges of E, and G^- is composed by all the negative edges of E. Using the algorithm given in Algorithm 1, two sets of communities CS^+ and CS^- are divided, in which CS^+ is the communities divided by G^+ and CS^- is the communities divided by G^-. The weak tie detection algorithm traverses each edges of E, if two end nodes of the edge belong to one community, this edge is regarded as the strong tie; otherwise, if two end nodes of the edge belong to two communities, this edge is regarded as the weak tie.

Algorithm 2 The algorithm of weak ties detection.

Input: $G = (V, E)$,V and E are the vertex set and edge set of the graph G
Parameters: CS^+, CS^- the positive and negative community set.
Output: U the community set.

1: $U \leftarrow \Phi$
2: $E = \{e_1, e_2, \cdots, e_m\}$
3: $m = |E|$
4: **for** $i = 1$ to m **do**
5:     $(s, t) \leftarrow e_i$
6:     **if** the vertec s,t belong to different communities in CS^+, CS^- **then**
7:         $U \leftarrow U \cup e_i$
8:     **end if**
9: **end for**
10: **Return** U

3.2   Feature Extraction

For each weak tie extracted by the above section, several attributes are extracted for the further sign prediction:

A. Jaccard similarity. The more similar two nodes are, the more possible the sign of the link connecting these two nodes is positive. The less similar two nodes are, the more possible the sign of the link connecting these two nodes is negative. It is calculated as:

$$JC(v_i, v_j) = \frac{|\Gamma(v_i) \cap \Gamma(v_j)|}{|\Gamma(v_i) \cup \Gamma(v_j)|} \tag{7}$$

where $\Gamma(\bullet)$ is the set of neighbors of $\bullet$ and $|\bullet|$ is the number of nodes in.

B. Negative outdegree ratio of the source node. The higher it is, the more possible the sign of the weak tie is negative. It is calculated as:

$$NOR(s) = \frac{d_{out}^-(s)}{d_{out}^-(s) + d_{out}^+(s)} \tag{8}$$

where s represents the source node of the weak tie, $d_{out}^-(s)$ is the negative out-degree of s, and $d_{out}^+(s)$ is the outdegree of s.

C. Negative indegree ratio of the target node. The higher it is, the more possible the sign of the weak tie is negative. It is calculated as:

$$NIR(t) = \frac{d_{in}^-(t)}{d_{in}^-(t) + d_{in}^+(t)} \tag{9}$$

where t represents the target node of the weak tie.

D. Positive link ratio between communities. The higher it is, the more likely the target weak tie is positive. It is measured as:

$$R^+(C_i, C_j) = \frac{P(C_i, C_j)}{N(C_i, C_j) + P(C_i, C_j)} \tag{10}$$

where $P(C_i, C_j)$ is the number of positive links between community C_i and community C_j, and $N(C_i, C_j)$ is the number of negative links between C_i and C_j.

E. Negative link ratio between communities. The higher it is, the more likely the target weak tie is negative. It is measured as:

$$R^-(C_i, C_j) = \frac{N(C_i, C_j)}{N(C_i, C_j) + P(C_i, C_j)} \tag{11}$$

3.3 Sign Predictor

Using the features extracted for each target weak tie, the SVM classifier is applied to predict the sign of the weak tie. Based on the featured extracted as shown in Sect. 3.2, a vector is generated for each target weak tie, i.e. $\mathbf{x} \in \mathbb{R}^5$ is used to describe the weak tie. Let be the sign of the weak tie, $y \in \{+1, -1\}$, in which $+1$ means the sign of the weak tie is positive, and -1 means the sign of the weak tie is negative. $D = \{(\mathbf{x}_1, y_1), (\mathbf{x}_2, y_2), \cdots, (\mathbf{x}_m, y_m)\}$ is used to train the classifier, in which $\mathbf{x}_i$ is the vector describing the ith training weak tie, $\mathbf{x}_i \in \mathbb{R}^5, i = 1, 2, \cdots, m$, m is the number of weak ties used for the training of SVM classifier, and y_i is the sign of the ith training weak tie. The sign of the weak tie is predicted as:

$$sign(f(\mathbf{x})) = sign(\omega^T \mathbf{x} + b) \tag{12}$$

where $sign(\bullet)$ is the sign of $\bullet$, ω and b are weight of the attributes and the bias respectively.

4   Experimental Results

The performances of the proposed method are measured on the real world application data Epinions dataset [9]. Epinions is an online review website where users can not only give their ratings on items but also point out their opinions to other users. If a user trusts another user, the sign of the link connecting these two users is regards as positive. If a user distrusts another user, the sign of the link connecting these two users is regards as negative. The Epinions dataset consists of 131828 nodes and 841372 directed links between these nodes, in which 85.3% links have positive signs and 14.7% links have negative signs.

Since the original dataset is sparse, the data are firstly preprocessed for better sign prediction. The data preprocessing keeps the nodes whose degree are bigger than 80, and removes the nodes whose degree are less than 80, as well as the connections pointing to these nodes. The remaining experimental dataset contains 1415 nodes and 113484 links, in which 99376 links are positive and 14108 links are negative. A positive network and a negative network are extracted from this experimental dataset for further sign prediction, in which the positive network contains all positive links of the experimental dataset and the negative network contains all negative links of the experimental dataset. The positive network consists of 1414 nodes and 99376 links, and the negative network consists of 1346 nodes and 14108 links.

Using the method given in Sect. 3.1, the weak ties of the experimental dataset are firstly detected. Based on the algorithm given in Algorithm 1, totally 16 communities are divided for the positive network and 31 communities are divided for the negative network. Based on the weak tie detection algorithm given in Algorithm 2, 1882 weak ties are detected between these communities, in which 1275 weak ties have positive signs and 607 weak ties have negative signs. We randomly select 70% of the weak ties to train the sign classifier and the remaining 30% of the weak ties are used to test the performances of the proposed method. The experiments are repeatedly held on the

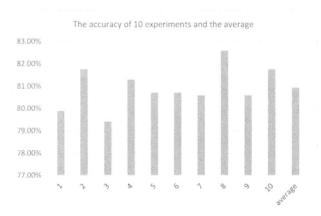

Fig. 2. The accuracy of the weak tie sign prediction

experimental data for ten times. The accuracy and the F1-score of the weak tie sign prediction are given in Figs. 2 and 3 respectively.

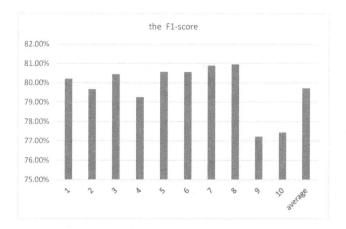

Fig. 3. The F1-Score of the negative sign prediction of the weak ties.

As shown in Fig. 2, the proposed method has high weak tie sign prediction accuracy. The average prediction accuracy of the 10 times experiments is 80.93%. For all experiments, the prediction accuracy is over 79%, and the prediction accuracy is more than 80% in 8 out of the 10 experiments. Since negative signs usually contain more information than positive signs [10], the performance of negative sign prediction is extremely important. We therefore measure the F1-score of the negative sign prediction for the weak ties, as shown in Fig. 3. The F1-score of the 10 times experiments is 79.72%. For all experiments, the F1-score is over 77%, and the F1-score is more than 79% in 8 out of the 10 experiments. Note that there is no existing work predicting the weak ties of signed network, so the performances of the proposed method could not be compared with the performances of other works.

5   Conclusions and Future Works

The sign prediction for weak ties of complex networks is a newly emerged research problem in the area of sign prediction. Weak ties are crucial bridges connecting tightly coupled nodes groups. The sign of the weak ties represents the relationships between two groups, which carries more information than the sign of strong ties in the complex networks. The paper propose a communited based sign predicting method to predict the sign of weak ties in complex network. The weak ties are firstly detected by community division. SVM classifier is trained to learn the relationship between the sign of the weak ties and the attributes related to the weak ties. The trained classifier is then used for the sign prediction of the unknown weak ties. Experimental results verifies the effectiveness of the proposed method in the real application data. Our future work will mainly focus on the performance improvement on the sign prediction of the weak ties. We will not only try to further improve the sign prediction accuracy, but also try to improve the F1-score of the negative sign prediction.

Acknowledgement. This research was supported by Nature Science Foundation of China (Grant No. 61672284), Natural Science Foundation of Jiangsu Province (Grant No. BK20171418), China Postdoctoral Science Foundation (Grant No. 2016M591841). This work was also supported by Open Project Foundation of Information Technology Research Base of Civil Aviation Administration of China (Grant No. CAAC-ITRB-201501 and Grant No. CAAC-ITRB-201602). Dr. Weiwei Yuan is the corresponding author of this paper.

References

1. Yuan, W., Guan, D., Lee, Y.K., et al.: Improved trust-aware recommender system using small-worldness of trust networks. J. Knowl. Based Syst. **23**(3), 232–238 (1981)
2. Wei, L., Xu, H., Wang, Z., et al.: Topic detection based on weak tie analysis: a case study of LIS research. J. Data Inf. Sci. **1**(4), 81–101 (2016)
3. Li, X., Fang, H., Zhang, J.: Rethinking the link prediction problem in signed social networks. In: AAAI, pp. 4955–4956 (2017)
4. Tang, J., Chang, Y., Aggarwal, C., et al.: A survey of signed network mining in social media. J. ACM Comput. Surv. (CSUR) **49**(3), 42 (2016)
5. Si, C., Jiao, L., Wu, J., et al.: A group evolving-based framework with perturbations for link prediction. J. Physica A Stat. Mech. Appl. **475**, 117–128 (2017)
6. Martnez, V., Berzal, F., Cubero, J.C.: A survey of link prediction in complex networks. J. ACM Comput. Surv. (CSUR) **49**(4), 69 (2016)
7. Nocaj, A., Ortmann, M., Brandes, U.: Adaptive disentanglement based on local clustering in small-world network visualization. J. IEEE Trans. Vis. Comput. Graph. **22**(6), 1662–1671 (2016)
8. Leicht, E.A., Newman, M.E.J.: Community structure in directed networks. J. Phys. Rev. Lett. **100**(11), 118703 (2008)
9. Massa, P., Avesani, P.: Trust-aware recommender systems. In: ACM Conference on Recommender Systems, pp. 17–24. ACM (2007)
10. Khodadadi, A., Jalili, M.: Sign prediction in social networks based on tendency rate of equivalent micro-structures. J. Neurocomput. **257**, 175–184 (2017)

Lake-Level Prediction Leveraging Deep Neural Network

Jinfeng Wen[1]([✉]) [iD], Peng-Fei Han[1], Zhangbing Zhou[1,2], and Xu-Sheng Wang[1]

[1] China University of Geosciences (Beijing), Beijing 100083, China
wenjinfeng127@163.com

[2] Computer Science Department, TELECOM SudParis, 91011 Evry, France

Abstract. Accurate estimation of water level dynamics in lakes at daily or hourly time-scales is important for the ecosystem and formulation of water resources policies. In this study, lake level dynamics of Sumu Barun Jaran are simulated and predicted at hourly time scale using Deep Learning (DL) model. Two mature machine learning methods, namely Multiple Linear Regression (MLR) and Artificial Neural Network (ANN), are also adopted for the comparison purpose. The result shows that the DL model preforms the best on three criteria, following by the three-layered Back-Propagation ANN model and MLR model.

Keywords: Lake level · Sumu Barun Jaran · Badain Jaran Desert
Deep learning · Artificial neural network

1 Introduction

Lakes, as the most abundant water resources that carries on land, are an important factor for impacting the human life and earth ecosystem. An accurate estimation of lake level dynamics in an efficient way is essential for effective assessments on water resources and environment in lakes. Generally, this estimation is a complicated mathematical problem. In the traditional methods of hydrology, physics-based numerical model and conceptual hydrological model are often used to simulate water level fluctuations [1]. However, this approach requires a variety of parameters with clear physical meaning, terrain data and boundary conditions, a lack of which may lead to poor model performance or increase the model uncertainty.

In recent years, the autoregressive integrated moving average (ARIMA) model and multiple linear regression model are usually used to define the trend or stochastic processes of variables, but neither of them consider the non-stationarity and non-linear characteristics of the data structure [2]. Artificial neural networks (ANNs) techniques have been applied to solve non-stationary and non-linear problems in time series analyses for the modeling of water level fluctuations [3]. However, because of the shallow number of layers of ANNs, the learning power of this model can hardly be applicable especially when spatial-temporal data are sensed with multiple features. Recently, deep learning is

© ICST Institute for Computer Sciences, Social Informatics and Telecommunications Engineering 2018
L. Wang et al. (Eds.): QShine 2017, LNICST 234, pp. 23–32, 2018.
https://doi.org/10.1007/978-3-319-78078-8_3

increasingly popular and accepted by researchers, and it can solve the tasks associated with artificial intelligence and achieve excellent results with efficient operations [4]. However, little research effort has been developed to solve the hydrological problem using the deep learning method at this moment.

In this study, we attempt to use different machine learning methods in estimating the lake level dynamics, for lakes in the Badain Jaran Desert, China. Note that the Deep learning (DL) model is constructed and applied to simulate and predict the lake level dynamics at hourly time scale for the first time, and the model performance is evaluated. Two mature machine learning methods, namely Multiple Linear Regression (MLR) and Artificial Neural Network (ANN), are also adopted for the comparison purpose. The result shows that these three models are appropriate for simulating and predicting lake level dynamics at hourly time scale, and the DL model preforms the best.

The rest of this paper is organized as follows. In Sect. 2, MLR, ANN and DL structures are introduced. In Sect. 3, the MLR, ANN with three-layered BP and DL models are applied and evaluated. Finally, the conclusion is being made in Sect. 4.

2 Prediction Models

Considering the variety of meteorological data, MLR, ANN and DL models are adopted to simulate and predict the lake level dynamics.

2.1 Multiple Linear Regression (MLR)

Multiple linear regression analysis is a multivariate statistical technique aimed to predict the lake level as a dependent variable, Y, by using a set of p predictor variables $(x_1, x_2, ..., x_p)$, as presented by Table 1.

Table 1. The partial meteorological and lake level data.

Time	TA($°C$)	TS$_{10}$($°C$)	TS$_{20}$($°C$)	RH(%)	WD(Deg)
2012 09-13 00:00	11.722	20.793	22.38	50.115	357.786
2012 09-13 02:00	10.314	20.602	22.479	60.253	3.004
2012 09-13 04:00	9.545	20.379	21.748	59.077	17.044
2012 09-13 06:00	9.373	20.544	22.157	61.716	342.339
Time	AP(hPa)	R$_n$(W/m^2)	WS(m/s)	P(mm)	H(m)
2012 09-13 00:00	888.409	−114.248	0.336	0	1179.086
2012 09-13 02:00	887.602	−114.823	0.579	0	1179.083
2012 09-13 04:00	886.987	−112.38	0.41	0	1179.082
2012 09-13 06:00	886.987	−114.248	0.616	0	1179.08

The main objectives of MLR are explanation and prediction. After the above two stages, the relationship between the lake level and the predictor variables is represented by the following equation:

$$y_i = b_0 + b_1 \times x_{1i} + b_2 \times x_{2i} + ... + b_p \times x_{pi} + e_i \tag{1}$$

where y_i is the predicted lake level values at time i, x_{1i} to x_{pi} are p predictor variables influencing lake level at time i, b_0 is the constant obtained from data training procedures, b_1 to b_p are the coefficients relating the p predictor variables to the variables of interest, and e_i is a random error term at time i.

The least squares criterion is applied to estimate the Eq. 1. The relationship between the nine predictor variables and the lake level as shown in Table 1 is expressed as follows:

$$\begin{aligned} H = b_0 &+ b_1 \times TA + b_2 \times TS_{10} + b_3 \times TS_{20} + b_4 \times RH + b_5 \times WD \\ &+ b_6 \times AP + b_7 \times R_n + b_8 \times WS + b_9 \times P \end{aligned} \tag{2}$$

2.2 Artificial Neural Networks (ANN)

Artificial neural network is a simple and efficient neural network and has been widely used in data fitting, prediction and classification. In this study, no matter how complicated the relationship between the data, ANN models can obtain satisfactory lake level values.

Neural Network (NN). Figure 1 illustrates a neural network with three layers. In each layer the circle with solid line represents a neuron that is a simple computational unit and has an input and output, denoted as z and a, respectively. Suppose that the number of layers of a neural network is L. The $z_k^{(l)}$ and $a_k^{(l)}$ denote the input and output of the kth neuron on the lth layer, respectively.

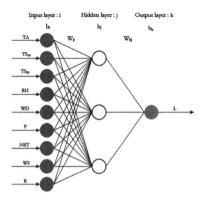

Fig. 1. Artificial neural network

The relationship between an input and output of neurons is usually described by an activation function $g(.)$ as follows:

$$a = g(z) \tag{3}$$

The sigmoid activation function:

$$g(z) = \frac{1}{1 + exp^{-z}} \tag{4}$$

or the hyperbolic tangent activation function:

$$g(z) = \frac{exp^z - exp^{-z}}{exp^z + exp^{-z}} \tag{5}$$

can be specified.

For the output layer about lake level, a linear transfer activation function:

$$g(z) = z \tag{6}$$

is adopted, which can avoid and correct the gradient disappearance problem.

A neuron receives signals from every neuron on the previous layer as the following:

$$z_k^{(l+1)} = \sum_{i=1}^{n_l} w_{ki}^{(l)} a_i^{(l)} + b_k^{(l)} \tag{7}$$

where $l \in \{1, L-1\}$, and $w_{ki}^{(l)}$ describe the relationship between the kth and the ith neurons on the $(l+1)$th and lth layers, respectively; $b_k^{(l)}$ is the bias associated with the kth neuron on the $(l+1)$th layer, and n_l is the number of neurons on the lth layer.

In our ANN model, the output of a neuron used to explain the lake level is the same with its input:

$$z_k^{(1)} = a_k^{(1)} (k \in \{1, n_1\}) \tag{8}$$

The output of the last layer can be denoted as $a^{(L)}$:

$$a^{(L)} = (a_1^{(L)}, \dots, a_{n_L}^{(L)}) \tag{9}$$

Suppose $x = (x_1, \dots, x_{n_1})^T$ is a representation of lake level predictor records in this paper, if the x is an input into a neural network:

$$z^{(1)} = x \tag{10}$$

a lake level output $a^{(L)}$ can be computed by this network (Eqs. 3 and 7). Therefore, a neural network implements a non-linear mapping $h_{w,b}(.)$ from an input $x = (x_1, \dots, x_{n_1})^T$ to an output $a^{(L)}$:

$$a^{(L)} = h_{w,b}(x) \tag{11}$$

where

$$b = b^{(l)} \tag{12}$$

is the set of biases, and

$$W = \{W^{(l)}\}(l \in \{1, L\}) \tag{13}$$

is the set of the weights of a NN in Eq. 7, where $b^l = \{b_j^{(l)}, 1 \leq j \leq n_l\}$ and $W^{(l)} = W_{ji}^{(l)}$.

A Back-Propagation Algorithm for Obtaining a NN. Suppose that

$$S = \{(x, y)\} \tag{14}$$

is a training set for a NN, where $x = (x_1, \ldots, x_{n_1})^T$ is the representation of a water level record, and y is the expected lake water level output with respect to x.

In a NN, some parameters W and b can be set through minimizing an objective function, namely, J, as presented by Eq. 15:

$$\mathbf{J(W,b)} = \frac{1}{N} \sum_{x \in S} \left(\frac{1}{2} \|h_{W,b}(x) - y\|^2\right) + \frac{\lambda}{2} \sum_{l=1}^{L-1} \sum_{i=1}^{n_l} \sum_{j=1}^{n_{l+1}} (w_{ji}^{(l)})^2 \tag{15}$$

where N is the number of samples in a training set S, and $\lambda \geq 0$ is a preset parameter. λ is commonly referred to as a weight decay parameter.

To obtain our NN from a training set, we initialize each parameter $w_{ji}^{(l)}$ and $b_i^{(l)}$ to a small random value near zero. Subsequently, two parameters W and b are iteratively optimized using a gradient descent method based on the objective function J in Eq. 15. This learning scheme is referred to as Back-Propagation (BP) algorithm.

2.3   Deep Learning (DL)

Deep learning is synonymous with deep neural networks (DNNs). In recent years, the DL model is adopted for solving the regression problems in several research areas. The combination of DL and lake data makes the problem better handled. In this paper, we abstract the more useful features by creating a multi-level and multi-neuron neural network, called the fully connected deep neural network, which automatically learns more appropriate weights and thresholds based on the structure of lake level data. The DNN basic structure is shown in Fig. 2.

This article trains the DL model mainly through the following two processes:

- First, our DL network uses the top-down supervised learning, which can be seen as a feature leaning process. Due to the constraints of the model capacity and the sparseness constraints, our DL model can learn the structure of the data itself. If the $n-1$ layer is obtained (Eq. 7), the output of this layer is the input as the nth layer (Eq. 8), and the nth layer is trained (Eq. 7) similarly.

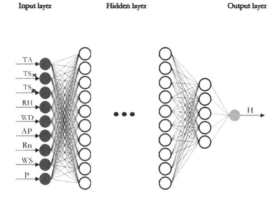

Fig. 2. Deep learning model.

– Then, the top-down and non-supervised learning is used in our DL network. The entire multi-layer model parameters are further fine-tuned (Eq. 15) based on the parameters obtained in the first step. Importantly, initial parameters of DL are not the same as the setting way of NN. In our DL model, the initial value corresponds to the global optimum by learning the structure of the input data, so that better results can be achieved.

2.4 Model Evaluation Criteria

The accuracy of the approximated three models' results is evaluated using the average relative error ($ARER$), the mean squared error ($RMSE$) and the coefficient of determination (R^2), and they are specified as follows:

- $ARER$: It reflects the overall forecast level of the data.

$$ARER = \overline{RER_i} \tag{16}$$

where RER_i is the radio between the absolute error of the index and the true value.
- $RMSE$: It is used to quantify the simulation results.

$$RMSE = \sqrt{\frac{\sum_{i=1}^{n}(e_i - t_i)^2}{n}} \tag{17}$$

- R^2: It indicates that there is a variation between the predicted value and the true value.

$$R^2 = \left(\frac{\sum_{i=1}^{n}(e_i - \overline{e_i})(t_i - \overline{t_i})}{\sqrt{(e_i - \overline{e_i})^2(t_i - \overline{t_i})^2}}\right)^2 \tag{18}$$

where e_i and t_i represent the model output and measured actual lake level value. $\overline{RER_i}$, $\overline{e_i}$ and $\overline{t_i}$ represent their average values, respectively, and n denotes the number of observations.

3   Study Area and Prediction Models Evaluation

3.1   Studying Area and Data Collection

As a typical arid region, the Badain Jaran Desert (BJD) is famous in the world for the presence of a number of lakes among the mega dunes. Due to the huge gap between precipitation and evaporation, the formation mechanism and evaluation trend of lakes become the important scientific problem concerned by researchers. Over the past decades, this issue has never reached a consensus, though a large number of scientists have conducted the scientific inquiry and survey. Therefore, to understand the formation mechanism of lakes, lake level fluctuations should be studied clearly. As shown in Fig. 3, the BJD ($39°20'-41°30'$N, $100°01'-103°10'$E) is located in the western Alxa Plateau in Inner Mongolia, China. It is the second largest desert in China and covers an area of $4.9 \times 10^4 \, \text{km}^2$ [5]. Consistent with the desert terrain, the overall flow of groundwater is from south to north and from east to west with hydraulic gradient between 0.8% and 7.9% [6]. About 100 lakes lie in the hinterland in BJD, but the lake area is generally less than $0.2 \, \text{km}^2$. A few of them are larger than $1 \, \text{km}^2$. The lakes in BJD are most salty with TDS between $1 \, \text{g/L}$ and $400 \, \text{g/L}$. The lake studied in this presentation is the second largest salt lake, Sumu Barun Jaran, with an area of $1.24 \, \text{km}^2$ and maximum depth more than $11 \, \text{m}$ [7].

In order to monitor the meteorological factors in Sumu Baran Jaran, a wooden bridge with steel structure was built in the lake to install an automatic weather station (Fig. 3c) since 2012, where the precipitation (P) is monitored by a self-recording pluviometer. The automatic weather station is used for measuring air temperature (TA), air relative humidity (RH), wind direction (WD), atmospheric pressure (AP), net radiation (R_n) and wind speed (WS). Water

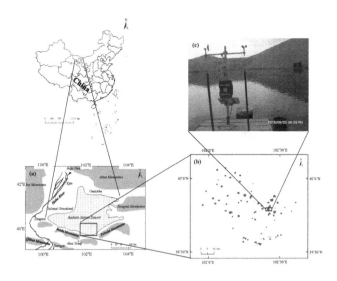

Fig. 3. Location of the study area (a), lakes (b) and weather station (c).

temperature at $10\,\mathrm{cm}$ (TS_{10}) and $20\,\mathrm{cm}$ (TS_{20}) depths are monitored by two sensors. The monitoring interval is 30 min. Near the bottom of the lake, a CDT-Diver sensor is installed to measure the conductivity, temperature and pressure once every $2\,\mathrm{h}$. After air pressure calibration, lake level (H) can be calculated using the pressure monitored by CDT-Diver sensor. This study collected the meteorological data and lake level data during the period from 00:00 on September 13, 2012 to 10:00 on October 28, 2012 with the interval of $2\,\mathrm{h}$.

3.2 Model Application

Training Models. In the DL network configuration, we build a six-layer deep neural network (including the input and output layers) as shown in Fig. 2. This network is a fully connected network. In addition, the number of neurons on the hidden layer is 10, 15, 10 and 5, respectively. The activation function of the neurons on the hidden layer is the hyperbolic tangent function. For the activation function of the output layer, rectified linear units function is applied. Importantly, our DL model supports the backward propagation and uses the random gradient descent algorithm for achieving the optimization of the weight.

In addition, the MLR and ANN models are applied to this problem for comparison. We carry out the MLR model training by giving the existing historical meteorological and lake level data, and the trained model is used to predict the future lake level changes. Nine variables serve as predictor variables as shown in Table 1. The ANN model is performed with a three-layer BP neural network as shown in Fig. 1, which is constructed by the LM optimization algorithm (Eq. 15) using MATLAB.

In this study, 528 hourly data during the period from 00:00 on September 13, 2012 to 22:00 on October 26, 2012 are used for the training purpose, and the result has been shown in Fig. 4(a).

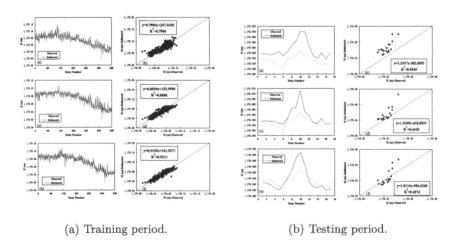

(a) Training period.   (b) Testing period.

Fig. 4. Observed and estimated lake level from 00:00 on September 13, 2012 to 22:00 on October 26, 2012 using MLR in (a) and (b), ANN3 in (c) and (d) and DL in (e) and (f).

Testing Models. The trained models are tested by predicting the lake level using 17 h data ranging from 00:00 on October 27, 2012 to 8:00 on October 28, 2012 as shown in Fig. 4(b).

3.3   Model Evaluation

In the training process, these three models can generate the accurate value of the average lake level (1179.07 m). In the testing procedure, on average, the lake level of observation is 1179.04 m, whereas the value calculated by MLR, ANN3, and DL are, 1179.05 m, 1179.05 m, and 1179.04 m, respectively. The average value modeled by DL is equal to the observation. On the whole, the MLR and ANN3 significantly overestimate the lake level for the testing period, while the DL performs the best.

The results of these three criteria for each of the models in the training and testing procedure are presented in Table 2. In the training process, the DL model obtains the highest value of R^2 (0.9211) and the smallest values of AREA (3.19E-06) and RMSE (0.005007). In the testing procedure, these models are acceptable according to the values of the ARER, RMSE and R^2. The DL model performs the best with the highest value of R^2 (0.6574) and smallest values of AREA (4.06E-06) and RMSE (0.001238).

Table 2. Models results

Model	ARER		RMSE		R^2	
	Training	Test	Training	Test	Training	Test
MLR	5.26E-06	8.59E-06	0.007983	0.011190	0.7906	0.5545
ANN3	4.27E-06	4.17E-06	0.006315	0.001316	0.8686	0.6420
DL	3.19E-06	4.06E-06	0.005007	0.001238	0.9211	0.6574

3.4   Discussion

Although the DL model established in this study performed better than the MLR and ANN3 models, the advantage is not very obvious because of a relatively small amount of data used in this study. The experimental settings should be considered for constructing the DL model, since these settings should affect the capabilities of the model to some extent in the training and testing processes, which should be set properly according to our requirements.

– *How to design a network structure.* The optimal number of hidden layers and neurons in each layer should be gotten according to the experience or comparative experimental results.

– *Selection of the activation function.* In this study, the linear activation function (Eq. 6) is selected to set the threshold as zero, which should significantly improve the convergence speed of the random gradient descent algorithm.
– *Selection of the optimization algorithms.* The stochastic gradient descent algorithm is chosen in this paper. In the large sample size circumstances, the samples only needs to be partially trained and this strategy can get a loss value within the acceptable range of the model.
– *How to set the rate at which the optimization algorithm moves in the search space.* If the learning rate is too large, it is possible to cross the optimal value. Otherwise, if the learning rate is too small, the efficiency of optimization may be too low, and the algorithm can not converge for a long time.

To summarize, a relatively simple framework of deep learning has been constructed in this study.

4 Conclusion

In this paper, we attempt to compare the DL model with the MLR and ANN3 models in simulating the hourly lake level dynamics in the Sumu Barun Jaran lake, Badain Jaran Desert, China. The performance of these models is evaluated with criteria including the average relative error, the mean squared error, and the coefficient of determination. Results indicate that the DL model performed the best on all of these criteria, and it has the potential to simulate and predict water level dynamics in rivers and groundwater systems. As the number of training samples increases, the DL model behaves better than other machine learning models with more efficient operation.

References

1. Gong, Y., Wang, X., Hu, B.X., Zhou, Y., Hao, C., Wan, L.: Groundwater contributions in water-salt balances of the lakes in the Badain Jaran Desert, China. J. Arid Land **8**(5), 694–706 (2016)
2. Nagesh, K.D., Rajib, M.: Bayesian dynamic modelling for nonstationary hydroclimatic time series forecasting along with uncertainty quantification. Hydrol. Process. **22**(17), 3488–3499 (2008)
3. Wei, C.-C.: Comparing lazy and eager learning models for water level forecasting in river-reservoir basins of inundation regions. Env. Modell. Softw. **63**, 137–155 (2015)
4. Li, X.-R., Pan, R.-Y., Duan, F.-Q.: Parameterizing stellar spectra using deep neural networks. Res. Astron. Astrophys. **17**(4), 036 (2017)
5. Wang, T.: Formation and evolution of Badain Jirin Sandy Desert, China. China J. Desert Res. **10**(1), 29–40 (1990)
6. Jing, Z., Wang, X.S., Jia, F.C., Guo-Min, L.I., Dong, Y.H.: New insights into the flow directions of groundwater in Western Alxa, Inner Mongolia. Geoscience **35**(3), 774–782 (2015)
7. Chen, T., Wang, X., Hu, X., Lu, H., Gong, Y.: Clines in salt lakes in the Badain Jaran Desert and their significances in indicating fresh groundwater discharge. J. Lake Sci. **27**(1), 183–189 (2015)

A Situation-Aware Road Emergency Navigation Mechanism Based on GPS and WSNs

Ruixin Ma[1], Qirui Li[1], Tie Qiu[4(⊠)], Chen Chen[2], and Arun Kumar Sangaiah[3]

[1] School of Software, Dalian University of Technology, Dalian 116620, China
{dlutwindows,lqrrey}@163.com
[2] State Key Laboratory of Integrated Services Networks, Xidian University,
Xi'an 710071, China
cc2000@mail.xidian.edu.cn
[3] School of Computing Science and Engineering, VIT University, Vellore, India
arunkumarsangaiah@gmail.com
[4] School of Computer Science and Technology, Tianjin University,
Tianjin 300350, China
qiutie@ieee.org

Abstract. Traffic congestion happens when emergencies occur. Traditional congestion algorithms evaluate traffic congestion only according to real-time vehicle speed, instead of comprehensive aspects. To address this shortcoming, we provide a new algorithm for congestion evaluation based on WSNs and GPS, which provide many sensor nodes to monitor and transmit traffic message in time. This paper takes more aspects for traffic into consideration, including congestion situation, danger condition and sudden road peak flow, and turns them into weights, which help to measure congestion intensity. According to congestion intensity, congestion field is established to navigate for the vehicles. Furthermore, we propose future prediction mechanism for vehicles. Finally, we do simulation with Matlab to evaluate the performance of the prediction mechanism, and results show that the performance of prediction mechanism is better than greedy algorithm. Moreover, a route will be recommended after a comprehensive evaluation about the distance, time, congestion and traffic lights number. In a word, the prediction mechanism for traffic can not only ensure the effectiveness of the navigation, but also protect drivers from the sudden peak flow, which brings convenience and comfortableness to drivers.

Keywords: Road congestion · Emergency navigation · Situation-aware

1 Introduction

Wireless Sensor Networks (WSNs) [5,7,12,16] has been got extensively applied currently because of its capability of providing a stable and reliable data prediction relatively [3,9,10,15,22,23,25]. But that is not enough, a stable navigation

© ICST Institute for Computer Sciences, Social Informatics and Telecommunications Engineering 2018
L. Wang et al. (Eds.): QShine 2017, LNICST 234, pp. 33–43, 2018.
https://doi.org/10.1007/978-3-319-78078-8_4

device between WSNs and vehicles is what we need. Global Position System (GPS) [2,11,14] plays an important role in our life and is widely applied in road traffic navigation. GPS navigators appear as the medium between WSNs and vehicles. In [2,11,15], great improvements have been made in the aspects of network stability for road navigation and real-time monitor for surrounding environment. However, it cannot play well in solving congestion situation, with the more and more complex road traffic situation, as a result of which, it is urgent to propose a new road navigation prediction mechanism. In this study, we build a communication network with WSNs and GPS. Traditional algorithms measure road congestion and navigate vehicles only with real-time driving speed, which fail to evaluate the road comprehensively. Multi-view aspects for road congestion are concerned in this paper to ensure the road measurement accurate. Besides, Traditional navigation mechanism cannot predict the future traffic condition, which can influence the final evacuation effect definitively, especially in sudden peak flow. This paper proposes the Future Prediction Mechanism for Road (FPMR). FPMR gets future traffic condition and total travel time by predicting the future arrival moment of the vehicles and recording it in the corresponding nodes list.

Many alternative roads can be offered by GPS. We calculate the total driving time, distance, congestion, and traffic number, instead of only road congestion condition, to choose the final road with smallest calculated result, which ensure the comprehensive measurement for emergency navigation.

The main contribution of this paper are as follows:

(1) Providing a new algorithm based on WSNs, which can measure the road congestion degree comprehensively.
(2) Proposing a prediction mechanism of FCRM, which predict future traffic condition to avoid future emergency congestion.
(3) Based on the driving time and traffic lights number that predicted by FCRM, this paper combines driving distance and road congestion to evaluate alternative roads and choose the final road, which is more humanize for drivers.

The remainder of this paper is organized as follows. We describe the theoretical foundation in Sect. 2 and introduce the algorithm detailed in Sect. 3, we present the experiment results in Sect. 4. Conclusion is given in Sect. 5.

2   Related Work

2.1   Background

Many articles mentioned the application of distributed sensor networks or GPS, and exploited one of them as basic network interactive platform for road traffic detection. Many of the traffic evacuation model that based on WSNs are proposed. In [1], it combined WSNs with smartphone, and built a new network model for vehicle navigation. This new model can realize real-time navigation, further, the thought of real-time was inspired by this model. [20] proposed the

Free-Oscillation navigation of OPEN based on WSNs, Eliminating reciprocating phenomenon on the maximum extent is the main contribution, we can call that reciprocating with circle phenomenon as random walk in road. It is common that random walk in road occurs. OPEN consider the dangerous situation for roads, this is instructive for us to avoid the random walk of road when navigation. Oscillation phenomenon that before and after moving driving mode [4] is legitimate sometimes. The feeling of experience is getting worse.

There were a great use of Optical flow on application areas to solve road traffic problems also. In [6], collecting road information based on the image information of road traffic, then getting the road vehicle traffic stream, measuring the road congestion condition final. [13] put forward the OF- MCMC method basing MCMC (Markov chain Monte Carlo) and improve the prediction accuracy of the optical flow. SURE [21] optimize predicted accuracy and distribution performance of optical flow vectors. In detail, SURE model obtain the road load condition for the current traffic through technical, after that, SURE analyze this load data to adjust vehicles. But they did not consider the future traffic condition else.

2.2   Problem Statement

(1) The effect of evacuation

Road traffic condition deteriorating more and more, low overall regulatory capacity and high time delay of the traffic network, inefficient travel phenomena occur, such as random walk in road. As shown in Fig. 1, random walk in road tends to cause greater congestion. Navigation system needs to be able to identify road congestion condition for all roads, and provides solution to avoid these congested road sections.

(2) The impact of local navigation failure

In WSNs, there may be temporary or permanent local node/link failures due to battery outage and node destroy. Once the connectivity destructed

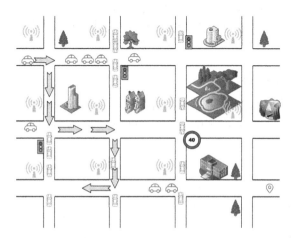

Fig. 1. The scene of the road random walk

between nodes, navigation failure. For this situation, we need to make timely treatment, and strive to minimize the impact of this situation. In this paper, the average node degree is above 6, which pledges the connectivity when the node battery outage or node damaged, ensure the data transmission and navigation affect.

3   Algorithm

In the network model, sensor nodes are placed at each intersection [8,17,24, 26] sensor node identify the dangerous road section through this two respects: (1) If one sensor node can not communicate with the other sensors node any more due to damaged or the other cause, WSNs set it to be a dangerous road section; (2) If sensors communication is normal, when a vehicle is traveling on the road, its running speed dropped to zero suddenly and continual for a long time, then signing to be dangerous. there are m junctions this model. Indexes can be represented as follows:

$$W_c = \left\{ W_c^j | j = 1, 2, ..., m \right\} \tag{1}$$

$$W_e = \left\{ W_e^j | j = 1, 2, ..., m \right\} \tag{2}$$

$$W_h = \left\{ W_h^j | j = 1, 2, ..., m \right\} \tag{3}$$

the concept of congestion can make use of the thought of congestion degree, Japanese uses, to calculate. By formula (4), wherein v represent the true speed, V stands for the standard road speed, we can call that speed limit.

$$W_c = \frac{v}{V} \tag{4}$$

The model of the 2D space that mentioned above mentioned has the ability to describe road conditions in manifold. Because the degree of each node is above 6 in our model setting. In this chapter, we focus on the deep description for the algorithm. Based on the above theories that have been told above, we introduce more detailed algorithm and specific steps next.

3.1   Network Model

The basic network model is shown in Fig. 2, in which WSNs and GPS are combined with. GPS sending all the possible and complete traffic routes to WSNs, WSNs finally choose.

3.2   Congestion Field

According to the current research situation at home and abroad. Europe is INRIX Index, United States is RCI and Japan DC is. This paper consider various road traffic conditions into parameters, and applied into algorithm. The

Fig. 2. Basic scene show

Table 1. Parameters in algorithm 1 and algorithm 2

Symbol	Description
R	The road
P_c	Sensor Network
$|PP_j|$	Euclidean distance
W_c	Parameter of road congestion
W_e	Parameter of road evacuation capacity
W_h	Parameter of traffic peak
W_d	Whether danger or not
I	Congestion Intensity
F_v	Congestion Potential

main idea of measurement road congestion algorithm is inspired by [18,19]. The main parameters are shown in the Table 1. Congestion Intensity (CI): Algorithm is based on the superposition principle. In detail, the using of Euclidean distance can reflect the character clearly that if further away from the congestion location, weaker of the user feelings for the congestion.

$$I = \sum_{j=1}^{m}(W_c^j + W_h^j - W_e^j)\frac{\overrightarrow{pp_j}}{|pp_j|^3} \tag{5}$$

As described as formula (5), this is a kind expression form of instantaneous congestion. But it is not enough that just use the instantaneous strength as the specific road congestion. Further, introducing the concept of Congestion Potential (CP). Congestion Potential: Congestion Potential (CP) is represented by Fv(p) in the formula, and it is based on the build-up of CI. Algorithm using infinite as a measure indicator when accumulated strength, infinite means safety to driver.

$$F_v(p) = \int_p^\infty \mathbf{I} dl \tag{6}$$

In order to avoid congestion, navigation mechanism need to select the smallest congestion value of the road as the re-road scheme, and this congestion value is viewed as an important measurement index to determine whether one alternative road to be chosen. As shown in the formula (7), we chosen the maximum Fv(p) after comparing all the sensor nodes of one road as the road congestion, specifically described as follows:

$$C_s(r) = max \{p \in r | F_v(p)\} \tag{7}$$

Table 2. Sensor data list

Name	Description
ID	Character a sensor or road uniquely
x	Definition the location with x
y	Definition the location with y
$Neighbors$	The adjacent intersection that connect with one road
$Readings$	The sensor reading
W_d	Whether danger or not
TL	Whether exist traffic light
$Type$	Road type, such as school factory
$Vnumber$	The vehicle number of the node

3.3 FCRM

If the current traffic condition of the driving road is not suitable to move forward any more, driver need to reconsider a new road. For the new road, this paper adds the time prediction mechanism of FPMR, which uses user's request time as the benchmark for the prediction time t_{start}. The start time of FPMR is the moment that vehicle requests, as a result, vehicle can avoid danger and reduce road random walk phenomenon so that repeated congestion can be avoided. Therefore, FPMR makes beneficial solutions for drivers to travel in traffic better. Firstly, according to the congestion situation to predict the driving speed, the driving speed is expressed as formula (8) to calculate,

$$v = V_{normal} * (1 - W_c) \tag{8}$$

V_{normal} represents the maximum speed that road allowed, the setting range of in (0, 1). Greater congestion index display, lower velocity, which turns that the reasonable of formula (8).

$$t_p = t_{start} + \sum_{j=1}^{|p|} \frac{s_p}{v_p} \tag{9}$$

In formula (9), p represents the predict node, $|p|$ is the section number of each alternative road. FPMR uses the superposition thought to predict the arriving moment and total driving time for every alternative roads. With regard to the peak flow, the arriving time t_p need to be judged by sensor node whether locate at the range that peak flow happen, thus reaching the purposes that forecast driving time and avoiding peak flow.

3.4 Overall Merit Method

After measuring the road congestion condition and the arrive moment of vehicles above, in the final evaluation for each alternative roads, we consider the following four aspects: total driving time, distance, congestion and traffic lights number. From the above formula of (8), (9), The total travel time T of every alternative roads can be described in the following:

$$T_r = t_{destination} - t_{start} \tag{10}$$

and total distance S_r:

$$S_r = \sum_{j=1}^{n} S_j \tag{11}$$

Traffic lights has influence on driving time and speed, but this index is often ignored. So this paper think about the influence caused by traffic lights into navigating program when evaluate re-road. The influences are reflected on vehicle velocity mainly, which reflects the comprehensive and humanized for road emergency navigation this paper. 60 s setting as a stage for the traffic lights. In the final road evaluation, all these road indicators are normalized, in order to control the difference influence that indicators bring on assessment. For each of the road, getting the comprehensive analysis and comparison, and choosing the most suitable way for users.

4 Simulation

According to introduced above, this paper simulated the specific program. The main process includes data initialization, congestion field establishing, the emergency evacuation road determining.

4.1 Simulation Initialization

In the simulation experiment, road condition is perceived by sensor nodes, which initialize the data entry for WSNs. When model working, sensor node detects the road data continually and receive drivers request when congestion occurs. WSNs establish congestion field, congestion field can make overall observation for traffic network more clear and the sensor list in the Table 2.

4.2   Results and Comparison

We add greedy algorithm navigation scheme to compare with our program called RENS. In this article, the selective method for alternative roads are based on the congestion field that established by WSNs. As shown in Fig. 3(a) is the greedy algorithm mechanism when navigating for drivers, it may cause the random road walk phenomenon in different degree. Random road walk may be caused time delay and bad satisfaction for drivers, so we consider that effect, which is one of the significant innovation of this paper. As shown in (b), it avoid the not ideal navigation condition that caused by the signal message of route after getting reasonable road indexes. In the experiment, we carried out holistic navigation for all the vehicles that running on the traffic network, reaching the balance for traffic network on whole level when evacuation for vehicles.

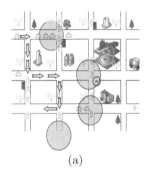

(a)   (b)

Fig. 3. There is the 2D space model that about the road traffic conditions for road navigation, (a) is based on the real time driving speed to measure road congestion, (b) is using RENS algorithm to establish congestion domain for the and select re-road

(1) Road damaged: Road quality should be pay attention. It is worrying that when driving on the damaged road, not only property damage for driver, seriously, a threat to the safety. In this paper, the basis network that combining WSNs with GPS as can perceives dangerous sections timely, and notifies basis network model to avoid damage to user. In Fig. 4, sensor node discover damaged road send this message to GPS, GPS formulate alternative road programs after removing damaged road, that is one of the superiority this paper.

(2) Peak flow In the experiment, we use various scene to simulate. It turn out the efficient that our program performed in different applied range.

As shown in Fig. 5, there are many difference scenes setting for this experiment comparison, RENS and GD use difference indexes of road to measure road condition. As the picture shows to us, GD did not navigate for road congestion very well. In the respect of time, distance and traffic light, our program has advantage after considering more influence factors.

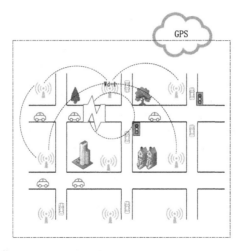

Fig. 4. A damage has exist in this model experiment

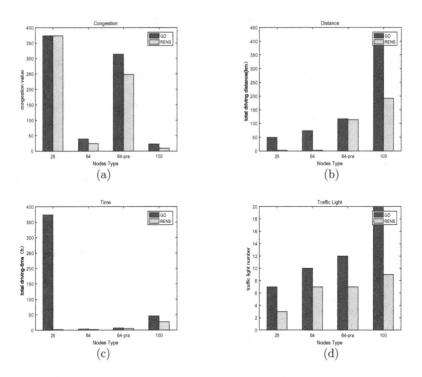

Fig. 5. In different comparison result, from the (a) (b) (c), we can see that more nodes number of the traffic network model, more stable of the RENS performance, and from (c), there are a better performance when RENS applied in the bigger scene.

5   Conclusion

It is an urgent problem needing to be solved that navigating emergency road congestion effectively. This paper proposed a navigation mechanism and consider variety of road indicators in our algorithm. FPMR plays an important role in predicting the future road traffic conditions, which can avoid two times congestion and random walk in road, it is the other innovation and breakthrough in our navigation mechanism. In the subsequent work, we devote to practical application in real life and combine with mechanical learning technology to analysis traffic data deeply. Putting forward to found the internal links on traffic, and solving the problem of the emergency road congestion better.

References

1. Aouami, R., Ouzzif, M., Rifi, M.: A new architecture for traffic congestion using smartphone and wireless sensor networks. In: 2016 3rd International Conference on Systems of Collaboration, pp. 1–5 (2016)
2. Bhuiyan, M.Z.A., Wang, G., Cao, J., Wu, J.: Sensor placement with multiple objectives for structural health monitoring. ACM Trans. Sens. Netw. (TOSN) **10**, 68 (2014)
3. Bondorf, S., Schmitt, J.B.: Boosting sensor network calculus by thoroughly bounding cross-traffic. In: 2015 IEEE Conference on Computer Communications (INFOCOM), pp. 235–243 (2015)
4. Buragohain, C.: Distributed navigation algorithms for sensor networks. In: 25th IEEE International Conference on Computer Communications (2006). https://doi.org/10.1109/INFOCOM.2006.191
5. Cheng, S., Cai, Z., Li, J., Gao, H.: Extracting kernel dataset from big sensory data in wireless sensor networks. IEEE Trans. Knowl. Data Eng. **29**, 813–827 (2017)
6. Giachetti, A., Campani, M., Torre, V.: The use of optical flow for road navigation. IEEE Trans. Robot. Autom. **14**, 34–48 (1998)
7. He, L., Yang, Z., Pan, J., Cai, L., Xu, J., Gu, Y.: Evaluating service disciplines foron-demand mobile data collectionin sensor networks. IEEE Trans. Mobile Comput. **13**, 797–810 (2014)
8. He, Z., Cai, Z., Yu, J., Wang, X., Sun, Y., Li, Y.: Cost-efficient strategies for restraining rumor spreading in mobile social networks. IEEE Trans. Veh. Technol. **66**, 2789–2800 (2017)
9. Gao, H., Zhang, X., Lifeng, A., Yuchao, L., Deyi, L.: Relay navigation strategy study on intelligent drive on urban roads. J. China Univ. Posts Telecommun. **23**, 79–90 (2016)
10. Hussein, A., Marín-Plaza, P., Martín, D., de la Escalera, A., Armingol, J.M.: Autonomous off-road navigation using stereo-vision and laser-rangefinder fusion for outdoor obstacles detection. In: 2016 IEEE Intelligent Vehicles Symposium (IV), pp. 104–109 (2016)
11. Li, M., Yang, Z., Liu, Y.: Sea depth measurement with restricted floating sensors. ACM Trans. Embed. Comput. Syst. (TECS) **13**, 1 (2013)
12. Lin, S., Zhou, G., Al-Hami, M., Whitehouse, K., Wu, Y., Stankovic, J.A., He, T., Wu, X., Liu, H.: Toward stable network performance in wireless sensor networks: a multilevel perspective. ACM Trans. Sens. Netw. (TOSN) **11**, 42 (2015)

13. Liu, Y., Lu, Y., Shi, Q., Ding, J.: Optical flow based urban road vehicle tracking. In: 2013 9th International Conference on Computational Intelligence and Security (CIS), pp. 391–395 (2013)

14. Liu, Y., Mao, X., He, Y., Liu, K., Gong, W., Wang, J.: Citysee: not only a wireless sensor network. IEEE Network **27**, 42–47 (2013)

15. Qiu, T., Zhang, Y., Qiao, D., Zhang, X., Wymore, M.L., Sangaiah, A.K.: A robust time synchronization scheme for industrial internet of things. IEEE Trans. Industr. Inf. (2017). https://doi.org/10.1109/TII.2017.2738842

16. Qiu, T., Zhao, A., Xia, F., Si, W., Wu, D.O.: ROSE: robustness strategy for scale-free wireless sensor networks. IEEE/ACM Trans. Netw. **25**(5), 2944–2959 (2017)

17. Qiu, T., Zheng, K., Han, M., Chen, C.L.P., Xu, M.: A data-emergency-aware scheduling scheme for internet of things in smart cities. IEEE Trans. Industr. Inf. (2017). https://doi.org/10.1109/TII.2017.2763971

18. Wang, C., Lin, H., Jiang, H.: Cans: towards congestion-adaptive and small stretch emergency navigation with wireless sensor networks. IEEE Trans. Mobile Comput. **15**, 1077–1089 (2016)

19. Wang, C., Lin, H., Zhang, R., Jiang, H.: Send: a situation-aware emergency navigation algorithm with sensor networks. IEEE Trans. Mobile Comput. **16**, 1149–1162 (2017)

20. Wang, L., He, Y., Liu, W., Jing, N.: On oscillation-free emergency navigation via wireless sensor networks. IEEE Trans. Mobile Comput. **14**, 2086–2100 (2015)

21. Wang, Y., Dong, Q.: Using optical flow with principal divection screen strategy for road navigation. In: 2016 9th International Symposium on Computational Intelligence and Design, vol. 2, pp. 52–55 (2016)

22. Yang, Z., Jian, L., Wu, C., Liu, Y.: Beyond triangle inequality: sifting noisy and outlier distance measurements for localization. ACM Trans. Sens. Netw. (TOSN) **9**, 26 (2013)

23. Zeng, K., Shu, Y., Liu, S.: A practical GPS location spoofing attack in road navigation scenario. In: Proceedings of the 18th International Workshop on Mobile Computing Systems and Applications, pp. 85–90 (2017)

24. Li, Z., Qian, C., Zun, G., Choi, Y.: A low latency, energy efficient MAC protocol for wireless sensor networks. Int. J. Distrib. Sens. Netw. (2015). https://doi.org/10.1155/2015/946587

25. Zheng, X., Cai, Z., Li, J., Gao, H.: A study on application-aware scheduling in wireless networks. IEEE Trans. Mobile Comput. **16**, 1787–1801 (2017)

26. Xiao, F., Wang, Z., Ye, N., Wang, R., Li, X.: One more tag enables fingrained RFID localization and tracking. IEEE/ACM Trans. Netw. **26**, 161–174 (2017). https://doi.org/10.1109/TNET.2017.2766526

Handoff Prediction for Femtocell Network in Indoor Environment Using Hidden Markov Model

Pengbo Yang, Xi Li$^{(\boxtimes)}$, Hong Ji, and Heli Zhang

Key Laboratory of Universal Wireless Communications, Ministry of Education,
Beijing University of Posts and Telecommunications,
Beijing, People's Republic of China
{yangpengboo,lixi,jihong,zhangheli}@bupt.edu.cn

Abstract. With the explosive growth of indoor data traffic, the indoor communication performance has become a popular research area in the future wireless network. Femtocells have been deployed to improve the network capacity and coverage in indoor environment. The complex building topology and user behavior may result in frequent handover and transmission interruption. Thus, we propose a mobility prediction scheme to optimize the handoff process in indoor environment using Hidden Markov Model (HMM). In this scheme, we set up the prediction model to find the optimized handoff Femtocell Access Point (FAP). A typical case of office scenario is studied as example. Considering the user behaviors, we divide the whole prediction time into several periods according to the working schedule and study the movement characteristics in each period. With the complex building topology, we generate all possible trajectories and predict the user's movement paths in these trajectories to improve the prediction accuracy. With the wall penetration loss influence, we revise the probability of connecting to FAP at the positions where have walls between FAP and connecting point. Eventually, we propose a mobility prediction scheme using HMM to forecast the next optimized handoff FAP. Simulation results show that the proposed scheme achieves a better performance compared with exiting schemes in terms of the handoff numbers and dwell time.

Keywords: Handoff prediction · Indoor environment · Femtocell
Hidden markov model

1 Introduction

With the explosive growth of mobile data traffic, it is predicted that mobile data traffic will be 49 exabytes per month by 2021, and most of them emerge at indoor environment [1–3]. It has become an important and interesting research area in future wireless network. The tradition cellular network has the bandwidth limitation and coverage issues in indoor environment. Therefore, femtocells have been proposed as a key solution to meet indoor users' requirements for providing a large variety of applications with better quality of service (QoS) [4]. Due to its short transmit-receive distance, femtocells can greatly lower transmit power and achieve a higher SINR. But with the short range coverage, there are many handoffs occured when user moves from the coverage of one Femtocell Access Point (FAP) to another. For optimizing the handoff process, researchers have paid great deal of attentions to the handoff optimization problem.

In indoor environment, unplanned deployment of femtocells usually suffers abrupt signal drop due to multi-path propagation, wall penetration loss, and shadowing. Unnecessary handoffs and ping-pong effects may happen frequently [5]. One of the effective solution is to predict the indoor users' accurate movement trajectories and the dwell time to find the next optimized FAP, which can reduce the unnecessary handoff numbers to provide the users with consistent service and high performance. However, the complex building topology and flexible user behavior make it difficult to accurately predict the movement.

In tradition cellular network, existing works mainly focus on speed and direction of the users to predict the paths. In [6], the authors propose a speed and service-sensitive handoff algorithm. It predicts the speed of mobile stations using Gauss-Markov mobility model to reduce unnecessary handoff for hierarchical cellular networks. In heterogeneous network, researchers have paid attention on handoff between macrocell and femtocell. In [5], the authors propose a self-adaptive handoff decision algorithm to address the issues of both macro-to-femto and femto-to-macro handoff. It is based on the user location history to assist the handoff decision-making. In indoor environment, the authors in [7] have used a standard markov chain model to predict the next location. But its prediction system is limited to the current state and current action to determine the next state, so the performance will degrade with increasing random movement. The authors in [8] propose a handoff framework using Hidden Markov Model (HMM), which adopts current and historical movement information of the users to predict the next location. However, the authors ignore the effect of time factors on the moving trajectory and use the random Way Point Mobility. It will not be suitable for indoor environment where users usually move along corridors. The authors in [9] propose a HMM based-tracking algorithm to accurately estimate the user's movement trajectory. The algorithm assumes that users move just along straight-line or circular path, which cannot reflect a real user movement behavior. Based on the discussion above, we note that existing works mainly use random way point model to predict the movement trajectory. But the complex building topology and user behavior will influence the user paths in indoor environment, so we consider the effect of space-time factors on the moving trajectory to improve the prediction accuracy.

In this paper, we focus on the user mobility prediction to optimize handoff process in indoor environment. The user behavior has different characteristics at different times and spaces. Taking the office environment as an example, we study the user movement. Then we propose a mobility prediction scheme based on users' behavior and movement information to optimize the handoff scheme

(MPOHS). In this scheme, we take the building topology and user behavior characteristics into account and divide the prediction time into several periods, according to the working schedule. In each period, we compute the state transition probability for accurate prediction. Then, we generate all possible trajectories to avoid non-existent predicted paths. And we divide the whole coverage area into grids to compute the connect probability to the FAP. Eventually, we propose the prediction scheme using HMM to forecast the optimized handoff FAP based on the history of the users' movement information. The proposed scheme is compared with existing schemes by simulation. The obtained results show that our scheme has a better performance in the terms of the handoff numbers and dwell time.

The rest of this paper is organized as follows. Section 2 describes the system scenario. In Sect. 3, we propose our handoff prediction scheme using HMM and compute the two probability matrixes. In Sect. 4, we give a detail description of our mobility prediction model to optimize the handoff process. Section 5 presents the simulation results and analysis, and Sect. 6 concludes our work.

2   System Description

We consider an indoor environment deployed with a set of N femtocells designated by F_i as depicted in Fig. 1 [10]. We divide the area into 2D-grid and each femtocell is installed in the center point of the grid, ensuring the signal can cover the whole area. At the initial state, the UEs are connected to one of the FAPs F_i. We can get the location of the UE at time t while it moving from one place to another by the localization system as a coordinate(x(t), y(t)). The handoff

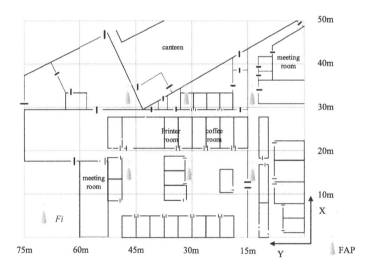

Fig. 1. Indoor environment map

occurs when UE moves from one area covered by F_i to another area covered by F_j during a communication.

Our purpose is to predict the optimized next FAP according to the previous and current positions of the UE. We can only observe the UE's position and have no information of which FAP the UE is connected to. Hence, we use the HMM as the most appropriate tool to solve the problem. We assume that all FAPs in the area are open access mode and have enough resource in the next FAP to confirm the handoff execution. In following section, we propose a scheme to predict the optimized next FAP using HMM.

3   Handoff Module Based on User Mobility Prediction

3.1   Hidden Markov Model

In this section, we give a brief overview of the HMM [11] and the method we used to solve the problem of handoff prediction. The HMM consists of a finite set of states (hidden variables), a sequence of emissions (observable variables), a finite set of state transition probabilities and a set of emission probabilities. In this model, the sequence of state transitions are hidden and can be only estimated through the sequence of emitted symbols. We can define the HMM as follows:

$S = \{S_1, S_2, S_3, ..., S_N\}$ is the set of hidden states in the system. Each state S_i represents a F_i which deployed at the center point of the grid.

$O = \{O_1, O_2, O_3, ..., O_T\}$ are the values of the observed sequences which defines the users' movement history.

$A = \{a_{i,j}\}$ are the state transition probabilities where $a_{i,j}$ denotes the probability of moving from state i to j.

$B = \{b_{ik}\}$ are the observation state probabilities where b_{ik} is the probability of emitting symbol O_k at state i.

$\Pi = \{\pi_i\}$ are the initial state probabilities where π_i indicates the probability of starting at state S_i.

For ease of use, this model is denoted as $\lambda = (\Pi, A, B)$.

3.2   State Transition Probability Distribution

The matrix A consists of the state transition probabilities, where $A = \{a_{i,j}\}$ is defined in above.

$$a_{i,j} = P(t_k == S_j | t_{k-1} == S_i) \tag{1}$$

where $a_{i,j}$ denotes the probability that the UE moving from the state S_i to the state S_j at next time slot. The indoor scenario is shown in Fig. 1. There are some popular areas such as coffee room, meeting room, printer room and canteen. The users' movement shows regularity according to the working schedule along the whole day. We assume that meeting usually takes place in the morning, the users move to canteen at noon, there will be another meeting takes place in the afternoon, and some other activities take place according to the schedule. The state transition probabilities will change at different time. So we divide the whole day into five periods, computing the matrix A at each period, as shown in Table 1. The division is suitable for most indoor office scenario. So we process the handoff prediction at different period using the appropriate matrix to improve the prediction accuracy.

Table 1. The state transition probability at each period

Period	Time interval	State transition probability matrix
t1	8:00–11:30	A1
t2	11:30–14:00	A2
t3	14:00–17:30	A3
t4	17:30–20:00	A4
t5	20:00–22:30	A5

3.3   Observation Probability Distribution

The matrix B consists of the observation probabilities, where $B = \{b_{ik}\}$ is defined in above.

$$b_{ik} = P(O_k | t_k == S_i) \tag{2}$$

where b_{ik} denotes the probability that the UE at geographical position O_k is connected to the FAP F_i, in state S_i at time t_k. The signal strength received by the UE changes according to the distance from observation to FAP. We divide the area covered by the FAP into grids, each grid represents an observation position. The authors in [8] distinguish the cover area into four signal level areas: high signal level area, medium signal level area, low signal level area and out of coverage area. It is reasonable and simple for calculating the observation probability. We refer to this coverage division idea.

It is important to notice that in indoor scenario, there are walls and other obstacles in the coverage area. The observation probability changes at different observations that belongs to the same signal level area. So we adjust the special positions observation probabilities to make it more accurate. As depicted in Fig. 2, the observation O_i and O_j belongs to Low signal level area, but there is a wall between O_i and FAP F_i, so the signal strength received at O_j is stronger than that at O_i. For that the grids we divide is small, so we assume that the walls only appear at the medium signal level area and low signal level area.

$$P_{O_k \epsilon M_{wb}} = b_{ik} \cdot \alpha \quad (0 < \alpha < 1) \tag{3}$$

$$P_{O_k \epsilon L_{wb}} = b_{ik} \cdot \beta \quad (0 < \beta < 1) \tag{4}$$

In (3) $P_{O_k \epsilon M_{wb}}$ denotes the probability connect to the FAP at the medium signal level area behind the wall. The parameter α is the coefficient to adjust the walls' influence. The same definition in (4) denotes the probability connect

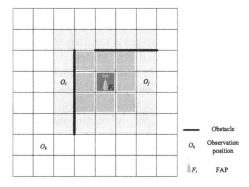

Fig. 2. The coverage of FAP and obstacle in the area

to the FAP at the low signal level area behind the wall, and the parameter β is the coefficient to adjust the walls' influence.

Now, we define all the parameters of the prediction system, the state transition probability matrix A, the observation probability matrix B, and the observation sequence of UE O. It is worth to notice that HMM can provide solution to three different problems [11]: calculating observation probability from observation sequence, decoding state sequence from observation sequence and adjustment of the HMM model to maximize the probability of the observation sequence. Our purpose is to select the optimized FAP, which we use the observation sequence of UE and the two matrixes we define in above to get the optimal state. Our problem is suitable to use the second scheme of HMM solutions, which decoding the most likely state sequence according to our observation sequence. The problem can be solved using the Viterbi algorithm.

4   Optimizing Handoff Based on Mobility Prediction Scheme

In this section, we introduce our mobility prediction based on users' behavior and movement information to optimize the handoff scheme (MPOHS). Our scheme predicts the user's next position based on the history movement information, combined with the indoor signal strength distribution to decide which optimized FAP to connect, to reduce the unnecessary handoff numbers. The MPOHS contains three major steps: initialization phase, prediction phase and handoff decision phase. In the initialization phase, we compute the two probability matrixes based on the training data. When a user comes to the coverage area, the prediction phase is activated to predict the user's next position. With the obtained prediction position, we can decide which FAP to connect in handoff decision phase.

4.1 Initialization Phase

The initialization phase is used to generate the state transition probability matrix A and the observation probability matrix B. In this phase, we generate the indoor scenario paths to train the users' movement trajectory according to the working schedule as defined in Table 1. In each period, we calculate the matrix A_i using (1), so we can acquire the needed five state transition probability matrixes. To calculate the observation probability matrix B, first we determine the values at signal level area where have no walls between FAP. Then we calculate the values at the signal level area behind the walls according to (2). Now we have the two probability matrixes and combine the history of users' movement information to predict the user's next movement position.

4.2 Prediction Phase

The prediction phase is activated at the time when a user comes to the coverage area, we add the current position to observation sequence. We calculate all the next possible position probabilities based on the two probability matrixes and the user's observation sequence using Viterbi algorithm. Then, we choose the maximum probability of all the next positions and output the position as the predict one.

4.3 Handoff Decision Phase

The handoff decision phase is used to decide which FAP to connect when we get the predict next position, we choose the optimized handoff FAP according to the observation probability matrix, which contains all position probabilities connect to the neighbor FAPs. If the predict optimized handoff FAP is the same with current connecting FAP, the user will still connect to the current FAP and go back to prediction phase. Otherwise, we execute the handoff process and handoff to the optimized FAP and then go back to prediction phase. The detail steps about our scheme is described at Algorithm 1.

5 Simulation Results and Discussions

In this section, we evaluate the performance of our handoff prediction scheme using HMM. We first describe the simulation scenario. Then we get the value of coefficient α and β through the simulation. We compare the benefits of our Scheme (MPOHS) with the OHMP [10] and Handoff to Nearest-neighbor Femtocell (HNF). The OHMP scheme optimizes handoff using HMM. It uses the random Way Point Mobility and ignores the walls' influence in the observation area. The HNF scheme chooses the nearest FAP to connect without any prediction procedures. We run multiple simulations and calculate the mean value of performance metrics.

Algorithm 1. Mobility Prediction to Optimize the Handoff Scheme(MPOHS)

1: Input:
 the transition probabilty matrix A=$\{A_1, A_2, A_3, A_4, A_5\}$
 the observation probability matrix B
 the current trajectory of the user,
 P=$< (O_1, t_1), (O_2, t_2), ...(O_k, t_k), ...(O_i, t_i) >$
 the current state FAP F_i
2: Output: predicted handoff FAP F_j
3: **for** $t = t_1, \cdots, t_i$ **do**
4:    choose matrix $A_i \epsilon A$
5: **end for**
6: T=1
7: **while** user is still in area **do**
8:    F_j=hmmviterbi(P,A,B)
9:    **if** $F_i == F_j$ **then**
10:       continue
11:    **else**
12:       handoff to F_j
13:    **end if**
14:    T=T+1
15: **end while**

5.1   Simulation Scenario

In our simulation scenario as depicted in Fig. 1, the FAPs are distributed in this 50 m * 70 m area. The users' movement in this scenario during the whole day is simulated. They move along the corridor from one position to the other with velocity that varied from 0.2 m/s to 1m/s. There are distributed 6 FAPs that has a transmission range of 15 m. In our mobility prediction scheme, we consider the walls influence. We compare the Received Signal Strength(RSS) in low signal level area and medium signal level area where behind the walls according to the RSS trace file [9]. We set the α to be 0.2 and the β to be 0.5

5.2   The Performance of Handoff

The handoff happens when the user moves from one FAP F_i area to the other FAP F_j area. We evaluate the handoff numbers in different periods according to the work schedule. Figure 3 shows that the handoff numbers increase when time goes on. Our handoff prediction scheme handoff numbers are less than the other two schemes, which we can find that our scheme average handoff number is 15, compared to 18 for OHMP and 27 for HNF. The handoff numbers increase with time goes on and our prediction scheme always has less handoff numbers. Figure 4 shows that the average handoff number in each period, and all the five periods show that our scheme is better than the other two scheme on handoff numbers. So that we can conclude that our prediction scheme reduces more unnecessary handoffs compared to OHMP and HNF. For that we consider the walls influence in indoor environment and the users' movement behavior along the whole day, it could get more accurate prediction information about the users' communication environment compared to OHMP, and more geographic position information to HNF. So we can get the optimized next handoff FAP, which can help to reduce the unnecessary handoffs.

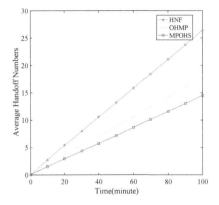

Fig. 3. Average handoff numbers

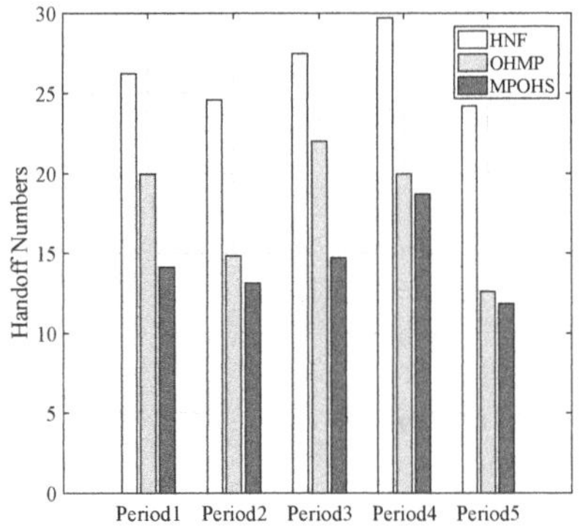

Fig. 4. Average handoff numbers in each period

5.3   The Performance of Dwell Time

The dwell time represents the amount time that user stays in a cell, where in this paper it means that user stays at the same FAP coverage area at continuous time slots. Figure 5 shows the dwell time at different period. It's obvious that our handoff prediction scheme enhance the dwell time compared to the other two schemes. At period 1 and 3, our scheme enhances the dwell time to 52.4%

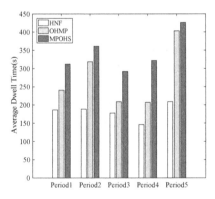

Fig. 5. Average dwell time

and 64.2% compared to HNF, and enhances the dwell time to 29.9% and 40.5% compared to OHMP. At period 2 and 4, our scheme enhances the dwell time to 173 s and 176 s compared to HNF, and enhances the dwell time to 43 s and 115 s compared to OHMP. At period 5, the dwell time is longer than the other periods, and our scheme enhances the dwell time to 217 s to HNF and 22 s to OHMP. We can conclude that our prediction scheme enhance the dwell time compared to the other two schemes. For that our scheme can have a good prediction of the user's movement and reduce unnecessary handoff, so it can enhance the time that users stay in the same coverage area.

6   Conclusion

In this paper, we propose a handoff prediction scheme using HMM. The HMM models FAP position as hidden states and the user's position as observation states. We consider the user's behavior along the whole day and compute five state transition probability matrixes at different period. Furthermore, we consider the walls influence at different signal level area and computing the observation probability matrix B. Then we use the users' movement information to predict the optimized FAP. The simulation results show that our prediction scheme has a better performance compared to HNF and OHMP, which reduces unnecessary handoff numbers and enhances the dwell time.

Acknowledgement. This paper is jointly sponsored by the National Natural Science Foundation of China for the Youth (Grant No.61501047) and the National Natural Science Foundation of China (Grant No.61671088).

References

1. Wen, J., Li, V.O.K.: Big-data-enabled software-defined cellular network management. In: 2016 International Conference on Software Networking (ICSN), pp. 1–5, May 2016
2. CISCO: Cisco visual networking index: Global mobile data traffic forecast update, 2016–2021, February 2017. http://www.cisco.com/c/en/us/solutions/collateral/service-provider/visual-networking-index-vni/mobile-white-paper-c11-520862.html
3. Chen, L., Yu, F.R., Ji, H., Liu, G., Leung, V.C.M.: Distributed virtual resource allocation in small-cell networks with full-duplex self-backhauls and virtualization. IEEE Trans. Veh. Technol. **65**(7), 5410–5423 (2016)
4. Knisely, D.N., Yoshizawa, T., Favichia, F.: Standardization of femtocells in 3GPP. IEEE Commun. Mag. **47**(9), 68–75 (2009)
5. Nasrin, W., Xie, J.: A self-adaptive handoff decision algorithm for densely deployed closed-group femtocell networks. In: 2015 12th Annual IEEE International Conference on Sensing, Communication, and Networking (SECON), pp. 390–398, June 2015
6. Zhu, X., Li, M., Xia, W., Zhu, H.: A novel handoff algorithm for hierarchical cellular networks. China Commun. **13**(8), 136–147 (2016)

7. Liu, G., Maguire Jr., G.: A class of mobile motion prediction algorithms for wireless mobile computing and communications. Mobile Netw. Appl. **1**(2), 113–121 (1996)
8. Cheikh, A.B., Ayari, M., Langar, R., Pujolle, G., Saidane, L.A.: Optimized handoff with mobility prediction scheme using HMM for femtocell networks. In: 2015 IEEE International Conference on Communications (ICC), pp. 3448–3453, June 2015
9. Laursen, T., Pedersen, N.B., Nielsen, J.J., Madsen, T.K.: Hidden Markov model based mobility learning fo improving indoor tracking of mobile users. In: 2012 9th Workshop on Positioning, Navigation and Communication, pp. 100–104, March 2012
10. Bauer, K., Anderson, E.W., McCoy, D., Grunwald, D., Sicker, D.C.: Crawdad dataset cu/rssi, May 2009. http://crawdad.org/cu/rssi/20090528
11. Rabiner, L., Juang, B.: An introduction to hidden Markov models. IEEE ASSP Mag. **3**(1), 4–16 (1986)

Self-organized Resource Allocation Based on Traffic Prediction for Load Imbalance in HetNets with NOMA

Jichen Jiang, Xi Li$^{(\boxtimes)}$, Hong Ji, and Heli Zhang

Key Laboratory of Universal Wireless Communications, Ministry of Education,
Beijing University of Posts and Telecommunications,
Beijing, People's Republic of China
{jiangjichen,lixi,jihong,zhangheli}@bupt.edu.cn

Abstract. With the development of mobile communication technology, the data traffic of wireless cellular network has grown rapidly in the past decade. Because of the various bandwidth-eager applications and users movement, load imbalance has become an increasing severe problem, impacting the user experience and communication efficiency. Especially, it may lead to the degrading of resource utilization and network performance. In this paper, we investigate this problem and propose a self-organized resource allocation algorithm that allocates the resource to somewhere that the resource is needed to deal with the load imbalance problem. The typical heterogeneous network with non-orthogonal multiple access (NOMA) is discussed. A traffic prediction model is applied to the NOMA system. Then the self-organized resource allocation is formulated as a mixed integer non-linear programming (MINP) problem aiming at maximizing the overall throughput. The optimization problem is hard to tackle so we propose an algorithm to obtain a suboptimal solution via quantum-behaved particle swarm optimization (QPSO) algorithm. To evaluate how the resource is allocated according to the data traffic requirements, an indicator called evolved balance factor (EBF) is proposed to jointly consider the resource utility and the distribution of data traffic. Simulation results show that the proposed algorithm achieves a better performance in the overall throughput compared with exiting schemes.

Keywords: Self-organized · Resource allocation · Traffic prediction
NOMA · Load imbalance

1 Introduction

As the mobile devices drastically increased over the past several years, the mobile data volume is experiencing an exponential growth. This growth not only increases the load pressure of the network, but also impacts resource utility. In order to face the challenge of providing higher data rate speed and system capacity, heterogeneous network with small cells and non-orthogonal multiple access

© ICST Institute for Computer Sciences, Social Informatics and Telecommunications Engineering 2018
L. Wang et al. (Eds.): QShine 2017, LNICST 234, pp. 55–65, 2018.
https://doi.org/10.1007/978-3-319-78078-8_6

(NOMA) technology are considered as the promising solutions to meet the users requirements and spectral efficiency [1–4]. In the NOMA-based heterogeneous networks (HetNets), due to the various bandwidth-eager applications and users movement, load imbalance is an important problem and may degrade the network performance obviously. Especially, the resource utility may be impacted. On one hand, the overall resource is short of use due to the rapidly increased throughput requirement; on the other hand, the traditional fixed resource allocation methods may result in low utility in local area. Therefore, how to allocate the resource properly according to the load imbalance condition is an interesting and necessary problem to investigate.

Resource allocation in NOMA and HetNets have many existing research results. Reference [1] proposes an optimal power allocation algorithm and an efficient user selection scheme for downlink NOMA system. The problem is formulated as an optimization problem that maximizes the weighted sum rate subjected to a power constraint and the algorithm is proved to be highly efficient through numeral results. Reference [5] provides an user paring and power allocation scheme in the 2-user NOMA system based on proportional fairness in which the proportional fairness is adopted as a key point to make tradeoff between transmission efficiency and user fairness. Reference [6] gives a complexity analysis on NOMA resource allocation and then provide an effective algorithm for multi-user power and channel allocation in NOMA system and propose a suboptimal solution combining Lagrangian duality and dynamic programming.

Load imbalance has attracted the researchers' attention with existing work, such as the handover to neighbor cells, traffic scheduling and base station turning on/off [7–9]. Traffic prediction is another effective method, based on which further steps could be carried out to deal with the possible load imbalance condition. Reference [10] proposes a resource allocation scheme that pre-download the files requested by users according to the user trajectory prediction procedure to minimize the maximal transmission completion time. Reference [11] proposes a predictive energy-aware network selection and resource allocation algorithm in which a tradeoff between power consumption and traffic delay is achieved. Reference [12] provides an AP access scheme for multiple APs in user-centric ultra dense networks in which the access rules highlight the QoS of users and the system EE and a grouping evaluation model is set up based on several network performance indicators.

As to the load imbalance in NOMA-based HetNets with small base stations (SBSs), it is just the beginning in the relative research fields. In this paper, we solve the problem by traffic prediction and then scheduling the resource accordingly. A self-organized resource allocation algorithm based on traffic prediction (SORA-TP) is proposed to allocate the resource to somewhere that the resource is needed to deal with the load imbalance problem. The traffic demand is predicted by minimum mean square error (MMSE) model which is suitable for online traffic prediction due to its simple and fast feature. Then SBSs can use the results of prediction to allocate the resource automatically aiming at maximizing the overall throughput. In order to evaluate the performance of the algorithm, an indicator called evolved balance factor (EBF) is derived which indicates how the resource is allocated with the predicted data traffic. Then we formulate this problem as a mixed integer non-linear programming (MINP) problem and solve it by quantum-behaved particle swarm optimization (QPSO) [13] algorithm. Simulation results reveal that the performance of the proposed algorithm outperforms the existing algorithms.

The rest of this paper is organized as follows. In Sect. 2, the system model and the studied scenario are introduced. Section 3 presents the problem formulation and describes the proposed self-organized resource allocation algorithm, followed by simulation results in Sect. 4. Section 5 concludes our work.

2   System Model

2.1   NOMA-Based HetNet

We consider a downlink two-tier HetNet with NOMA where several users are randomly distributed in each cell, as shown in Fig. 1. The user set is denoted as $\mathcal{K}$, $\mathcal{K} = \{1, 2, \cdots, K\}$. Total bandwidth is W and is divided into N resource blocks (RB). The RB set is defined as $\mathcal{N} = \{1, 2, \cdots, N\}$, each with bandwidth B, $B = W/N$. The set of SBSs is defined as $\mathcal{J}$, $\mathcal{J} = \{1, 2, \cdots, J\}$. Factor g_{kj}^n is used to describe the channel gain between user k and SBS j on RB n. We assume that the SBS allocates the power to all RBs equally but each users are assigned with different power which is denoted as p_{kj}^n. Single antenna is used for both transmission and reception. Thus the received signal for user k with SBS j in n-th RB is given as

$$y_{kj}^n = \sqrt{p_{kj}^n} g_{kj}^n \xi_{kj}^n + \sum_{i=n+1}^{N} \xi_{ij}^n \sqrt{p_{ij}^n} g_{kj}^n + w_{kj}^n \tag{1}$$

where w_{kj}^n is the noise, ξ_{kj}^n is an indicator that describes the relationship between user k with SBS j RB n which is defined as

$$\xi_{kj}^n = \begin{cases} 1 & \text{user } k \text{ is served by SBS } j \text{ in RB } n \\ 0 & \text{otherwise} \end{cases}$$

In downlink NOMA, successive interference cancellation (SIC) is applied in user receivers. Users with better channel quality employ SIC to remove the inference from other users that have lower CQIs. For example, in Fig. 1, user 1 has better channel quality and the channel quality of user 2 is lower. So SIC receiver has to be used on user 2 to remove the interference from the transmission to user 2 while user 1 can decode the signal directly without SIC. We assume that users are defined in the descending order of signal-to-interference-plus-noise ratio (SINR) as $\gamma_1 \geq \gamma_2 \geq \gamma_3 \geq \cdots \geq \gamma_n \geq \gamma_{n+1} \geq \cdots \geq \gamma_N$. So user k can successfully decode the signal of user l if $\gamma_k > \gamma_l$. So the post-processing SINR for user

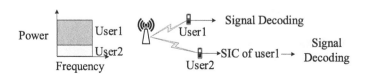

Fig. 1. System model of the studied network with NOMA

k with SBS j in RB n is denoted as

$$\gamma_{kj}^n = \frac{p_{kj}^n g_{kj}^n}{\sum\limits_{i=n+1}^{N} p_{ij}^n g_{kj}^n + 1} \tag{2}$$

Assuming the signal is successfully decoded at user receiver and no error propagation occurs, the data rate for user k with SBS j in RB n can be written as

$$R_{kj}^n = B \log(1 + \gamma_{kj}^n) \tag{3}$$

2.2 Prediction Model with MMSE

Minimum Mean Square Error (MMSE) predictor is a simple and fast traffic prediction model in both theory and practice, which is suitable for the real time application and dynamic network environment [14]. The mathematical description of MMSE is shown as:

$$D_{t+1} = w_n D_t + \cdots + w_1 D_{t-n+1} + N_t \tag{4}$$

where n is the order of regression and N_t is white noise.

$\{D_t\}$ denotes a random linear process and D_{t+1} can be described with a linear combination of current and previous value of $\{D_t\}$. $\widehat{W}$ is a factor that describes the estimated weight vector, therefore the above equation can be changed to

$$\widehat{D}_{t+1} = \widehat{W} D' + N_t \tag{5}$$

where $\widehat{D}_{t+1}$ is the predicted value of D_{t+1}.

The expected value of squared errors is given by

$$E[e_t^2] = E[(D_{t+1} - \widehat{D}_{t+1})^2] \tag{6}$$

By minimizing the expected squared errors, the weight vector can be derived as

$$\widehat{W} = \Gamma G^{-1} \tag{7}$$

where G is the auto correlation matrix and Γ is an autocorrelation vector as given by

$$G = \begin{bmatrix} \rho_0 & \rho_1 & \cdots & \rho_{n-1} \\ \rho_1 & \rho_0 & \cdots & \rho_{n-2} \\ \vdots & \vdots & \ddots & \vdots \\ \rho_{n-1} & \rho_{n-2} & \cdots & \rho_0 \end{bmatrix} \tag{8}$$

$$\Gamma = \begin{bmatrix} \rho_n \cdots \rho_1 \end{bmatrix} \tag{9}$$

Autocorrelations ρ_k can be obtained by

$$\rho_k = \frac{\sum\limits_{t=1}^{n-k}(D_t - \overline{D})(D_{t+k} - \overline{D})}{\sum\limits_{t=1}^{n}(D_t - \overline{D})^2} \tag{10}$$

3   Problem Formulation and Algorithm Design

3.1   Traffic Prediction

In this subsection, we introduce the traffic prediction procedure with MMSE as mentioned above. The data traffic of each SBS at each time t is recorded as the input of our MMSE traffic prediction model. Then the mean value of the input sequence is calculated and so as the autocorrelation of the sequence. According to the autocorrelation matrix, the next-time traffic can be estimated. The predicting traffic value of SBS_j is $\widehat{D}_{j,t+1}$ which is given by

$$\widehat{D}_{j,t+1} = \widehat{w}_j D_{j,t} + \cdots + \widehat{w}_1 D_{j,t-n+1} + N_t \tag{11}$$

The computing procedure is summarized in Algorithm 1.

3.2   Self-organized Resource Allocation Algorithm

To cope with the imbalance problem of resource allocation in NOMA system and low resource utility problem brought by fixed allocation, we propose a self-organized resource allocation algorithm in which the network resource is allocated automatically according to the traffic load predicted by the prediction

---

Algorithm 1. Traffic Prediction Based on MMSE

1: Initialization:
   a)$D_{j,t}$ describes the current traffic of SBS_j and $D_{j,t-1}, D_{j,t-2}, \cdots, D_{j,t-n+1}$ denotes previous observation of traffic on SBS_j
   b)$\{D_j\} = \{D_{j,t}, D_{j,t-1}, D_{j,t-2}, \cdots, D_{j,t-n+1}\}$ denotes the set of current and previous traffic
2: **for** $j = 1, 2, \cdots, J$ **do**
3:    Calculate the mean value $\overline{D}$ of $\{D_j\}$
4:    Calculate the autocorrelations ρ_k according to (10)
5:    Obtain the matrix G and Γ based on the calculated ρ_k
6:    Calculate $\widehat{W}$ according to (7)
7:    Obtain the estimated traffic $\widehat{D}_{j,t+1}$ of time $t+1$ according to (5)
8: **end for**

---

model. The overall data rate is taken as the maximization goal which can be formulated as follows:

$$\max \sum_{k,n,j} r_{kj}^n x_{kj}^n$$

$$s.t. \quad x_{kj}^n \in \{0,1\}, k \in \mathcal{K}, j \in \mathcal{J}, n \in \mathcal{N}$$

$$\sum_k p_{kj}^n < p_j^n, k \in \mathcal{K}, n \in \mathcal{N} \tag{12}$$

$$\sum_{i,n} r_{ij}^n > D_{j,t+1}, i \in \mathcal{I}, j \in \mathcal{J}, n \in \mathcal{N}$$

$$\sum_k \sum_n p_{kj}^n < p_{tot}, k \in \mathcal{K}, n \in \mathcal{N}$$

where p_n represents the power allocated to n-th RB, p_{tot} represents the total transmission power.

Note that problem (12) is a non-linear integer programming problem which is a NP-hard problem that can not be solved in linear time scale, so we can derive a suboptimal solution for problem via QPSO algorithm.

QPSO has three major parts consist of particle position, fitness function and evolution equation. The solution to our problem is the particle position which contains two parts, the RB allocation and the power allocation for each SBS. Assuming that there are P particles, and the position of the p particle is expressed as:

$$Q_p = (Q_{p,1}, \cdots, Q_{p,j}, \cdots, Q_{p,J}) \tag{13}$$

where, $Q_{p,j}$ denotes the result of the resource allocation for SBS_j, it can be written as:

$$Q_{p,j} = (x_{11}^j, \cdots, x_{KN}^j, p_{11}^j, \cdots, p_{KN}^j) \quad \forall j \in \mathcal{J} \tag{14}$$

where x_{kn}^j denotes that $user_k$ is connected with SBS_j on RB_n and p_{kn}^j is the corresponding transmission power.

The fitness function is derived from the formulated problem which is used to evaluate the performance of each particle. In this paper, the fitness function is the overall data rate of the system which is given as:

$$\mathbb{F}(x_{kn}^j, p_{kn}^j) = \sum_{k,n} r_{kn}^j x_{kn}^j \tag{15}$$

In QPSO, the evolution equation of particle p ($p = 1, \cdots, P$) is given as:

$$\begin{cases} \mathbf{Q}_p(m+1) = \mathbf{B}_p(m) + b|\mathbf{L}_{best}(m) - \mathbf{Q}_p(m)| \cdot ln(\frac{1}{u}) \\ \qquad\qquad \text{if } r \geq 0.5 \\ \mathbf{Q}_p(m+1) = \mathbf{B}_p(m) - b|\mathbf{L}_{best}(m) - \mathbf{Q}_p(m)| \cdot ln(\frac{1}{u}) \\ \qquad\qquad \text{if } r < 0.5 \end{cases} \tag{16}$$

where, m denotes the iteration time; b is the contraction-expansion coefficient, which can be used to control the algorithm convergence rate; u and r are both random variables between 0 and 1; and $\mathbf{L}_{best}(m)$ is the mean best position of all particles in the m iteration, which can be obtained by

$$\mathbf{L}_{best}(m) = \frac{1}{P} \sum_{p=1}^{P} \mathbf{B}_p^{pbest}(m) \tag{17}$$

where $\mathbf{B}_p^{pbest}(m)$ is the best position of the p-th particle in the m-th iteration. The $\mathbf{B}_p(m)$ in (16) is called local attractor of particle p in the m-th iteration, which can be given as:

$$\mathbf{B}_p(m) = \alpha \mathbf{B}_p^{pbest}(m) + (1 - \alpha)\mathbf{G}_{best}(m), \tag{18}$$

where α is a random variable varies from 0–1, and $\mathbf{G}_{best}(m)$ is the global best position of all particles in the m-th iteration. The detailed procedure of the proposed self-organized resource allocation algorithm based on traffic prediction (SORA-TP) is summarized in Algorithm 2.

3.3   Derivation of Evolved Balance Factor

Because the proposed algorithm illustrates a self-organized resource allocation method that automatically allocates the resource based on the result of traffic prediction, so more resource is allocated to the SBSs that have heavier traffic load as predicted. To evaluate this characteristic of the proposed algorithm, we take joint consideration of the overall data traffic distribution and the resource utility and derive the EBF as follows

$$\psi = \eta \lg \mathbb{F}(x_{kn}^j, p_{kn}^j) \tag{19}$$

where η denotes the spectrum utility which is given as follows:

$$\eta = \frac{\sum\limits_{k,n} r_{kn} x_{kn}}{W} \tag{20}$$

With the proposed factor, the performance of the algorithm can be evaluated efficiently.

Algorithm 2. SORA-TP Algorithm

1: Initialization:
   a)Set user number K, SBS number J, number of subcarriers N
   b)The maximum number of iterations M, number of particles P
   c)The position of each particle $\mathbf{P}_p(j)$, $j \in \mathcal{J}$, set of best position of each particle $\mathbf{B}_p^{pbest}(1) = \mathbf{Q}_p(1)$, and according to the fitness function choose a best position from $\mathbf{B}_p^{pbest}(1)$ as $\mathbf{G}_{best}$, $best_{fit} = \mathbb{F}(x(1), p(1))$
   d)Set the initial traffic value sequence $\{D_{j,t}\}$ for each SBS_j at time t
2: **for** $j = 1, 2, \cdots, J$ **do**
3:     Calculate $D_{j,t+1}$ according to (5)-(10)
4: **end for**
5: **for** $m = 1, \cdots, M$ **do**
6:     **for** $p = 1, \cdots, P$ **do**
7:         Calculate $\mathbf{L}_{best}(m)$ and $\mathbf{B}_p(m)$ according to (17) and (18), respectively
8:         Calculate $\mathbf{L}_{best}(m) - \mathbf{Q}_p(m)$, set random variable b, u, r
9:         **if** $r < 0.5$ **then**
10:            $\mathbf{Q}_p(m+1) = \mathbf{B}_p(m) - b|\mathbf{L}_{best}(m) - \mathbf{Q}_p(m)| \cdot ln(\frac{1}{u})$
11:        **else**
12:            $\mathbf{Q}_p(m+1) = \mathbf{B}_p(m) + b|\mathbf{L}_{best}(m) - \mathbf{Q}_p(m)| \cdot ln(\frac{1}{u})$
13:        **end if**
14:        Calculate the fitness function $\mathbb{F}(x_{kn}^j, p_{kn}^j)$ according to (15)
15:        **if** $best_{fit} < \mathbb{F}(x_{kn}^j, p_{kn}^j)$ **then**
16:            Update the $best_{fit}$ value to $\mathbb{F}(x_{kn}^j, p_{kn}^j)$, and $\mathbf{G}_{best}(m) = \mathbf{B}_p^{pbest}(m)$
17:        **else**
18:            $best_{fit} = best_{fit}$, $\mathbf{G}_{best}(m) = \mathbf{G}_{best}(m)$
19:        **end if**
20:    **end for**
21: **end for**
22: Output the $\mathbf{G}_{best}$, and obtain the resource allocation scheme according to the $\mathbf{G}_{best}$

---

4 Simulation Results and Discussions

In this section, simulation results are presented to illustrate the performance of the proposed algorithm. We consider a two-layer HetNet with 9 SBSs covered by one MBS. And there are 5 to 25 users randomly distributed in this area. System bandwidth is 4.5 MHz and subcarrier bandwidth is 180 kHz, accordingly. Inter site distance of SBSs is 40 m. Thermal noise is -174 dBm/Hz and the maximum transmit power is limited to 1 W. To express the simulation results better, we also run the simulation of the resource allocation algorithm without traffic prediction (RA-NOMA) and resource allocation algorithm with orthogonal multiple access (RA-OMA) as contrast.

Figure 2 compares the throughput performance of the above three algorithms with the number of users. With the increase in the number of users, overall throughput of the three algorithms increases as well, for the reason that data rate is brought by users. The proposed algorithm has higher throughput compared to the other two resource allocation schemes. The reason is that in our proposed algorithm, the resource is allocated to SBSs according to the results of traffic

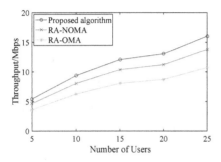

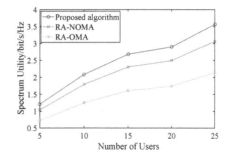

Fig. 2. Overall throughput versus the number of users

Fig. 3. Spectrum utility versus the number of users

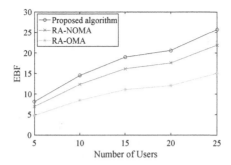

Fig. 4. EBF versus the number of users

prediction, so heavier the traffic load is, more resource will be allocated to the SBS. We can also see from the result that the throughput performance of RA-NOMA is better than RA-OMA. To explain, NOMA has higher resource utility than the orthogonal frequency division multiple access (OFDMA) and the SIC at the end of receiver can reduce the interference so SNR increased.

Figure 3 shows the curves of spectrum utility performance of different algorithms. The spectrum utility of the RA-OMA scheme is lowest because OFDMA system wastes some spectrum resources to avoid the interference. As the number of users increases, the spectrum utility becomes higher due to the increasing data rate brought by users. As for the proposed algorithm, the resources are allocated to where the traffic load is heavy, so the efficiency of resource utilization is higher than the comparison scheme.

Figure 4 describes the value of EBF with the number of users. The RA-OMA scheme has the worst EBF performance because neither the resource utility is efficient nor the throughput is high. It is noticeable that the EBF of the proposed algorithm is obviously higher than the other algorithm which denotes that the resource allocation in our proposed algorithm is adjusted automatically according to the distribution of data traffic load and achieves a better performance compared with other schemes.

5 Conclusion

In this paper, a resource allocation algorithm called SORA-TP in a two-tier HetNets with NOMA is proposed. To allocate the resource properly, a MMSE traffic prediction model is used which is appropriate for on-line traffic prediction. Then the resource allocation problem is formulated as a mixed integer non-linear programming (MINP) problem aiming at maximizing the overall throughput based on the prediction results. The optimization problem is difficult to solve in linear time scale so we propose an algorithm to obtain a suboptimal solution via QPSO algorithm. In order to illustrate the relationship between the predicted traffic and the allocated resource, a factor called EBF is derived which considers both resource utility and the overall throughput. The simulation results show that the proposed algorithm is efficient and outperforms the comparison schemes.

Acknowledgments. This paper is jointly sponsored by the National Natural Science Foundation of China (Grant No. 61671088) and the National Natural Science Foundation of China for the Youth (Grant No. 61501047).

References

1. Datta, S.N., Kalyanasundaram, S.: Optimal power allocation and user selection in non-orthogonal multiple access systems. In: 2016 IEEE Wireless Communications and Networking Conference, pp. 1–6, April 2016
2. Dai, L., Wang, B., Yuan, Y., Han, S., I, C., Wang, Z.: Non-orthogonal multiple access for 5G: solutions, challenges, opportunities, and future research trends. IEEE Commun. Mag. **53**(9), 74–81 (2015)
3. Wang, Y., Ren, B., Sun, S., Kang, S., Yue, X.: Analysis of non-orthogonal multiple access for 5G. China Commun. **13**(Supplement 2), 52–66 (2016)
4. Fang, F., Zhang, H., Cheng, J., Leung, V.C.M.: Energy-efficient resource allocation for downlink non-orthogonal multiple access network. IEEE Trans. Commun. **64**(9), 3722–3732 (2016)
5. Liu, F., Mahonen, P., Petrova, M.: Proportional fairness-based user pairing and power allocation for non-orthogonal multiple access. In: 2015 IEEE 26th Annual International Symposium on Personal, Indoor, and Mobile Radio Communications (PIMRC), pp. 1127–1131, August 2015
6. Lei, L., Yuan, D., Ho, C.K., Sun, S.: Joint optimization of power and channel allocation with non-orthogonal multiple access for 5G cellular systems. In: 2015 IEEE Global Communications Conference (GLOBECOM), pp. 1–6, December 2015
7. Hagos, D.H., Kapitza, R.: Study on performance-centric offload strategies for LTE networks. In: 6th Joint IFIP Wireless and Mobile Networking Conference (WMNC), pp. 1–10, April 2013
8. Zhang, S., Gong, J., Zhou, S., Niu, Z.: How many small cells can be turned off via vertical offloading under a separation architecture? IEEE Trans. Wireless Commun. **14**(10), 5440–5453 (2015)
9. Jin, Z., Pan, Z., Liu, N., Li, W., Wu, J., Deng, T.: Dynamic pico switch on/off algorithm for energy saving in heterogeneous networks. In: 2015 IEEE 81st Vehicular Technology Conference (VTC Spring), pp. 1–5, May 2015

10. Yao, C., Guo, J., Yang, C.: Achieving high throughput with predictive resource allocation. In: 2016 IEEE Global Conference on Signal and Information Processing (GlobalSIP), pp. 768–772, December 2016
11. Yu, H., Cheung, M.H., Huang, L., Huang, J.: Power-delay tradeoff with predictive scheduling in integrated cellular and Wi-Fi networks. IEEE J. Sel. Areas Commun. **34**(4), 735–742 (2016)
12. Liu, Y., Li, X., Ji, H., Zhang, H.: A multiple APs cooperation access scheme for energy efficiency in UUDN with NOMA. In: 2017 IEEE Conference on Computer Communications Workshops (INFOCOM WKSHPS), pp. 1–5, May 2017
13. Sun, J., Fang, W., Wu, X., Palade, V., Xu, W.: Quantum-behaved particle swarm optimization: analysis of individual particle behavior and parameter selection. Evol. Comput. **20**(3), 349–393 (2012)
14. Li, J., Wang, X., Yu, R., Jia, J.: The adaptive routing algorithm depending on the traffic prediction model in cognitive networks. In: 2010 First International Conference on Pervasive Computing, Signal Processing and Applications, pp. 319–322, September 2010

A Short Review on Sleep Scheduling Mechanism in Wireless Sensor Networks

Zeyu Zhang[1], Lei Shu[1,2(✉)], Chunsheng Zhu[3], and Mithun Mukherjee[1]

[1] Guangdong Provincial Key Lab of Petrochemical Equipment Fault Diagnosis,
Guangdong University of Petrochemical Technology, Maoming 525000, China
zeyu-zhang@outlook.com, mithun.mukherjee@outlook.com
[2] School of Engineering, University of Lincoln, Lincoln, UK
lshu@lincoln.ac.uk
[3] Department of Electrical and Computer Engineering,
The University of British Columbia, Vancouver, Canada
cszhu@ece.ubc.ca

Abstract. As a common train of thought to save energy, sleep scheduling which turns sensor nodes on and off has become a significant method to prolong the lifetime of wireless sensor networks (WSNs). In recent years, many related sleep scheduling mechanisms with diverse emphases and application areas for WSNs have been proposed. This paper reviews those mechanisms and further classifies them in different taxonomies as well as provides an insight into them.

Keywords: Sleep scheduling · Wireless Sensor Networks (WSNs)
Insight

1 Introduction

In wireless sensor networks (WSNs) [1–4], most sensor nodes generally have to rely on unrechargeable power sources, e.g., batteries, to provide the necessary power. For certain cases, e.g., outdoor monitoring, it is even difficult to replace the batteries that run out of power. Thus, the power management of sensor nodes is very crucial for WSNs. To address the energy shortage which is generally a bottleneck restricting the applications of WSNs [5], substantial attention have been devoted to sleep scheduling approaches, which have long been used in a wide variety of devices to save energy consumption and prolong the lifetime of equipments, such as air-conditioning compressors, pumps and electric motors [6].

Specifically, as for WSNs, most existing hardware, e.g., CC2420, can support several modes, i.e., transmission mode, idle mode and sleep mode [7]. The power consumption for idle listening is in the same order for transmitting. In other words, if the radio keeps listening for incoming messages, most of the battery energy will be consumed. For example, as much as tens to thousands times the current consumed energy can be drained if the sensor nodes are in the idle listening state for a certain period [8]. Thus, the major goal of sleep scheduling mechanism in WSNs is to reduce the energy consumption of idle listening state on the condition of guaranteeing network connectivity.

© ICST Institute for Computer Sciences, Social Informatics and Telecommunications Engineering 2018
L. Wang et al. (Eds.): QShine 2017, LNICST 234, pp. 66–70, 2018.
https://doi.org/10.1007/978-3-319-78078-8_7

2   Sleep Scheduling

Sleep scheduling means that there is a ratio between the wake up time length in a predefined period and the total length of the period [9]. For example, for a period which is 1 s, if one node stays active for 0.1 s and sleeps for 0.9 s, then the ratio is 0.1.

Sleep scheduling mechanisms for WSNs can be classified into three categories generally, i.e., synchronous schemes, semi-synchronous schemes, and asynchronous schemes.

- **Synchronous Schemes:** For synchronous schemes, such as S-MAC [10], T-MAC [11], sleeping nodes wake up at the same time periodically to communicate with one another, which means the network has to keep a global synchronization.
- **Semi-Synchronous Schemes:** Regarding semi-synchronous schemes (e.g., [12–14]), sensor nodes are generally grouped into clusters. In the same cluster, sensor nodes wake up or go to sleep at the same time. But clusters act together with others asynchronously.
- **Asynchronous Schemes:** In terms of asynchronous schemes, such as [15–17], each sensor node has its own wake-up and sleep schedule.

3   Recent Research

There are a few surveys (e.g., [8]) about sleep scheduling in the last four years. This section summarizes the main conclusions after reviewing recent papers published from 2015 to 2017 about sleep scheduling for WSNs, as shown in Table 1. From the table, we can further observe that most papers focus on the asynchronous scheduling schemes. And machine learning is more widely applied into this field.

4   Future Directions

Sleep scheduling for WSNs aims at saving the energy consumption of WSNs. We list some potential directions in terms of this topic.

1. **Mobile relays and sinks for WSNs:** Sensor nodes around the sink node ran out of energy easily, which can lead to energy hole. Mobile relays and sinks can mitigate this kind of problem. The mobile relay or mobile sink, just like a mobile robot, can travel around to gather information, which offers a good trade-off between energy consumption, latency and delivery delay.
2. **Clustering for WSNs:** For semi-synchronous sleep scheduling schemes, network is generally divided into several clusters, and cluster heads are responsible for communicating with other clusters. In such a way, the cluster heads might need to consume more energy compared with normal sensor nodes. Therefore, how to save the energy consumption for cluster heads is very important.

Table 1. Analysis of recent sleep scheduling mechanisms for WSNs

	Aim	Network structure	Energy	Solution	Advantages
Kordafshari et al. [18]	Trade-off between energy conservation and network throughput	Static	Non-rechargeable battery	Evolutionary game theory	Achieve a stable and optimal schedule
Ye et al. [9]	Multi agent	Static	Non-rechargeable battery	Fussy logic and Q-learning algorithm	Dynamical adjustment
Mosta-faei et al. [19]	Partial coverage and preserve connectivity	Static	Non-rechargeable battery	Learning automation	Adaptive control, global optimization and robustness
Chen et al. [20]	Reduce to-sink data transmission delay while lifetime is improved	Static	Non-rechargeable battery	Comparison and adjust duty-cycle	Dynamic adjustment and consider energy hole
Kumar et al. [21]	Minimize the active time period of every node	Multi-channel and static	Non-rechargeable battery	Integer linear programming	Less energy consumption and minimize the network latency
Wang et al. [12]	Sleep scheduling for critical nodes	Grouped and static	Non-rechargeable battery	Depth first search-based algorithms and k-means cluster algorithm	Maintain group-connectivity
Fang et al. [13]	Trade-off between energy harvesting and data transmission	Static, multi-sink, and tree-based	Rechargeable battery and solar energy	Comparative and random scheduling	Lower control overhead and avoid energy hole
Khalil et al. [11]	Energy hole and data recovery	Mobile, tree topology	Non-rechargeable battery	Oriented method based on TDMA	Less data collision and save transaction time
Chen et al. [22]	Desired area coverage and balance energy consumption	Static	Rechargeable battery and solar energy	Reinforcement learning	Dynamic scheduling and high coverage ratio
Xie et al. [23]	Trade-off among the network lifetime, transmission delay and packet loss ratio	Static	Non-rechargeable battery	Based on residual energy	Adjustable schedule
Oller et al. [15]	Decrease overhearing and idle listening	Static	Non-rechargeable battery	Wake-up radio	Reduce unnecessary energy waste
Baba et al. [16]	Improve the energy efficiency	Static	Replaceable battery	Progressive sleep scheduling and opportunistic routing	Less energy overhead and increase the routing quality
Gupta et al. [17]	Minimize the number of active nodes in a field of interest	Three dimensions and static	Non-rechargeable battery	Estimate the probability of a sensor being redundant	Lower energy waste and maintain sensing coverage
Xu et al. [24]	Make some nodes sleep and maintain monitoring accuracy	Clustering and static	Non-rechargeable battery	Sentinel nodes and select the cluster head randomly	Effectively balance the energy consumption and extend network lifetime

3. **Energy Harvesting for WSNs:** As a common train of thought to prolong the network lifetime, sleep scheduling can only save energy consumption but cannot generate energy. Thus, energy harvesting becomes a promising area, which can further mitigate the problem of energy shortage.
4. **Wireless charging for WSNs:** Wireless charging provides a convenient way to power electrical devices, which can become a very helpful method to supply the energy.
5. **Cloud computing for WSNs:** Cloud computing can be utilized to process the data and share the data processing results with users. Therefore, cloud computing can be incorporated into WSNs to reduce the energy consumption in terms of delivering data to WSN users.
6. **Cross-layer design for WSNs:** Compared to the layered approaches, cross-layer design might achieve better energy efficiency, via utilizing the interaction among different layers.

Acknowledgments. This work is supported by China Maoming Engineering Research Center on Industrial Internet of Things (No. 517018) and major international cooperation projects of colleges in Guangdong Province (No. 2015KGJHZ026) and Science and Technology Planning Project of Guangdong Province (No. 2017A050506057).

References

1. Zhu, C., Yang, L.T., Shu, L., Rodrigues, J.J.P.C., Hara, T.: A geographic routing oriented sleep scheduling algorithm in duty-cycled sensor networks. In: 2012 IEEE International Conference on Communications (ICC), pp. 5473–5477. IEEE (2012)
2. Zhu, C., Yang, L.T., Shu, L., Duong, T.Q., Nishio, S.: Secured energy-aware sleep scheduling algorithm in duty-cycled sensor networks. In: 2012 IEEE International Conference on Communications (ICC), pp. 1953–1957. IEEE (2012)
3. Zhu, C., Shu, L., Hara, T., Wang, L., Nishio, S., Yang, L.T.: A survey on communication and data management issues in mobile sensor networks. Wirel. Commun. Mobile Comput. **14**(1), 19–36 (2014)
4. Zhu, C., Yang, L.T., Shu, L., Leung, V.C.M., Hara, T., Nishio, S.: Insights of top-k query in duty-cycled wireless sensor networks. IEEE Trans. Ind. Electron. **62**(2), 1317–1328 (2015)
5. Akyildiz, I.F., Su, W., Sankarasubramaniam, Y., Cayirci, E.: Wireless sensor networks: a survey. Comput. Netw. **38**(4), 393–422 (2002)
6. Ye, W., Heidemann, J., Estrin, D.: An energy-efficient MAC protocol for wireless sensor networks. In: The 21st Annual Joint Conference of the IEEE Computer and Communications Societies (INFOCOM), vol. 3, pp. 1567–1576. IEEE (2002)
7. Texas Instruments: Cc2420: 2.4 GHz IEEE 802.15. 4/ZigBee-ready RF transceiver, vol. 53 (2006). http://wwww.ti.com/lit/gpn/cc2420
8. Carrano, R.C., Passos, D., Magalhaes, L.C., Albuquerque, C.V.: Survey and taxonomy of duty cycling mechanisms in wireless sensor networks. IEEE Commun. Surv. Tutorials **16**(1), 181–194 (2014)
9. Ye, D., Zhang, M.: A self-adaptive sleep/wake-up scheduling approach for wireless sensor networks. IEEE Trans. Cybern. **48**(3), 979–992 (2017)
10. Zhu, C., Chen, Y., Wang, L., Shu, L., Zhang, Y.: SMAC-based proportional fairness backoff scheme in wireless sensor networks. In: The International Wireless Communications and Mobile Computing Conference (IWCMC), pp. 138–142 (2010)

11. Khalil, M.I., Hossain, M.A., Mamtaz, R., Ahmed, I., Akter, M.: Time efficient receiver oriented sleep scheduling for underwater sensor network. In: 2017 IEEE International Conference on Imaging, Vision & Pattern Recognition (icIVPR), pp. 1–6. IEEE (2017)

12. Wang, D., Mukherjee, M., Shu, L., Chen, Y., Hancke, G.: Sleep scheduling for critical nodes in group-based industrial wireless sensor networks. In: 2017 IEEE International Conference on Communications Workshops (ICC Workshops), pp. 694–698. IEEE (2017)

13. Fang, W., Mukherjee, M., Shu, L., Zhou, Z., Hancke, G.P.: Energy utilization concerned sleep scheduling in wireless powered communication networks. In: 2017 IEEE International Conference on Communications Workshops (ICC Workshops), pp. 558–563. IEEE (2017)

14. Wang, Y., Chen, H., Wu, X., Shu, L.: An energy-efficient SDN based sleep scheduling algorithm for WSNs. J. Netw. Comput. Appl. **59**, 39–45 (2016)

15. Oller, J., Demirkol, I., Casademont, J., Paradells, J., Gamm, G.U., Reindl, L.: Has time come to switch from duty-cycled MAC protocols to wake-up radio for wireless sensor networks? IEEE/ACM Trans. Netw. **24**(2), 674–687 (2016)

16. Baba, S.B., Rao, K.M.: Improving the network life time of a wireless sensor network using the integration of progressive sleep scheduling algorithm with opportunistic routing protocol. Indian J. Sci. Technol. **9**(17), 1–6 (2016)

17. Gupta, H.P., Rao, S.V., Venkatesh, T.: Sleep scheduling protocol for k-coverage of three-dimensional heterogeneous WSNs. IEEE Trans. Veh. Technol. **65**(10), 8423–8431 (2016)

18. Kordafshari, M., Movaghar, A., Meybodi, M.: A joint duty cycle scheduling and energy aware routing approach based on evolutionary game for wireless sensor networks. Iran. J. Fuzzy Syst. **14**(2), 23–44 (2017)

19. Mostafaei, H., Montieri, A., Persico, V., Pescapé, A.: A sleep scheduling approach based on learning automata for WSN partial coverage. J. Netw. Comput. Appl. **80**, 67–78 (2017)

20. Chen, Z., Liu, A., Li, Z., Choi, Y.-J., Li, J.: Distributed duty cycle control for delay improvement in wireless sensor networks. Peer-to-Peer Netw. Appl. **10**(3), 559–578 (2017)

21. Kumar, S., Kim, H.: Low energy scheduling of minimal active time slots for multi-channel multi-hop convergence wireless sensor networks. In: 2017 International Conference on Computing, Networking and Communications (ICNC), pp. 1051–1057. IEEE (2017)

22. Chen, H., Li, X., Zhao, F.: A reinforcement learning-based sleep scheduling algorithm for desired area coverage in solar-powered wireless sensor networks. IEEE Sens. J. **16**(8), 2763–2774 (2016)

23. Xie, R., Liu, A., Gao, J.: A residual energy aware schedule scheme for WSNs employing adjustable awake/sleep duty cycle. Wirel. Pers. Commun. **90**(4), 1859–1887 (2016)

24. Xu, Z.-Y., Zhao, S.-G., Jing, Z.-J.: A clustering sleep scheduling mechanism based on sentinel nodes monitor for WSN. Int. J. Smart Home **9**(1), 23–32 (2015)

Semi-fragile Watermarking Algorithm Based on Arnold Scrambling for Three-Layer Tamper Localization and Restoration

Bin Feng[1,2], Xiangli Li[1], Yingmo Jie[1,2], Cheng Guo[1,2(✉)], and Huijuan Fu[3,4]

[1] School of Software Technology, Dalian University of Technology, Dalian 116620,
People's Republic of China
{fengbin,guocheng}@dlut.edu.cn, dllgdxlxl@foxmail.com,
jymsf2015@mail.dlut.edu.cn
[2] Key Laboratory for Ubiquitous Network and Service Software of Liaoning Province,
Tuqiang Street, Dalian 116620, People's Republic of China
[3] School of Information Management, Wuhan University, Wuhan 430014,
People's Republic of China
huijuanfu@163.com
[4] School of Information Engineering, Jiangxi University of Science and Technology,
Ganzhou 341000, People's Republic of China

Abstract. To protect the content integrity, authenticity and improve the effect of tamper localization and recovery, this paper designs and implements a semi-fragile watermark based on Arnold transformation, which is used to localize and recover tamper of confused image and plain-image. The sender encodes the watermark into the 2-bit least significant bit of the pixel of the original image, and the authentication watermark consists of the pixel value comparison result and the parity check code; the recovery watermark is the pixel value of the Torus image block. In the detection side, the plain-image adopts the stratified idea, carries on the three-level tamper localization and recovery, the third-party authentication institution can detect tamper of the scrambled image using the layer detection method, the receiver will detect the positioning result again. The experimental results show that the proposed algorithm can accurately locate tamper and realize the content recovery and effectively prevent the vector quantization attack. Compared with other algorithms, this algorithm has better effect of tamper localization and recovery.

Keywords: Semi-fragile watermark · Arnold scrambling
Hierarchical tamper localization · Tamper recovery
Torus self-isomorphism mapping

1 Introduction

In order to protect the integrity and authenticity of image, this paper proposes a new semi-fragile digital watermarking algorithm based on the literature [1,2],

© ICST Institute for Computer Sciences, Social Informatics and Telecommunications Engineering 2018
L. Wang et al. (Eds.): QShine 2017, LNICST 234, pp. 71–80, 2018.
https://doi.org/10.1007/978-3-319-78078-8_8

which is used for image content integrity authentication, and according to the algorithm [3], we change our method for better effect.

In this chapter, we propose the related work of our method. We shall study the related work and change some parts of them to suit for our algorithm preferably [4].

1.1 Torus Automorphism Mapping

Torus isomorphic mapping is a typical chaotic map. In this method, a point is mapped to another different point, and for each point there is only one corresponding mapping point.

$$\begin{bmatrix} x_{n+1} \\ y_{n+1} \end{bmatrix} = A \times \begin{bmatrix} x_n \\ y_n \end{bmatrix} \pmod{N} \tag{1}$$

A is a matrix of 2×2, like $\begin{bmatrix} a & b \\ c & d \end{bmatrix}$ and $\det A = 1$.

In this paper, we use this for the selection of watermark embedded position. Since the sequence of image blocks is a one-dimensional sequence, the Torus mapping is transformed into a one-dimensional transformation formula.

$$X^{'} = f(X) = (k \times X) \bmod N + 1 \tag{2}$$

$X, X^{'} (\in [1, N])$ are respectively the current serial number and the mapping number; $k (\in [0, N-1])$ must be a prime number and belong to a private key; $N (\in Z - \{0\})$ is the total number.

1.2 Arnold Image Scrambling Algorithm

Arnold Scrambling is proposed by Russian mathematician Vladimir l. Arnold, also known as cat face transformation. Arnold scrambling has a periodicity, and after multiple transformations, the image will become very chaotic, but after specific transformations, re-transformed into the initial image. Such transformation can be used as image encryption [9].

In Arnold scrambling, the image is digitized into a matrix, and the rows and columns of its elements correspond to the values of the arguments, and the values of the elements represent image information. The position (x', y') of the matrix in one transformation is

$$\begin{bmatrix} x' \\ y' \end{bmatrix} = \begin{bmatrix} 1 & 1 \\ 1 & 2 \end{bmatrix} \times \begin{bmatrix} x \\ y \end{bmatrix} \pmod{N} \tag{3}$$

$x, y \in \{0, 1, 2, \cdots, N-1\}$ indicates the position of the pixel before transformation. Digital images can be seen as a two-dimensional matrix, and after Arnold transformation, the pixel position will be rearranged, so the image will appear chaotic to achieve the effect of scrambling encryption.

2   Proposed Method

In this paper, based on the literature [1,5], our algorithm is proposed for hierarchical tamper localization and restoration, which can be applied to both plain-image and scrambling images. Wherein tamper localization is based on the three-layer detection [1], and the effective recovery depends on the pixel information embedded in the Torus mapping block. The three-layer localization is carried out directly on the plain-image, and the tamper of the scrambling image can be detected on the cloud side, and we can decrypt the result and carry on the secondary detection for a better effect. The following sections describe the process of the watermark embedding, plain-image tamper detection, confused image tamper localization and recovery [6,8].

2.1   Based on Block Watermark Embedding

In this section, the original image is preprocessed to generate the watermark, and the watermark is embedded according to the Torus automorphism mapping. The watermark is embedded in the lowest 2 bits of each pixel.

2.1.1   Pretreatment

Assuming the original image I is 256 gray levels, its size is $M \times M$, where M is a multiple of 2. The image is segmented and the block mapping sequence $A \to B \to C \to D \to \ldots \to A$ is obtained by the Torus automorphism transformation. Each letter in the sequence represents a separate block. That means the pixel value of block A is embedded in block B, the pixel value of block B is embedded in block C, and so on.

Firstly, we divide the image I into 2×2 blocks and number them. Secondly, calculate their Torus mapping blocks.

2.1.2   Watermark Generation and Embedding

Assuming A and B are a pair of Torus automorphism mapping blocks in the image I.

The watermark of the image block B is represented by an array(v, p, r), where v, p are one bit, and r is 6 bits determined by the pixel value of A. The generation of watermark and the embedding process are as follows:

Step 1 : The 2-bit LSB of the pixels of B is set to zero.
Step 2 : Generates authentication watermark v of the block B.

$$v = \begin{cases} 1 \ B_{14} > B_{23} \\ 0 \ B_{14} \le B_{23} \end{cases} \tag{4}$$

Step 3 : Calculate the 6 bit MSB average B_{avg} of image block B.
Step 4 : Calculate the quantity N of 1 in B_{avg}, and the parity watermark p.

$$p = \begin{cases} 1 \ N \to Even \\ 0 \ N \to Odd \end{cases} \tag{5}$$

Step 5 : The average A_{avg} of the 6 bit MSB of the image block A is as the recovery watermark r.

Step 6 : The watermark (v, p, r) are composed of 8 bits, and then embedded into the 8-bit LSB of the four pixels of the image block B.

Repeat the above steps (1) to (6) for the other blocks, obtain the embedded image I'.

2.2   Arnold Transformation

Divide the embedded image I' into 2×2 image blocks, and take the image block A for an example.

Step 1 : The coordinate of the first pixel point of the block A are (x_A, y_A), and the other coordinates are calculated as $(x_A, y_A + 1), (x_A + 1, y_A), (x_A + 1, y_A + 1)$.

Step 2 : Assume the private key is (a, b, N), and after Arnold transformation, the coordinate (x_A, y_A) is converted to $(x_A{}', y_A{}')$.

$$\begin{bmatrix} x_A{}' \\ y_A{}' \end{bmatrix} = \begin{bmatrix} 1 & b \\ a & ab+1 \end{bmatrix} \begin{bmatrix} x_A \\ y_A \end{bmatrix} \quad (\text{mod } M) \tag{6}$$

Step 3 : The pixels $(x_A, y_A + 1), (x_A + 1, y_A), (x_A + 1, y_A + 1)$ of the block A are respectively converted into $(x_A{}', y_A{}' + 1), (x_A{}' + 1, y_A{}'), (x_A{}' + 1, y_A{}' + 1)$.

The Arnold scrambling image I'_{arnold} can be obtained by repeating the above steps (1) to (3) on other image blocks.

2.3   Tamper Detection

2.3.1   Tamper Detection of Plain-Images

The tampered image I'_w is detected in three layers. In the first layer, we detect the 2×2 image blocks. And in the second layer, we mark the independent 4×4 blocks that has more than one marked 2×2 block. In the third layer, mark the independent blocks according to the surrounding image blocks.

In the first detection, the image I'_w is divided into independent 2×2 image blocks. Take the block B' as an example and the specific steps are as follows:

Step 1 : The watermark (v, p) in the image block B' is extracted according to the embedding rules.

Step 2 : Set the 2 bit LSB of the pixels of B' to 0, and calculate the average pixel value B'_{avg} of B'.

Step 3 : Calculate the quantity N' of 1 in B'_{avg} and the parity code p'.

Step 4 : If $p' = p$, the image block B' is authenticated, otherwise the image block is marked.

Step 5 : When the parity code p' is verified, the image block B' is evaluated for the watermark v'.

Step 6 : If $v' = v$, the image block B' is authenticated, otherwise the image block B' is marked.

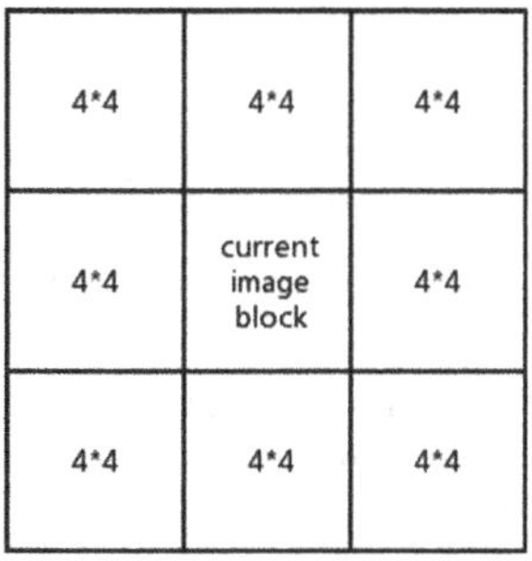

4*4	4*4	4*4
4*4	current image block	4*4
4*4	4*4	4*4

Fig. 1. Secondary tampering localization image block

Repeat the above steps (1) to (6) for other image blocks of I'_w, and the detection result I_{locate} is acquired.

In the second detection, the localization image I_{locate} is divided into independent 4×4 image blocks and each individual image block is divided into four 2×2 image blocks. And mark each individual 4×4 image block that has more than one marked 2×2 block, and finally obtain the second localization image I'_{locate}.

In the third detection, the second localization image I'_{locate} is divided into non-overlapping 4×4 image blocks, and as shown in Fig. 1, the image block is marked where there are more than five marked image blocks of the eight surrounding blocks. After that, we get the final localization image I''_{locate}.

2.3.2 Tamper Detection of Scrambled Images

Assume the scrambled image I'_{Arnold} requires tamper detection in an unsafe third party, the insecure cloud detection system is A_{cloud}, and the local security detection system is B_{locate}, then the first layer of the confused image is detected in the cloud detection system. A_{cloud} send detection results to the local security detection system for 2, 3 layer detection. The specific steps are as follows:

Step 1 : At the cloud system, calculate the localization image I_{locate}^{cloud} like Sect. 2.3.1.

Step 2 : In the local detection system, use the private key to decrypt I_{locate}^{cloud} to get the localization image $I_{locate}^{location}$.

Step 3 : In the second detection, the localization image $I_{locate}^{location}$ is divided into independent 4×4 image blocks and it is detected whether there is a marked independent 2×2 image block in each individual 4×4 image block. And finally get the second localization image $I'^{location}_{locate}$

Step 4 : In the third detection, the localization image $I'^{location}_{locate}$ is divided into 4×4 image blocks. Mark the image block where there are more than five marked surrounding image blocks, and finally get the localization image $I''^{location}_{locate}$.

2.4 Tampering Recovery

After the above tamper detection, we need to recover the image. So assume the image block B' has a tamper mark, and take B' for an example.

$Step\ 1$: The image block C' is calculated according to the key k of the Torus transformation.

$Step\ 2$: If the image block C' is not marked with tamper, extract the recovery watermark r, shift r left twice, and get r' to recover the image block B'.

$Step\ 3$: The pixel value of the image block B' is replaced with r'.

$Step\ 4$: If the image block C' has a tamper mark, the image block B' is re-marked.

Repeat the steps (1) to (4) for all the image blocks, and finally obtain the recovery image $I_{recover}$. Because there are some image blocks that are not recovered, preform the following operations.

$Step\ 1$: Calculate the average $B'_{surroud}$ of the surrounding recovered image blocks around the image block B'

$Step\ 2$: Recover the image block B' according to $B'_{surround}$.

The above operations (1) to (2) are performed for each unrecovered image blocks to obtain the final recovery image $I'_{recover}$.

3   Results and Analysis

In this paper, the gray images Peppers, Lena, Plane, Baboon are used as test images. The peak signal to noise ratio and the structure similarity of the image are used to measure the ability of localization and recovery [7].

3.1 Peak Signal-to-Noise Ratio and Image Structure Similarity

3.1.1 Peak Signal-to-Noise Ratio

Assume the images are the reference image f and the test image g, whose size is $M \times N$, the calculation formula between f and g is as follows.

$$MSE(f,g) = \frac{1}{MN} \sum_{i=1}^{M} \sum_{j=1}^{N} (f_{ij} - g_{ij})^2 \qquad (7)$$

$$PSNR(f,g) = 10\log_{10}(255^2/MSE(f,g)) \qquad (8)$$

When MSE approaches zero, the PSNR is near infinity, that indicates higher PSNR provides higher image quality. The peak signal-to-noise ratio can reflect the mean square error between the watermark image and the original image. The larger value shows the smaller difference between the embedded image and the original image.

3.1.2 Image Structure Similarity

Structured similarity is not designed using a traditional error summation method, but by modeling any image distortion as a combination of three factors, which are correlation loss, luminance distortion, and contrast distortion. Assume the images are the reference image f and the test image g whose size is $M \times N$, the formula is as follows.

$$
\begin{cases}
l(f,g) = \frac{2\mu_f\mu_g + C_1}{\mu_f^2 + \mu_g^2 + C_1} \\[2mm]
c(f,g) = \frac{2\sigma_f\sigma_g + C_2}{\sigma_f^2 + \sigma_g^2 + C_2} \\[2mm]
s(f,g) = \frac{\sigma_{fg} + C_3}{\sigma_f\sigma_g + C_3}
\end{cases}
\tag{9}
$$

$$
SSIM(f,g) = l(f,g) \times c(f,g) \times s(f,g)
\tag{10}
$$

μ_f, μ_g are the average of the reference image f and the test image g, σ_f, σ_g stand for their standard deviation, σ_f^2, σ_g^2 are their variance, σ_{fg} is the covariance. In order to avoid the above formula denominator to 0, C_1, C_2 and C_3 are constants. In general, $C_1 = (K_1 \times L)^2$, $C_2 = (K_2 \times L)^2$, $C_3 = C_2/2$. Usually, $K_1 = 0.01$, $K_2 = 0.03$, $L = 255$.

We use the peak signal to noise ratio and structured similarity of the image to measure the image quality. Figure 2 shows the original image of Lena, Peppers, Plane and Baboon, and the image after adding watermark. As shown in Table 1, this method increases the PSNR after embedding the watermark, and this paper has great superiority in embedding the watermarking invisibility.

As we can see, the performance of our algorithm has the high peak signal-to-noise ratio and image structure similarity, which reflect the mean square error between the watermark image and the original image. The larger value shows the smaller difference between the embedded image and the original image.

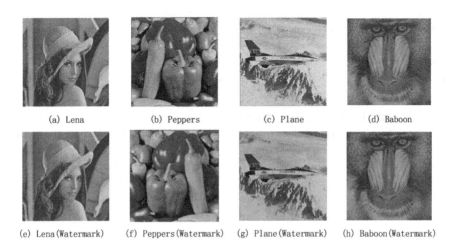

(a) Lena   (b) Peppers   (c) Plane   (d) Baboon

(e) Lena (Watermark)   (f) Peppers (Watermark)   (g) Plane (Watermark)   (h) Baboon (Watermark)

Fig. 2. The effect of the images embedded watermark

Table 1. The $PSNR$ and $SSIM$ of images

Image	Lena	Peppers	Plane	Baboon
PSNR	47.16	47.10	47.29	47.53
SSIM	0.9795	0.9825	0.9777	0.9930

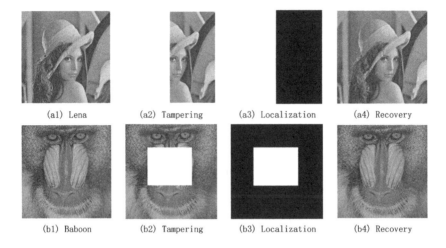

(a1) Lena   (a2) Tampering   (a3) Localization   (a4) Recovery

(b1) Baboon   (b2) Tampering   (b3) Localization   (b4) Recovery

Fig. 3. The effect of localization and recovery

3.2   Test and Analysis

3.2.1   Result in Plain-Image

As shown in Fig. 3(a2), (b2) are the tampering image after attack and Fig. 3(a3), (b3) are the localization results. And Fig. 3(a4), (b4) are the recovery results, we can see this method has a great advantage in resisting attack.

After the shear attack, we can see that the image Lena has the half lost and our algorithm can localize the attack precisely and perfectly. Besides, through recovery of our method, the image has very little difference compared with the original image, which shows that our algorithm has unparalleled superiority.

3.2.2   Result in Scrambling Image

The algorithm can directly locate the scrambling image, and it has the same effect compared with the plain-image. The experimental results are shown in Fig. 4. As we can see, tamper can be localized in the scrambling image and the image can be recovery accurately, that is a great innovation, and the result in the scrambling image is still as well as the plain-image

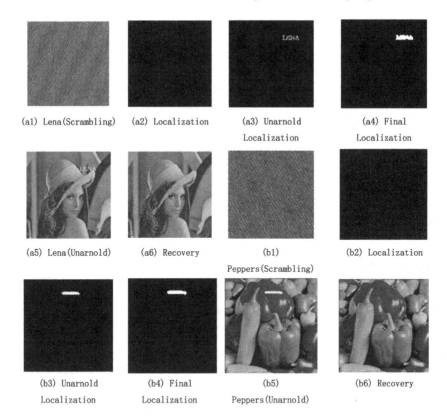

Fig. 4. Localization and recovery of scrambling image

4   Conclusion

This paper presents a semi-fragile image digital watermarking algorithm for plain-image and scrambling image. The main features of this algorithm include the following aspects:

(1) The hierarchical idea is used to locate the tampering position, and it has better anti-shear attack ability, and adds a recovery watermark for tampering recovery. The authentication watermark is composed of the parity check code and the comparison result; the recovery watermark is the average pixel value.

(2) The embedded algorithm uses the well-known spatial domain LSB algorithm. The aim is to improve the tampering recovery effect. The algorithm is simple in principle, has higher localization accuracy and better recovery effect.

(3) This paper use three layers to detect and localize tamper. In this algorithm, the experimental verification can detect the location of tampering in the image, and can effectively recover the tampering content, and can effectively prevent the vector quantization attack.

(4) This algorithm can directly localize tamper in the scrambling conditions, and it can detect tamper without revealing the plain-image, greatly improve privacy and security of the image.

Acknowledgements. This paper is supported by the National Science Foundation of China under grant No. 61401060, 61501080, 61572095 and 61771090, the Fundamental Research Funds for the Central Universities' under No. DUT16QY09, and the Social Science Foundation of Jiangxi Province, China No. 15JY48.

References

1. Celik, M.U., et al.: Hierarchical watermarking for secure image authentication with localization. IEEE Trans. Image Process. **11**(6), 585 (2002). A Publication of the IEEE Signal Processing Society
2. Potdar, V.M., Han, S., Chang, E.: A survey of digital image watermarking techniques (2005)
3. Cox, I.J., Kilian, J., Leighton, F.T., et al.: Secure spread spectrum watermarking for multimedia. IEEE Trans. Image Process. **6**(12), 1673–1687 (1997). A Publication of the IEEE Signal Processing Society
4. Walton, S.: Information authentication for a slippery new age. Dr. Dobbs J. **20**(4), 18–26 (1995)
5. Fridrich, J., Goljan, M.: Images with self-correcting capabilities. In: Proceedings of the International Conference on Image Processing, ICIP 1999, vol. 3, pp. 792–796. IEEE (2002)
6. Sikder, I., Dhar, P.K., Shimamura, T.: A semi-fragile watermarking method using slant transform and LU decomposition for image authentication. In: International Conference on Electrical, Computer and Communication Engineering, pp. 881–885. IEEE (2017)
7. Hore, A., Ziou, D.: Image quality metrics: PSNR vs. SSIM. In: International Conference on Pattern Recognition, pp. 2366–2369. IEEE (2010)
8. Liu, Q., Jiang, X., et al.: A unified digital watermark algorithm based on singular value decomposition and spread spectrum technology. Acta Electron. Sin. **4**, 621–624 (2005)
9. Arnold, V.I.: Geometrical Methods in the Theory of Ordinary Differential Equations, 2nd edn., 351 pp. Springer, New York (1988). https://doi.org/10.1007/978-1-4612-1037-5. Rota, G.C. Adv. Math. **80**(2), 269 (1990)
10. Qiu, T., Zhao, A., Xia, F., Si, W., Wu, D.O.: ROSE: robustness strategy for scale-free wireless sensor networks. IEEE/ACM Trans. Networking **25**(5), 2944–2959 (2017)
11. Qiu, T., Qiao, R., Wu, D.O.: EABS: an event-aware backpressure scheduling scheme for emergency internet of things. IEEE Trans. Mobile Comput. **17**(1) (2017). https://doi.org/10.1109/TMC.2017.2702670
12. Guo, C., Zhuang, R., Jie, Y., Ren, Y., Wu, T., Choo, K.-K.R.: Fine-grained database field search using attribute-based encryption for E-healthcare clouds. J. Med. Syst. **40**(11), 235:1–235:8 (2016)

Quality and Reliability

A Comprehensive Analysis of Video Service Quality on IQIYI from Large-Scale Data Sets

Yao Guo[1(✉)], Qiujian Lv[2], Fang Liu[1], Jie Yang[1], and Zhe Gao[3]

[1] Beijing Laboratory of Advanced Information Networks,
Beijing Key Laboratory of Network System Architecture and Convergence,
Center for Data Science, BUPT, Beijing 100876, China
{2013211938,lindaliu,janeyang}@bupt.edu.cn
[2] Institute of Information Engineering, Chinese Academy of Sciences,
Beijing 100093, China
lvqiujian@iie.ac.cn
[3] Technology Research Institute, Aisino Corporation, Beijing 100086, China
gaozhe@aisino.com

Abstract. With the proliferation of online video, measuring the quality of the video service has become a vital aspect for improving user's experience. Recent work shows that measurable quality metrics such as buffering, bitrate, and video resolutions impact user's experience, but none of them reveal the real relationships between these metrics and user's actual experience. This paper attempts to solve the problem above. We use IQIYI as the sample, and our large-scale dataset consists of 7 days real Internet traffic in a northern city of China. We quantify user's experience at per-video level (or view). Using Apache Spark, we extract some video events and calculate several quality metrics. In order to investigate the relationship between the metrics and user's experience, we use the FP-Growth algorithm to mining the implicit association rules and get some interesting results.

Keywords: IQIYI · Apache Spark · Video quality
User's experience · FP-Growth algorithm

1 Introduction

In the past few years, video streaming has become one of most popular Internet services. In China, the number of online video service users has reached 565 million, accounting for 75.2% of the total number of Internet users in 2017 [1]. IQIYI is one of the most popular online video service providers in China. According to a report [2] issued in 2016, IQIYI has accounted for 51% of the market share in the online video industry, having the largest amount of monthly active users comparing other companies such as Tencent and Youku.

© ICST Institute for Computer Sciences, Social Informatics and Telecommunications Engineering 2018
L. Wang et al. (Eds.): QShine 2017, LNICST 234, pp. 83–93, 2018.
https://doi.org/10.1007/978-3-319-78078-8_9

As video distribution over the Internet becomes mainstream, user's demands on video qualities have dramatically increased. Different from other services on the Internet, online video streaming tends to occupy more traffic and bandwidth, and is easier to be disturbed by external factors such as network congestion, causing terrible experience. In this context, analysis of video service quality is paramount for content providers.

Quality of Experience (QoE) in HTTP video streaming is a well-known and largely investigated topic. Recent work [3,4] shows that measurable quality metrics, such as buffering, joining time, bitrate, and frequency of bitrate switching, impact user experience. Unfortunately, converting these observations into a quantitative QoE metric turns out to be challenging since these metrics are interrelated in complex, and can be unpredictable [5]. Some researchers [5] address these challenges through casting QoE inference as a machine learning problem. However, they have not revealed the implicit interrelation between the video metrics and user's experience yet, and the understanding of video QoE is just limited to a simple qualitative understanding of how individual metrics impact engagement (e.g., playing time) in some other works [6].

To solve the problems above, this paper quantifies user's experiences at a per-video level and introduce the FP-Growth algorithm to mine the implicit association rules between the quality metrics and user's experience. To improve the quality of the analysis, this paper uses large-scale traffic records from a leading Chinese Online video service IQIYI, which is similar to Youtube. Considering the huge size of data, we apply the Apache Spark to analyze the quality of IQIYI video service. Overall, the contributions of this paper can be summarized as follows:

(1) We analyze the interactive processes of watching an IQIYI video in detail. We distinguish the video events using Spark from massive data, which are extracted from real network traffic records collected from a metropolitan city that represent the activities of more than 223,800 people in seven days.
(2) We extract some video parameters and calculate video quality metrics about IQIYI;
(3) Using FP-Growth algorithm, we get some association rules between quality metrics and user's experience, and we verify the findings.

The rest of paper is structured as follows. We present some related work in Sect. 2. After this, we analyze the process of playing an IQIYI video and give some features of its request URI, then we filtered the HTTP packets of IQIYI. Based on the work before, we calculate some video quality metrics in Sect. 3. In Sect. 4, we try to analyze some relationships between different video quality metrics and give some conclusions.

2   Related Work

At present, with regard to video quality, there are two main research directions, which focus on the network transmission side and the user side respectively.

QoS-based video quality prediction: The measurements of QoS focus on the network transmission side. QoS metrics uses available network diagnostic parameters, such as traffic jitter, arrival time, and packet loss, which are easy to measure at any point inside the delivery network [7], and ITU-T has given some standards [8]. The advantage of QoS-based metrics is that these models are designed to be easily deployed at any point in the distribution network. The disadvantage is that QoS models do not have access to two pieces of important information: (1) how the video originally looked and sounded, and (2) what the end-user sees and hears. This limits the ability of QoS models to predict quality as perceived by the end user.

Measuring end-user's quality perception: The measurements of QoE focus on the user side. Subjective video quality tests and objective video quality metrics provide established techniques for end-user point-of-view. Subjective methods for video quality assessment are considered the most accurate and reliable way [9], and ITU-T has already given some standards [10]. However, these methods are non-real-time, terrible in portability and applicability between different service providers. Many researchers turn to the objective assessment approach and get some results. Some found that the initial buffering duration, buffering length, buffer location and bit rate were the key factors affecting video quality [3,4]. Authors in [6,11,12] showed that the percentage of time spent in buffering had the largest impact on user engagement in some special video contents, while authors in [13] showed that initial buffering latency was preferred to stalling by around 90% of users. Unfortunately, the state of the art in their understanding of video QoE was limited to a simple qualitative understanding of how individual metrics impacted engagement. In this context, the researchers continued to introduce different types of regression models [14] and classification models [15], and further explore the user's experience. Besides, some researchers have attempted to map the objective quality of service (QoS) metrics acquired in the network transmission side directly to the subjective QoE evaluation [9]. However, they all didn't point out the implicit association rules between the quality metrics and user's experience.

Apart from the previous works, this paper is to investigate the implicit relationships between quality metrics and how these metrics influence user's experience in user side.

3 Analysis of IQIYI Video Metrics

3.1 Data Description

The traffic data we used is collected by our self-developed Traffic Monitoring System [14]. The system can monitor packets and aggregate them into records. Each record contains a lot of useful information about user's requests to the Internet. The dataset used ranges from February 21 to February 26,2017 (Monday - Sunday), covering about 223,800 users. Moreover, the size of datasets is about 4TB.

3.2 Data Filtering

A complete IQIYI video interactive process usually includes: select the video and click the play button on the web page, starting to request video resources, starting playing the advertisement, ending playing the advertisement, downloading the initial video cache, downloading the subsequent video cache while playing, starting buffering, ending buffering, channel conversion and playing the next video, etc.

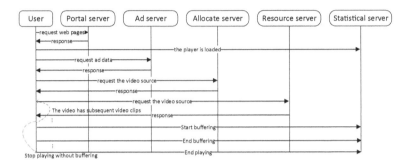

Fig. 1. IQIYI video interactive process.

As shown in the Fig. 1, a playing process needs several servers to participate in. By experimenting and reproducing the interactive process many times, we find some features of its domain names of different servers. For example, almost all IQIYI's domain names end with "qiyi.com" or "iqiyi.com". The statistical server, which collects the status information of the video during playback, its domain name is fixed to "msg.71.am". The allocation server is responsible for scheduling video resources and getting their specific locations to the client side, and its domain name is also fixed to "data.qiyi.com". All videos' URIs, including advertisement, start with "/videos/". We also find that there are many differences in the request URI when using different platforms to watch an IQIYI video, such as Windows OS and Android OS, which is worthy of our attention when conducting an experiment.

Based on the IQIYI's hosts we find above, we can easily filter the data about IQIYI from the massive data. But there are still some redundant records we don't need in calculating the quality metrics. We just need to extract key records about the video event during playing such as downloading data event. In this case, we use the regular expression to finish this work.

3.3 Video Metrics Calculation

In this part, we calculate the video quality metrics at a per-video level (or view).

Joining Time. When we decide to watch a video and click the playing button on the web, we can't see the video contents at once, which has an impact on user's experience. Based on the description of Fig. 1, the joining time T_j is defined as the time interval between the time when the user clicks the playing button and the time the video starts to play, including the time T_1 to init buffer and the time T_2 to play the advertisement. We define:

$$T_j = T_1 + T_2 \qquad \cdot \qquad (1)$$

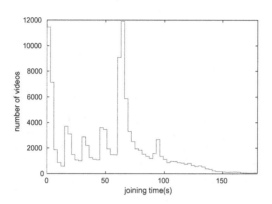

Fig. 2. The histogram of video joining time

Six peaks appear in Fig. 2, and the interval time between peaks is about 15s. Actually, the peak is caused by advertisement playing. In IQIYI, each advertisement's time length is fixed to fifteen seconds strictly, and the number of the advertisements being played is decided by the length of the video. A User, who chooses a video length at about 45 min, usually needs to watch four advertisements before the video starts to play. That means the user needs to wait at least 60 s.

Video Resolution. Video resolution is one of the most intuitive metrics. Through capturing the video list information the allocation server sends to the client, we know IQIYI provides five kinds of video resolutions. According to the status of the network, the player requests the proper resolution to download.

The IQIYI's statistical server plays a role as a monitoring station, which collects the status of the video player cyclically, and we call this detection signal as the heartbeat signal. In the request URI of the heartbeat signal, the parameter called defi is discovered to be the flag of a video's resolution.

IQIYI defines the resolution over "896 * 504" as high resolution. The pie in Fig. 3 reports that 73% of views are at the resolution "896 * 504". Due to the fact that an important factor limiting the resolution is the quality of the network, so we can infer that the resolution of "896 * 504" is the best compromise between the clarity of a video and quality of network when watching a video in the IQIYI platform.

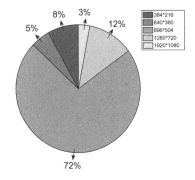

Fig. 3. The distribution of video's resolution

Buffering Ratio and Buffering Frequency. Buffering Ratio is represented as a percentage. It is the fraction of the total session time spent in buffering. The player goes into a buffering state when the video buffer becomes empty and moves out of buffering (back to playing state) when the buffer is replenished. It is worth to note that the buffering ratio doesn't take the number of buffering events into account. Although the buffering ratios of a video is same, the number of buffering events may vary. The author in [12] gives the conclusion that multiple buffering events have the different influence on user's engagement comparing to a single buffering event, causing more users to stop the playing process.

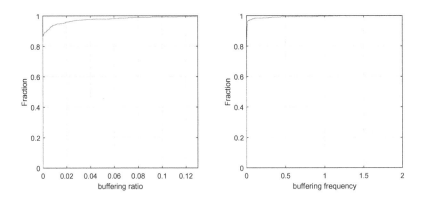

Fig. 4. The CDF of buffering ratio and buffering frequency

As expected in Fig. 4, most viewing sessions experience good quality, both having a very low buffering ratio and low buffering frequency. We note that the possibility of buffering during playback in IQIYI is small since we only find about thirty thousand buffering records from the traffic data collected in seven days.

4   Correlation Between Quality Metrics and Experience

This section aims to investigate the implicit relationships between the quality metrics and user's experience based on the results discovered in Sect. 3. The relationships between the quality metrics and the effective user experience can be extremely complex, and the quality metrics themselves have subtle interdependencies and have implicit tradeoffs. For example, some research has shown that although switching bit rate to adapt to the bandwidth condition can reduce buffering effectively, the high rates of bit rate switching annoy users to some extent.

4.1   Settings and Assumptions

Unlike other video providers such as YouTube that streams short videos, IQIYI typically provides TV series usually length at about 45 min. Figure 5 shows the distribution of the lengths of the videos being played in seven days. It is clear that users prefer to choose the TV series when using IQIYI platform. In order to eliminate the impact of user's bias on QoE, we filter the videos length at 40 min to 50 min to analyze in the following experiments. We also note that the impact of joining time can be ignored when the video length is fixed and has been playing, as explained in Sect. 3.

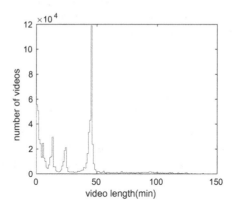

Fig. 5. The histogram of video length

Then, we point out how we distinguish the videos that are abandoned due to poor viewing experiences from the massive records. As other researchers [12], we also adopt the video abandonment to do this work. Besides, we take the dragging events into account for complementary. When a user drags the process bar during playback, we infer that the user has poor engagement, which also reflects user's experience. After making these assumptions, we introduce the FP-Growth algorithm.

4.2   FP-Growth Algorithm

In order to obtain the relationship between the video metrics and user experience, we implement the FP-Growth algorithm to mine [16] the implicit association rules.

The FP-growth algorithm is proposed by Han et al., and aims at mining frequent patterns without candidate generation. The FP stands for the frequent pattern. Given a dataset of transactions, the first step of FP-growth is to calculate item frequencies and identify some frequent items. The second step of FP-growth uses a suffix tree (FP-tree) structure to encode transactions without generating candidate sets explicitly, which is usually expensive to generate. After the second step, the frequent itemsets can be extracted [17]. The Spark.mllib provides a parallel implementation of FP-growth.

4.3   Analysis of Association Rules

To implement the RDD-Based FP-Growth API, we need to provide two parameters called *Support* and *Confidence*. *Support* is an indication of how frequently the itemset appears in the dataset, and *Confidence* is an indication of how often the rule has been found to be true. As related works show buffering events have the largest impact on user's experience, we concentrate on finding the rules related to buffering events. Based the analysis results discovered in Sect. 3, we have realized that the possibility of buffering during playback in IQIYI is small, and this indicates a small supportance value of rules including buffering events. Through extensive experiments, we find 0.17% is the threshold of *Support*. We set *Confidence* at a high level, 90%, to enhance accuracy. To verify the correctness, we calculate *lift* of the rules we have found. The *lift* is defined as:

$$lift\,(X \Rightarrow Y) = \frac{supp\,(X \cup Y)}{supp\,(X) \times supp\,(Y)} \tag{2}$$

If the rule had a lift of 1, it would imply that the probability of occurrence of the antecedent and that of the consequent are independent of each other. When two events are independent of each other, no rule can be drawn involving those two events [18].

We use eight letters to represent different video events or quality metrics shown in Table 1. Then, we get some preliminary results shown in Table 2. Finally, we calculate these rule's *lift* to verify correctness.

From Table 2, we see that:

Line 1: When users watch a high-resolution video and drag the process bar during playing, 94.6% of them tend to switch the channel or stop playing this video. We infer that the dragging behavior can be a signal that user is losing interest or meets some terrible video events, such as buffering when watching a high-resolution video.

Line 2: When users meet a buffering event in IQIYI, there is a great possibility that they have chosen a high-definition video.

Table 1. Definition of the symbols

Symbols	Definition	Attributes
A	Suffering buffering events	Video quality
B	Playing fluently	Video quality
C	Users drag the process bar	Video event
D	User don't drag the process bar	Video event
E	Switch channels or click to stop	Video event
F	Keep playing session	Video event
G	High-resolution videos	Video quality
H	Low-resolution videos	Video quality

Table 2. Mining results

Rules	Confidence	lift
$[C, G] \Rightarrow E$	94.62%	1.034
$[A] \Rightarrow G$	92.10%	1.032
$[A, G] \Rightarrow E$	96.77%	1.072
$[B, G] \Rightarrow D$	95.91%	1.047

Line 3: Encountering some buffering events while watching a high-resolution videos can have a great impact on the user's experience. We note that if the extent of buffering is severe, the player of IQIYI will stop the playing process automatically.

Line 4: It indicates that if users lose interest in the video contents or have a bad experience, they will drag the process bar or just stop the playing process. Watching a high-resolution video fluently means a good user experience, and 95.1% of users won't drag the process bar during playing.

5   Conclusion

In this paper, we investigate the video service quality of IQIYI in detail. We analyze the interactive processes when watching an IQIYI video in detail and find some features of IQIYI's hosts and request URIs. We distinguish the video events from large scale traffic records using Spark and calculate the quality metrics of IQIYI. Finally, we try to find out the implicit association rules between quality metrics and user's experience and get some findings. Our analysis provides a better understanding in quality metrics and user's experience. Further, improvements may be achieved by taking more metrics into account and investigating user's experience in more dimensions.

Acknowledgment. This work is supported in part by the National Natural Science Foundation of China (61671078, 61701031), Director Funds of Beijing Key Laboratory of Network System Architecture and Convergence (2017BKL-NSAC-ZJ-06), and 111 Project of China (B08004, B17007). This work is conducted on the platform of Center for Data Science of Beijing University of Posts and Telecommunications.

References

1. CNNIC: The 40th China statistical report on internet development. http://www. cnnic.net.cn/hlwfzyj/hlwxzbg/hlwtjbg/201708/P020170807351923262153.pdf. Accessed July 2017
2. China Economic Net: Video market tripartite confrontation. IQIYI occupies 51% of the market share. http://www.ce.cn/cysc/tech/gd2012/201702/13/t20170213_20160241.shtml. Accessed Feb 2017
3. Shunmuga Krishnan, S., Sitaraman, R.K.: Video stream quality impacts viewer behavior: inferring causality using quasi-experimental designs. IEEE/ACM Trans. Netw. **21**(6), 2001–2014 (2013)
4. Yu, F., Chen, H., Xie, L., Li, J.: Impact of end-user playout buffer dynamics on http progressive video QoE in wireless networks, vol. 136, no. 5, pp. 1996–2001. IEEE (2014)
5. Balachandran, A., Sekar, V., Akella, A., Seshan, S., Stoica, I., Zhang, H.: A quest for an internet video quality-of-experience metric. In: ACM Workshop on Hot Topics, Networks, pp. 97–102 (2012)
6. Dobrian, F., Awan, A., Zhan, J., Zhang, H.: Understanding the impact of video quality on user engagement. In: ACM SIGCOMM 2011 Conference, pp. 362–373 (2011)
7. Staelens, N., Pinson, M., Corriveau, P., De Turck, F., Demeester, P.: Measuring video quality in the network: from quality of service to user experience. In: 9th International Workshop on Video Processing and Consumer Electronics (VPQM 2015), pp. 5–6 (2015)
8. Seitz, N.: ITU-T QoS standards for IP-based networks. IEEE Commun. Mag. **41**, 82–89 (2003)
9. Moldovan, A.N., Ghergulescu, I., Muntean, C.H.: A novel methodology for mapping objective video quality metrics to the subjective MOS scale (2014)
10. BT ITU-R: Methodology for the subjective assessment of the quality of television pictures. EBU Technical Review (2015)
11. Hoßfeld, T., Seufert, M., Hirth, M., Zinner, T., Tran-Gia, P., Schatz, R.: Quantification of Youtube QoE via crowdsourcing. In: IEEE International Symposium on Multimedia, pp. 494–499 (2012)
12. Nam, H., Kim, K.H., Schulzrinne, H.: QoE matters more than QoS: why people stop watching cat videos. In: IEEE INFOCOM 2016 - the IEEE International Conference on Computer Communications, pp. 1–9 (2016)
13. Hossfeld, T., Egger, S., Schatz, R., Fiedler, M., Masuch, K., Lorentzen, C.: Initial delay vs. interruptions: between the devil and the deep blue sea. In: Fourth International Workshop on Quality of Multimedia Experience, pp. 1–6 (2012)
14. Rodriguez, D.Z., Abrahao, J., Begazo, D.C., Rosa, R.L., Bressan, G.: Quality metric to assess video streaming service over TCP considering temporal location of pauses. IEEE Trans. Consum. Electron. **58**(3), 985–992 (2012)
15. Balachandran, A., Sekar, V., Akella, A., Seshan, S., Stoica, I., Zhang, H.: Developing a predictive model of quality of experience for internet video. ACM SIGCOMM Comput. Commun. Rev. **43**(4), 339–350 (2013)

16. Verhein, F.: Frequent pattern growth (FP-growth) algorithm. University of Sydney, January 2018
17. Apache: Docs of frequent pattern mining RDD-based API. https://spark.apache.org/docs/latest/mllib-frequent-pattern-mining.html. Accessed July 2016
18. Wikipedia: Association rule learning. https://en.wikipedia.org/wiki/Association_rule_learning. Accessed Aug 2017

Contact Quality Aware Routing for Satellite-Terrestrial Delay Tolerant Network

Wenfeng Shi, Deyun Gao$^{(\boxtimes)}$, Huachun Zhou, Qi Xu, and Guanglei Li

School of Electronic and Information Engineering, Beijing Jiaotong University,
Beijing 100044, China
{14111038,gaody,hchzhou,15111046,15111035}@bjtu.edu.cn

Abstract. In space delay tolerant network (DTN), the absence of adequate nodes makes the communication opportunities precious. If the messages are transmitted using a path which exists high bit error, it can increase the delivery delay and reduce the delivery ratio. Therefore, how to distinguish the contact quality and select a path with little bit error is crucial to improve the network performance. In this paper, we propose a contact quality aware routing which operates cooperatively with Licklider Transmission Protocol (LTP). We use the processing signals in LTP to reflect the contact quality. Further more, we propose a contact quality based forwarding scheme to select a path which exists little bit error. The enhancements are verified using a test-bed with 15 simulation nodes. The experiments show that the proposed schemes can reduce the delivery delay, increase the delivery ratio and improve the throughput.

Keywords: Space delay tolerant network · LTP
Contact quality aware routing

1 Introduction

With the development of space technology, how to build a satellite relay network to support the communication becomes crucial. However, the long delivery delay, frequent link disruption in satellite networks prevent the traditional TCP/IP protocols from being adopted. What's more, the high asymmetry channel rate in deep space networks is also a severe challenge to TCP/IP protocol when faced with large scale of processing signals. Thanks to the ability of batting with such tough features, DTN is extremely fit for satellite networks [1]. DTN inserts an overlay called bundle layer below the application layer to realize the reliable communication. Meanwhile, DTN introduces the convergence layer protocols such as UDPCL [2] and LTPCL to realize the communication between bundle layer and the transport layer.

Among these convergence layer protocols, the performance of LTP is proved most outstanding when faced with high asymmetry channel rate and high bit errors [3,4]. The application data is divided into bundles and delivered as the

© ICST Institute for Computer Sciences, Social Informatics and Telecommunications Engineering 2018
L. Wang et al. (Eds.): QShine 2017, LNICST 234, pp. 94–103, 2018.
https://doi.org/10.1007/978-3-319-78078-8_10

units in bundle layer. In order to reduce the processing signals, several bundles are aggregated into LTP blocks according the preset block length. Then the block will be divided into segments which are encapsulated as data part of transport layer protocols.

LTP adopts a retransmission mechanism which depends on the import session, export session, checkpoints and report segments to realize the reliable transmission for blocks. The sender in LTP will create an export session and send the block during that session. Meanwhile, the receiver will create an import session to receive the block. When the block is received completely, the export session and the import session will be closed. The block will be flagged with offset. The receiver can identify the missing data according to the offset. When the receiver receives a checkpoint, it will respond a report segment to notice the sender of the missing data. Then the sender will retransmit the missing data. The process will continue until the block has been transmitted correctly. LTP has drawn many attention such as the performance analyse [4], the model evaluation [5]. However, the research of LTP in other aspects such as how to use LTP to identify the link quality has received very little attention.

Contact Graph Routing (CGR) [6] is a routing scheme developed for the networks whose topology is dynamic but predictable, such as the satellite networks. Due to that the orbit and trajectories of space nodes are fixed, it can acquire the communication information such as the duration previously. CGR calculates routes depends on these pre-acquired communication information. The main factor considered by CGR when select the path is the earliest bundle arrival time. Despite that many attentions have been paid on the research of CGR, such as the performance improvement [7] and the contact plan design [8], the contact quality based selection scheme receives very little attention.

In deep space network, the satellite nodes are usually sparse. This makes the communication opportunities very precious. Meanwhile, the space environment features such as the electromagnetic interference can bring high bit error to satellite links. If the data is transmitted using a path which is suffering high bit error, it can incur a lot of retransmission and cause a great waste of transmission opportunities. Although the LTP protocol can handle the bit error, the retransmission can lead to a sharp increase in delivery delay. What's more, if the delivery delay exceeds the bundle residual survival time, it can even incur data loss and reduce the deliver ratio. Therefore, how to distinguish the contact quality and select a path with little bit error is crucial to improve the network performance.

Considering above, in this paper we use DTN and LTP to deal with the tough space network environment and propose a contact quality aware routing which cooperates with LTP protocol to select a high quality path for data. Since a higher bit error can incur more retransmission, we use the processing signal numbers in LTP during one session to represent the contact quality. Meanwhile, an updating mechanism is also proposed to update the contact quality dynamically. When computing routes, we take both the contact quality and the earliest bundle arrival time into consideration. The main contributions of this paper are summarized as follows:

(1) A contact quality aware routing which contains contact quality detecting scheme and contact quality based forwarding scheme is proposed to select a path which exists little bit error.

(2) The performance of the proposed method is verified on a testbed with 15 simulation nodes and experimental results prove that the schemes can reduce the delivery delay, increase the delivery ratio and improve the throughput.

The remainder of the paper is organized as follows: In Sect. 2, we introduce the details of contact quality aware routing. In Sect. 3, we present the experiments on our test-bed. In the last part, we summarize the works in this paper.

2 Contact Quality Aware Routing

When LTP provides reliable transmission for blocks, the sessions are determined by the original block numbers. However, the checkpoints and report segments will be increased with the rise of bit error. Therefore, we can use the checkpoint and report segment numbers to reflect the contact quality. By combining the contact quality with delay information, contact quality aware CGR could select a delivery path which exists little bit error. The contact quality aware routing includes contact quality detection scheme and contact quality based forwarding scheme. Satellites will use contact quality detection scheme to detect the contact quality and update the contact quality timely. The contact quality based forwarding scheme is used to select a path with little bit error.

2.1 Contact Quality Detection

When the sender requires reliable services, LTP will adopt a retransmission mechanism which is enabled by the checkpoints and report segments. When the transmission of the data is completed, both the associated import session and export session will be closed. When there exists bit error, the segments could suffer retransmissions, both the report and checkpoint numbers will be increased which is caused by the retransmission processes. However, the export sessions and the import sessions are mainly determined by the block numbers, the bit error has no influence on the session numbers. Thus, the ratio of checkpoint and export session numbers as well as the ratio of report segment and import session numbers can be used as the identification of the contact quality. We create a list to record the checkpoint, export session, report segments and import session for each neighbor node respectively.

Let f_c denote the ratio of checkpoint numbers and import sessions. It can reflect the contact quality in the sender node. Let f_r denote the ratio of report segments and import sessions. It can reflect the contact quality in the receiver. The contact quality factor f_c and f_r are calculated as

$$f_c = \frac{\sum checkpoint}{\sum exportsession} \tag{1}$$

$$f_r = \frac{\sum report}{\sum importsession} \tag{2}$$

Algorithm 1. Contact quality detecting

Input:
    contact quality recording list
Output:
    contact quality updating message
1: Open contact quality recording list
2: **for all** neighbor nodes in contact quality recording list **do**
3:     Calculate $f_c = \frac{\sum checkpoint}{\sum exportsession}$ $f_r = \frac{\sum report}{\sum importsession}$
4:     **if** $f_c > f_r$ **then**
5:       $C=f_c$
6:     **else**
7:       $C=f_r$
8:     **end if**
9:     Open contact plan, compare the value of C with contact quality v recorded in the contact plan
10:     **if** $\frac{|C-v|}{v} > updatingratio$ **then**
11:       $v=C$, send contact updating message to other nodes
12:     **end if**
13: **end for**
14: **return** contact quality updating message;

When there exists no bit error, the value of f_c and f_r can be 1. When there exists bit error, the value of f_c and f_r will be increased with the rise of bit error.

We modify the contact plan to add quality weight C to identify the contact quality. We compare the value of f_c and f_r periodically and select the higher one as the value of contact quality weight C. In order to reduce the updating message numbers, we use a changing ratio to determine whether to send contact updating messages to the other nodes. We calculate the change ratio of the C between the prior recorded contact quality v. When the changing ratio is larger than a preset value, an updating message will be sent to other nodes. In this paper the change ratio is set to 4%. When the nodes identify the change of C, they will send a contact quality updating message to other nodes in the network. In order to distinguish the updating message from the user message, we use the reserved flag of Bundle protocol to mark the updating messages. The contact quality updating algorithm is showed in Algorithm 1. The contact quality detection period is set to 5 s.

2.2 Contact Quality Based Forwarding

In the original CGR, the key factor considered when nodes select path is the earliest arrival time, without considering the contact quality. Although LTP protocol could deal with the bit error using its retransmission scheme, it can cause the increase of retransmissions when select a lower quality path. This will incur a long delivery delay. Thus, by coordinating with the contact quality detection scheme described in part A, we can select a path with little bit error to reduce the delivery delay.

Algorithm 2. Contact quality aware forwarding

Input:
    contact plan, bundles
Output:
    forwarding path
1: **while** nodes receive bundles **do**
2:     **if** bundle is contact quality updating message **then**
3:         update the contact quality in contact plan
4:     **else**
5:         compute all the candidate paths using CGR,
           compute $f_{quality} = \prod_{i=s}^{r} u_{i,i+1} a_{i,i+1}$ of all the path
6:     **end if**
7:     **for all** the potential paths **do**
8:         select the path with the earliest arrival time as the delivery path
9:         **if** there exists paths with the same earliest arrival time **then**
10:           select the one with the lowest $f_{quality}$ as the delivery path
11:           **if** there exists paths withe the same $f_{quality}$ **then**
12:             select the one with the lowest hop count as the delivery path
13:             **if** there exists paths with the same hop count **then**
14:                select the one with the lowest neighbor node number as the delivery path
15:             **end if**
16:           **end if**
17:         **end if**
18:     **end for**
19: **end while**
20: **return** the delivery path;

Let $u_{i,j}$ denote whether satellite i could communicate with satellite j at time t. Let $a_{i,j}$ denote the contact quality weight between satellite i and j. The value of $u_{i,j}$ can only be 0 or 1. Then the path quality factor from the sender s to the receiver r could be denoted as

$$f_{quality} = \prod_{i=s}^{r} u_{i,i+1} a_{i,i+1} \tag{3}$$

The contact quality aware CGR is to select the lowest path quality factor $f_{quality}$ from all the potential paths.

For nodes in satellite networks, when receiving a bundle, they will firstly identify whether the bundle is a contact quality updating message according to the reserved bundle flag. If it is, they will update the contact quality information in its contact plan. If not, they will select a path for the message using the processes as follows:

Firstly, nodes will compute all potential paths for bundles using CGR. Along with the path computation, the earliest arrival time of each potential path which considers of the queue delay and OWLT will also be calculated. OWLT is the propagation delay among nodes configured in the contact plan. Then nodes will compute the contact quality factor $f_{quality}$ of each available path use Eq. (3). When select paths, nodes will select a path with the lowest arriving time. If the arriving time of the bundles is the same, then they will select a path with the lowest $f_{quality}$ and queue the bundles into the neighbor node on the path. In this way, nodes could avoid all the bundles being concentrated to one path which has the highest contact quality. If there exists two paths with the same value of $f_{quality}$, then nodes will select the one which has the lowest hop count. If there exists two paths with the same hop count, then nodes will select the path whose neighbor node number is lower. The contact quality aware forwarding scheme is showed in Algorithm 2.

3   Performance Evaluation

In this section, we produce a satellite terrestrial test-bed with 15 Linux nodes to evaluate the performance of the contact quality aware routing. In this paper, we mainly focus on the enhancements of CGR, the communication details of the satellite terrestrial network are presented in our previous works in [9]. Figure 2 is the moon-earth experimental topology which contains a moon satellite ChangE, three China's relay satellites Tianlian [10], and the terrestrial network which is made up of core and mobile access networks.

The height of ChangE satellite is 1938 km from moonscape and the orbit inclination is 90. The parameter of the three Tianlian satellites and the gateway which locates at JiuQuan are shown in Table 1. We use STK [11] to obtain the delay and contact information among these nodes according to the orbit parameters. The contacts and the propagation delay among these nodes are shown in Table 2. The space nodes adopt the BP/LTP/UDP/IP protocol which is realized using ION.3.3.1 [12], a software developed by NASA to implement the DTN protocols.

Table 1. Parameters of the satellites and gateway

Satellite	Height	Longitude	Latitude
Tianlian01	42371 km	76.95 E	0
Tianlian02	42371 km	176.71 E	0
Tianlian03	42371 km	16.65 E	0
Jiuquan	0	103.316 E	41.118 N

The experiments include two parts. We evaluate the performance of contact quality aware CGR(CGR-CA) by comparing with CGR-ETO [7] which is a typical improvement of CGR. In the first part, we compare the delivery ratio and the delivery delay of CGR-CA and CGR-ETO when faced with different link bit error. In the second part, we evaluate the throughput of the system at the receiver.

Table 2. Contact information of satellites

Start node	End node	Start time	End time	Delay
ChangE	Tianlian01	0	1000 s	1400 ms
ChangE	Tianlian02	0	1000 s	1400 ms
ChangE	Tianlian03	0	1000 s	1400 ms
Tianlian01	Tianlian02	0	86400 s	300 ms
Tianlian01	Tianlian03	0	86400 s	300 ms
Tianlian02	Tianlian03	0	86400 s	300 ms
Jiuquan	Tianlian01	0	86400 s	300 ms
Jiuquan	Tianlian02	0	86400 s	300 ms

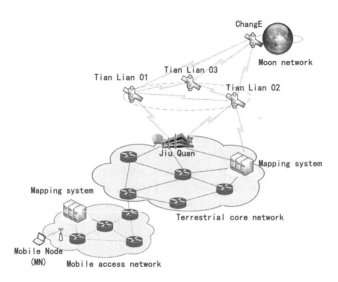

Fig. 1. Experimental topology

3.1   The Impacts of Bundles with Different Bit Errors

We use ChangE to send data to the mobile node (MN) which is located in the mobile access network. The channel rate of the links between ChangE and Tanlians is asymmetrical, the rate of links between Tianlians and gateway is symmetrical. In the links between ChangE and Tianlians, the data channel rate is set to 250 kbyte/s and the ACK channel rate is set to 500 byte/s. In the links between Tianlians and gateway, both the data channel rate and the ACK channel rate are set to 250 kbyte/s. We use the ChangE to send a bundle to MN every second. The bundle size is set to 200 kbyte. The experimental duration is 1000 s. The priority of the files is set to bulk, standard and urgent in turn. In DTN, the urgent bundle will be firstly transmitted and the bulk will be transmitted in the last turn. The bit error of links among Tianlian satellites and gateway are set to 10^{-7}, the bit error of links among Tianlian satellites and ChangE are varying.

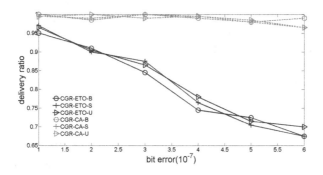

Fig. 2. The delivery ratio of bundles with different bit error

In Figs. 2 and 3 we compare the performance of contact quality aware CGR with CGR-ETO when faced with different bit errors. The bit error of the link between ChangE and Tianlian02 is set to be varying from 10^{-7} to $6*10^{-7}$. The bit error of link between ChangE and Tianlian03 and the link between ChangE and Tianlian01 is set to 5 times and 10 times of the bit error of the link between ChangE and Tianlian02 respectively. The time to live(TTL) of bundles are set to 8 s. Since the Tianlian03 has no direct link to gateway and the node number of Tianlian01 is smaller than Tianlian02, CGR-ETO will select Tianlian01 as the next delivery node. However, the bit error on the link between Tianlian01 and the ChangE is higher than that of the link between Tianlian02 and ChangE. While considering the contact quality factor, CGR-CA can select tianlian02 as the next delivery node.

From the figs we can see that the delivery ratio will be decreased with the increase of bit error when nodes adopt CGR-ETO. This is because that with the increase of bit error, more data will suffer retransmission. This can increase the delivery delay. When delivery delay exceeds the residual survival time, the bundles can suffer data loss. However, when nodes adopt CGR-CA, all the bundles can be delivered through a path with little bit error. This can reduce the

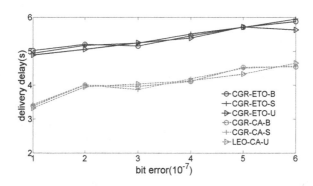

Fig. 3. The delivery delay of bundles with different bit error

retransmission. From Fig. 2 we can see that the contact quality aware CGR can increase the delivery ratio as high as 30% against CGR-ETO. From Fig. 3 we can conclude that CGR-CA can reduce almost 25% of the delivery delay compared with CGR-ETO. This is because that contact quality aware CGR can select a path with high quality which could reduce the retransmissions.

3.2   The Impacts of Throughput

In this part, we evaluate the throughput of CGR-CA and CGR-ETO. The TTL of bundles are set to 20 s. The bit error of the link between ChangE and Tianlian02 is set to be $3*10^{-7}$. The bit error of link between ChangE and Tianlian03 and the link between ChangE and Tianlian01 is set to 5 times and 10 times of the bit error of the link between ChangE and Tianlian02 respectively.

Figure 4 shows the throughput acquired at the MN. We can see that the throughput of MN when nodes adopt CGR-CA is more stable than that when nodes adopt CGR-ETO. This is because that CGR-ETO haven't considered the contact quality factor and select Tianlian01 as the next hop node. The bundles can suffer more retransmission.

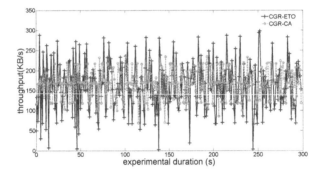

Fig. 4. The throughput at the receiver

4   Conclusion

In this paper, we focused on the contact quality based routing selection problem in satellite terrestrial network and proposed a contact quality aware CGR to deal with the impact of bit error. When compute routes, our design considers both the contact quality and the delay information to select a path with little bit error. To show the effectiveness of our design, we built a test-bed with 15 Linux nodes and implemented our proposed algorithm. The extensive experimental results demonstrate that the contact quality aware CGR can increase the delivery ratio, reduce the delivery delay and improve the throughput.

Acknowledgement. This work was supported in part by NSAF of China under Grant No. U1530118, National Basic Research Program of China (973 program) under Grant No. 2013CB329101, and National High Technology of China (863 program) under Grant No. 2015AA015702.

References

1. Caini, C., Cruickshank, H., Farrell, S., Marchese, M.: Delay-and disruption-tolerant networking (DTN): an alternative solution for future satellite networking applications. Proc. IEEE **99**(11), 1980–1997 (2011)
2. Kruse, H., Ostermann, S.: UDP convergence layers for the DTN bundle and LTP protocols. IETF Draft (2008)
3. Wang, R., Burleigh, S.C., Parikh, P., Lin, C.-J., Sun, B.: Licklider transmission protocol (LTP)-based DTN for cislunar communications. IEEE/ACM Trans. Netw. **19**(2), 359–368 (2011)
4. Bezirgiannidis, N., Tsaoussidis, V.: Packet size and DTN transport service: evaluation on a DTN testbed. In: International Congress on Ultra Modern Telecommunications and Control Systems, pp. 1198–1205, October 2010
5. Lu, H., Jiang, F., Wu, J., Chen, C.W.: Performance improvement in DTNs by packet size optimization. IEEE Trans. Aerosp. Electron. Syst. **51**(4), 2987–3000 (2015)
6. Araniti, G., Bezirgiannidis, N., Birrane, E., Bisio, I., Burleigh, S., Caini, C., Feldmann, M., Marchese, M., Segui, J., Suzuki, K.: Contact graph routing in DTN space networks: overview, enhancements and performance. IEEE Commun. Mag. **53**(3), 38–46 (2015)
7. Bezirgiannidis, N., Caini, C., Tsaoussidis, V.: Analysis of contact graph routing enhancements for DTN space communications. Int. J. Satell. Commun. Network. **34**(5), 695–709 (2016). sAT-15-0048.R1
8. Fraire, J.A., Madoery, P.G., Finochietto, J.M.: Traffic-aware contact plan design for disruption-tolerant space sensor networks. Ad Hoc Netw. **47**, 41–52 (2016)
9. Feng, B., Zhou, H., Li, G., Li, H., Yu, S.: SAT-GRD: an ID/Loc split network architecture interconnecting satellite and ground networks. In: 2016 IEEE International Conference on Communications (ICC), pp. 1–6, May 2016
10. Jiasheng, W.: Proposal for developing China's data relay satellite system. Spacecraft Eng. **2**, 002 (2011)
11. Satellite tool kit (STK) (2015). http://www.agi.com/products/stk/
12. Interplanetary overlay network (ION) (2015). https://sourceforge.net/projects/ion-dtn/

Joint Optimization of Latency Monitoring and Traffic Scheduling in Software Defined Heterogeneous Networks

Xu Zhang, Weigang Hou$^{(\boxtimes)}$, Lei Guo$^{(\boxtimes)}$, Siqi Wang, Qihan Zhang,
Pengxing Guo, and Ruijia Li

College of Computer Science and Engineering, Northeastern University,
Shenyang 110819, China
{houweigang,guolei}@cse.neu.edu.cn

Abstract. Since the current Internet is only able to provide best-effort services, the quality of service (QoS) for many emerging businesses cannot be well guaranteed. Meanwhile, due to the privatization of networks management, multi-vendor heterogeneous networks are difficult to provide end-to-end QoS assurance on demand. Therefore, heterogeneous devices from different vendors also bring new challenges to the flexible control of network equipment. Software defined network (SDN) is an emerging paradigm which separates the network's control logic from the underlying routers and switches. In this paper, we design a monitoring loop of link latency by using both LLDP and Echo probing modules. Then, a dynamic routing algorithm is proposed to select optimized transmission path based on the information of link latency. In addition, we develop a routing application assorted with the monitoring mechanism by extending the RYU controller. We implement our solution in a semi-practical SDN testbed. Finally, the overall feasibility and efficiency of the proposed solution are experimentally verified and evaluated.

Keywords: SDN · Latency monitoring · Traffic engineering · QoS
Heterogeneous network

1 Introduction

In the traditional IP network, all packets are switched by using best-effort way. Since best-effort service model reduces the overhead and the cost at the network layer without losing reliability and robustness, this architecture can perfectly provide data transmission in the case of conventional applications (voice, video, etc.). However, with the rapid development of the Internet, there have been a large number of new types of business, e.g., VoIP, HDTV, Multimedia service, and so on. This kind of traffic has stringent delay requirements which cannot be guaranteed in the best-effort Internet. Although the Internet Engineering Task Force (IETF) has proposed several quality of service (QoS) architecture such as Integrated Services (IntServ) [1] and Differentiated Services (DiffServ) [2], these

© ICST Institute for Computer Sciences, Social Informatics and Telecommunications Engineering 2018
L. Wang et al. (Eds.): QShine 2017, LNICST 234, pp. 104–113, 2018.
https://doi.org/10.1007/978-3-319-78078-8_11

proposals are not very successful. They have not been deployed on a large scale commercial environment because they all need to make fundamental changes to the top layer of a distributed hop-by-hop routing architecture without a global view. Meanwhile, some solutions based on multi-protocol label switching (MPLS) [3] and border gateway protocol (BGP) [3] are explored to address the problem that is severely lacking on the information of the available network resources (e.g., network delay information) from an end-to-end perspective. However, these schemes do not have good re-configurability and adaptability. More particularly, with the expansion of network scale, multi-vendor devices coexist on the Internet [4]. Therefore, the network architecture of the current Internet is inflexible for the rapid development and deployment of network services supporting multiple application requirements.

Software defined network (SDN) [5] is one of the latest revolutions in the networking field, which allows network administrators to manage network services through the abstraction of underlying network functionality [6–8]. To efficiently apply QoS policies [9–12], it is important to obtain the latency information in a SDN-based packet network. In [13], authors presented a measurement scheme of the link latency, but they did not give a routing solution to schedule traffic. Note that, both the network measurement and the traffic engineering are important. If operators want to provide differentiated services for various users through the SDN solution, it is essential to design the monitoring mechanism and develop the traffic scheduling algorithm.

In this paper, we first focus on designing a monitoring mechanism of link delay by using both link layer discovery protocol (LLDP) monitoring module and Echo monitoring module. Then, we propose a dynamic shortest delay routing algorithm, i.e., SDRA, in order to meet the QoS requirements of different traffic. In addition, we develop a routing application assorted with both the monitoring mechanism and the SDRA traffic scheduling by extending the RYU controller. We implement our solution in a semi-practical SDN testbed. Finally, the overall feasibility and efficiency of the proposed solution are experimentally verified and evaluated. In the four-node four-link network (n4s4) topology, we measure the link latency detected by the delay monitoring module, and this demonstrates the feasibility of the monitoring mechanism. Moreover, the performance of the SDRA scheme under different traffic loads is also quantitatively evaluated based on the simulated NSFNET network in term of the end-to-end delay, compared with the minimum hop routing algorithm (MHRA). It is beneficial for us to verify the efficiency of our SDN-based delay solution.

The contributions of this work can be summarized as follows,

(1) We design a monitoring mechanism to measure the link delay in multi-vendor heterogeneous network. And experimental presentation demonstrates the feasibility of the monitoring mechanism.
(2) We propose a delay-aware SDRA algorithm to provide the end-to-end QoS guarantees based on a centralized network view. It is able to choose the optimized path according to the network status in real time.

(3) We develop a SDN-based shortest delay application by extending RYU controller. The efficiency of overall solutions is evaluated in a semi-practical SDN platform.

2   Problem Statement and Analysis

In this section, we first describe the network architecture and the key notations used for the problem formulation. Then, we introduce the system model. Finally, we formulate mathematically our problem in term of providing an end-to-end shortest delay guarantee.

2.1   Network Architecture

The SDN architecture can be depicted as a composition of three planes, as shown in Fig. 1. Each plane has its own specific functions. The data plane corresponds to the multi-vendor heterogeneous devices, which only are responsible for the data forwarding. Different from traditional networks, the control plane is stripped from the underlying forwarding device. The control plane controls all network devices and abstracts the underlying network resources by using the OpenFlow protocol. This is a key characteristic of SDN network, which makes it possible to allocate network resources of multi-vendor heterogeneous devices based on a centralized controller. The management plane is the set of applications that use algorithms or protocols to implement network control and distribute the operations logic to the underlying devices. For instance, the SDRA application maintains a routing policy to provide the end-to-end QoS service by utilizing the proposed solution.

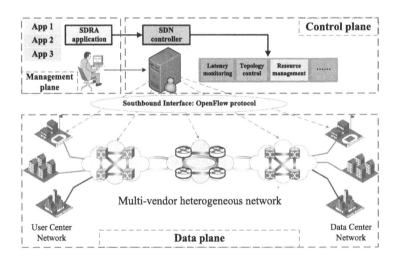

Fig. 1. Network architecture.

2.2 Notation Definitions

(1) u, v: index of OF-Switch, $u, v \in \{1, 2, 3, ..., N\}$.

(2) K: the number of shortest paths.

(3) P_K: the set of K shortest paths.

(4) P^k: the kth shortest path from source node to destination node, where $k \in \{1, 2, 3, ..., K\}$.

(5) $B_{e(u,v)}$: the total bandwidth capacity of link $e(u, v)$.

(6) $B^f_{e(u,v)}$: the free bandwidth capacity of link $e(u, v)$.

(7) H: the maximum number of path length, and we regard that a path is unreachable if its length is more than H hops.

(8) T^{lldp}_c: a time cycle of LLDP process, and it is constant value.

(9) T^{echo}_c: a time cycle of Echo process, and it is constant value.

(10) $T_{e(u,v)}(t)$: the delay of link $e(u, v)$ at time t, and we assume that $T_{e(u,v)}(t) = T_{e(v,u)}(t)$.

(11) $T^{lldp}_{e(u,v)}(t)$: the delay of a LLDP process about link $e(u, v)$ at time t, where $\forall t \in \{t_1, t_2, t_3, ..., T^{lldp}_c\}$. The process is defined as: first, the controller sends Packet-Out message to OF-Switch u for guiding OF-Switch u forwarding LLDP packet. Then, LLDP packet is transmitted to OF-Switch v through link $e(u, v)$. Finally, OF-Switch v sends Packet-In message to the controller when it receives the LLDP packet.

(12) $T^{echo}_u(t)$: the delay of an Echo process about OF-Switch u at time t, where $\forall t \in \{t_1, t_2, t_3, ..., T^{echo}_c\}$. The process is that the controller sends Echo Request message to the OF-Switch u for checking the latency between the controller and OF-Switch u. Then, when the OF-Switch u receives the message, it immediately returns an Echo Reply message to the controller.

(13) $e(u, v)$: binary variable, taking 1 if that exists a link between node u and v ($u \neq v$), and 0 otherwise.

(14) $\varphi^{P^k}_{e(u,v)}$: binary variable, taking 1 if the kth shortest routing path includes link $e(u, v)$ and 0 otherwise.

(15) α_p: binary variable, taking 1 if the path p is selected as the working path and 0 otherwise.

2.3 System Model

We model the network of packet switching by a graph $G(V, E)$, in which $V = \{v_1, v_2, ..., v_N\}$ denotes the set of OpenFlow-enabled switches and $E = \{e_1, e_2, ..., e_M\}$ is the set of bidirectional edges between OF-Switches. N is the total number of OF-Switches in the network, while M is the total number of edges in the network. Note that, $e(u, v)$ taking 1 if that exists a link between node u and v ($u \neq v$), and 0 otherwise. In a SDN-based packet network, it consists of a controller and multiple OF-Switches. All OF-Switches are responsible for forwarding data packet only. The control function of the network belongs to the upper controller, and OpenFlow protocol is utilized to communicate between the controller and OF-Switch. More specifically, the network is dynamic, and the status information changes over time. Let $G'(V', E', t)$ represent the network graph at time t, where $\forall t \in \{t_1, t_2, t_3, ..., T_c\}$, and T_c denotes a cycle time of probing network status. Meanwhile, let $T_{e(u,v)}(t)$ denotes the delay of link $e(u, v)$ at time t, and we assume that it is invariant in a cycle T_c. Therefore, we are able to dynamically generate the graph $G'(V', E', t)$ when let $T_{e(u,v)}(t)$ be the weight of the edge in the packet network. In addition, every delay-sensitive service requirement is represented by a 5-tuple: $\langle s, d, x, b_x, t_x \rangle$, where s is a IP address of source host, d is a IP address of destination host, x represents a type index of the delay-sensitive traffic, b_x is the bandwidth requirement, and t_x is the maximum number of latency requirement level.

2.4 Problem Formulation

In reality, the status of packet switching network is varies with time. However, we can investigate the optimal delay problem at a particular time t. Our objective is to minimize the transmission delay. Mathematically, our problem can be formulated as follows (1).

$$Minimize : \sum_{k=1}^{K} \sum_{u=1}^{N} \sum_{v=1}^{N} \left(T_{e(u,v)}(t) \times \varphi_{e(u,v)}^{P^k} \right) \tag{1}$$

$$\sum_{u=1}^{N} \sum_{v=1}^{N} \left[e(u,v) \cdot \varphi_{e(u,v)}^{P^k} \cdot b_x \right] - \sum_{v=1}^{N} \sum_{u=1}^{N} \left[e(v,u) \cdot \varphi_{e(v,u)}^{P^k} \cdot b_x \right] = \left\{ \begin{array}{l} b_x, \ if \ u = s, \\ -b_x, \ if \ u = d, \\ 0, \ otherwise. \end{array} \right. \tag{2}$$

$$\varphi_{e(u,v)}^{P^k} \cdot b_x \leq B_{e(u,v)}^{f} \tag{3}$$

$$\sum_{u=1}^{N} \sum_{v=1}^{N} \varphi_{e(u,v)}^{P^k} \leq H \tag{4}$$

$$T_{e(u,v)}^{lldp}(t) \leq T_{c}^{lldp} \tag{5}$$

$$T_{u}^{echo}(t) \leq T_{c}^{echo} \tag{6}$$

$$\sum_{p \in P_K} \alpha_p = 1 \tag{7}$$

$$\frac{1}{2} \left[T_{e(u,v)}^{lldp}(t) + T_{e(v,u)}^{lldp}(t) - T_{u}^{echo}(t) - T_{v}^{echo}(t) \right] = T_{e(u,v)}(t) \tag{8}$$

The constraint (2) states that for all nodes of the network, the outgoing traffic should be equal to incoming traffic except for the source and the destination nodes. Equation (3) represents that the residual bandwidth of each link along the routing path should be higher than the bandwidth requirement of the traffic. Equation (4) limits the path length no longer than H hops. Equations (5) and (6) ensure the effectiveness of the probing time for the both LLDP and Echo processes. Equation (7) ensures that, for each service request, only one candidate path is selected as the working path. Equation (8) calculates the delay of the link according to the probing results from the monitoring module.

3   SDN-Based Delay Solution

3.1   Monitoring Mechanism

Our latency monitoring mechanism consists of the LLDP monitoring module and the Echo monitoring module. LLDP monitoring module is used to obtain the delay of the link discovery process, while Echo monitoring module is responsible for detecting the propagation latency between the controller and the switch. The link discovery process is achieved based on sending a specially crafted packet (i.e., LLDP data packet) through a link from the controller and back while the adjacent switch has no matched flow entry. The controller guides the switch 1 to send LLDP packet through a particular port via a Packet-Out message, and records the current timestamp. Then, the packet is transmitted from the switch 1 to the switch 2 along link 1→2. Since there is no flow entry to match the packet in the switch 2, switch 2 sends Packet-In message to the controller. The controller calculates the latency of LLDP process about link 1→2 when receiving the Packet-In message from switch 2. Similarly, we can get the latency of LLDP process about link 2→1. Let $T^{lldp}_{e(s1,s2)}$ and $T^{lldp}_{e(s2,s1)}$ denote the delay of the above two processes, respectively. In addition, we can also describe the process of Echo monitoring module. Firstly, the controller sends the Echo Request message encapsulated timestamp to the switch. The switch returns the Echo Reply message back to the controller when it receives the Echo Request message. Then, the Echo Monitoring module retrieves the timestamp from the Echo Reply message, and deduces the latency how long it takes for the packet to complete its journey between the controller and the switch. Note that, let T^{echo}_{s1} and T^{echo}_{s2} represent the propagation latency between the controller and the switch 1 and 2, respectively. Thus, we have above four variables. The latency of link S1↔S2 will be $T^{link}_{e(s1,s2)} = T^{link}_{e(s2,s1)} = 1/2 \times (T^{lldp}_{e(s1,s2)} + T^{lldp}_{e(s2,s1)} - T^{echo}_{s1} - T^{echo}_{s2})$, where we assume that the delay of link S1→S2 is equal to link S2→S1.

3.2   Delay-Aware Heuristic Algorithm

We illustrate the detailed procedure of the dynamic SDRA algorithm by using Fig. 2. First, we have constructed a virtual network graph with the edge weight that is the link delay. Based on the virtual network graph, Dijkstra's algorithm is used to calculate the best path from source node A to destination node F, which is A→C→D→F with cost 5. This path becomes the first shortest delay path. Meanwhile, node A becomes the spur node with a root path of itself. The edge A→C is removed because it coincides with the root path. Dijkstra's algorithm is used to compute the spur path again, which is A→B→D→F with a cost of 8. Then, the node C becomes the spur node, while A→C is the root path. We remove the edge C→D from the graph since it coincides with the root path. And, the spur path C→E→F can be obtained by using Dijkstra. The total path is the sum of root path and spur path, i.e., A→C→E→F with cost 7. Finally, we remove the edge D→F, and let node D become the spur node. Another potential path A→C→D→E→F is drawn with a cost of 8. Note that, A→C→E→F is

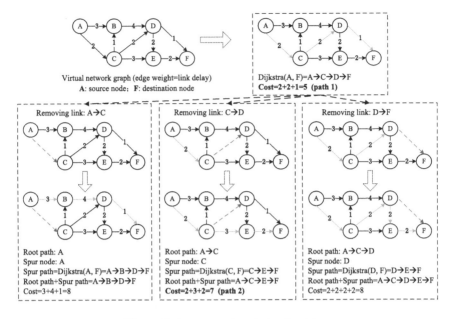

Fig. 2. Delay-aware heuristic algorithm.

chosen to become the second path because it has the lowest cost of 7. Repeat the above iterative process, so that we can dynamically calculate the k-shortest delay path between any two nodes. The purpose of multiple paths is to achieve the fault tolerance of the network, the detailed process can be found in our previous work [14,15].

The time complexity of the algorithm is dependent on the Dijkstra algorithm used in the computation of the spur paths. Dijkstra's algorithm has a worse case time complexity of $O(N^2)$, but using a Fibonacci heap it becomes $O(M + N \log N)$. Since our algorithm makes Kl calls to the Dijkstra in computing the spur paths, where l is the length of spur paths. In a network graph, the value of l is N at the worst case. Therefore, the total time complexity of our algorithm is approximate $O(KN(M + N \log N))$, which is polynomial.

4   Experimental Results and Discussions

To evaluate the feasibility and efficiency of the proposed solution, we first establish a SDN testing environment by utilizing the RYU controller (2 processors, 2 GB memory, and independent network adapter) and the Mininet (2 processors, 2 GB memory, and independent network adapter). The IP address of the controller is 192.168.100.100, whereas the 192.168.100.20 represents the IP address of the mininet.

Next, in our experiments, we focus on a 4-node 4-link 5-host network topology for verifying the feasibility of our SDRA solution. Meanwhile, we also define a scenario to evaluate the delay parameters of the network. That is a simulation of the client-server model in the real network, i.e., the Host 1 (client) sends the traffic requests to Host 2 and 3 (servers) at the same time. Then, we record the latency of all links in the topology, shown in Fig. 3. In addition, Fig. 4 quantitatively shows the histogram of the end-to-end delay, processing delay and path delay, respectively. We can see that the end-to-end delay is about 15 milliseconds (ms), which consist of the processing delay of the controller, the forwarding delay of the switch and the transmission delay of path. The processing latency of the controller here is the time duration from receiving a traffic request to distributing Flow-Mod message. The path delay is the sum of the delays of all links that the traffic passes from client to server. Therefore, we thank to the introduction of SDN-based delay scheme, the network can achieve dynamic delay balance (e.g., service requests of the host 1→2 and the host 1→3 dynamically select different paths to implement shortest transmission delay).

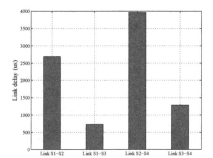 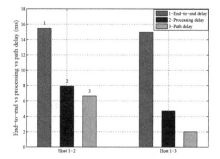

Fig. 3. The link latency.   **Fig. 4.** End-to-end vs processing vs path.

Finally, we conduct a lot of dynamic experiments based on the NSFNET topology [8]. In this experiment, the traffic request is randomly generated between any two nodes. The MHRA algorithm is also compared with the proposed SDRA algorithm in term of both the maximum end-to-end delay and the maximum path delay. As shown in Figs. 5 and 6, the MHRA mechanism makes it possible to achieve a delay control similar to that of SDRA at light traffic loads. However, when the number of traffic request keeps increasing, MHRA increases significantly. This is because a lot of traffic congestion occurs on the shortest path. As a result, the MHRA deteriorates the quality of data transmission. Conversely, the SDRA can turn to the idle path to ease the network pressure and thus ensure the quality of service. With the increasing number of services, the advantage of the proposed SDRA will be more highlighted. The results indicate that the SDN-based delay solution can dynamically select the optimized path to reduce the delay of data transmission, which verifies its feasibility and efficiency.

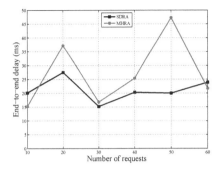
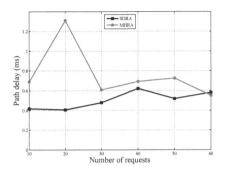

Fig. 5. The maximum end-to-end delay.   **Fig. 6.** The maximum path delay.

5   Conclusions

Traditional IP networks were complex and very hard to manage, hence it was difficult to configure the network based on predefined policies or very hard to reconfigure the network adaptive to faults and load variation. Meanwhile, multi-vendor heterogeneous networks also brought new challenges to the flexible control of network device for providing the end-to-end QoS service on demand. Therefore, in this paper, we investigated how to utilize SDN to guarantee the QoS of applications. We first formulated mathematically our problem in term of providing the end-to-end shortest delay. Then, we designed a monitoring mechanism of link latency by using both LLDP and Echo probing modules. Next, a dynamic routing algorithm was proposed to select optimized transmission path based on the information of link latency. More importantly, we developed a routing application that had the monitoring mechanism through extending the RYU controller, and our solution was achieved in a semi-practical SDN testbed. Finally, we quantitatively evaluated the performance of the overall system in terms of the end-to-end delay, the path delay, and the processing latency of the controller. The experimental results showed the system's overall feasibility and efficiency.

Acknowledgements. This work is supported by the National Nature Science Foundation of China under Grant 61401082, in part by the General Armament Department and Ministry of Education United Fund under Grant 6141A0224-003, in part by the Fundamental Research Funds for the Central Universities under Grant N161604004 and Grant N161608001, and in part by National Scholarship Foundation of China.

References

1. Braden, R., Clark, D., Shenker, S.: Integrated services in the internet architecture: an overview, June 1994
2. Blake, S., Black, D., Carlson, M., Davies, E., Wang, Z., Weiss, W.: An architecture for differentiated services, December 1998

3. Rosen, E., Rekhter, Y.: BGP/MPLS VPN, March 1999
4. Hou, W., Ning, Z., Guo, L., Chen, Z., Obaidat, M.: Novel framework of risk-aware virtual network embedding in optical data center networks. IEEE Syst. J. **PP**(99), 1–10 (2017). https://doi.org/10.1109/JSYST.2017.2673828
5. Kreutz, D., Ramos, F., Verissimo, P., Rothenberg, C., Azodolmolky, S., Uhlig, S.: Software-defined networking: a comprehensive survey. Proc. IEEE **103**, 14–76 (2015)
6. Hou, W., Ning, Z., Guo, L., Zhang, X.: Temporal, functional and spatial big data computing framework for large-scale smart grid. IEEE Trans. Emerg. Top. Comput. **PP**(99), 1–11 (2017). https://doi.org/10.1109/TETC.2017
7. Hou, W., Tian, G., Guo, L., Wang, X., Zhang, X., Ning, Z.: Cooperative mechanism for energy transportation and storage in internet of energy. IEEE Access **5**, 1363–1375 (2017). https://doi.org/10.1109/ACCESS.2017.2664981
8. Zhang, X., Guo, L., Hou, W., Wang, S., Zhang, Q., Guo, P., Li, R.: Experimental demonstration of an intelligent control plane with proactive spectrum defragmentation in SD-EONs. Opt. Express **25**(20), 24837–24852 (2017)
9. Ning, Z., Hu, X., Chen, Z., Zhou, M., Hu, B., Cheng, J., Obaidat, M.: A cooperative quality-aware service access system for social internet of vehicles. IEEE Internet Things J. (2017). https://doi.org/10.1109/JIOT.2017.2764259
10. Ning, Z., Xia, F., Ullah, N., Kong, X., Hu, X.: Vehicular social networks: enabling smart mobility. IEEE Commun. Mag. **55**(5), 49–55 (2017)
11. Hou, W., Ning, Z., Guo, L.: Green survivable collaborative edge computing in smart cities. IEEE Trans. Ind. Inform. (2018). https://doi.org/10.1109/TII.2018.2797922
12. Hou, W., Zhang, R., Qi, W., Lu, K., Wang, J., Guo, L.: A provident resource defragmentation framework for mobile cloud computing. IEEE Trans. Emerg. Top. Comput. **6**(1), 32–44 (2015). https://doi.org/10.1109/TETC.2015.2477778
13. Phemius, K., Bouet, M.: Monitoring latency with OpenFlow. In: International Conference on Network & Service Management, pp. 122–125 (2013)
14. Zhang, X., Hou, W., Guo, L., Wang, S., Sun, Y., Yang, X.: Failure recovery solutions using cognitive mechanisms for software defined optical networks. In: 2016 15th International Conference on Optical Communications and Networks, pp. 1–3 (2016)
15. Zhang, X., Guo, L., Hou, W., Zhang, Q., Wang, S.: Failure recovery solutions using cognitive mechanisms based on software defined optical network platform. Opt. Eng. **56**(1), 1–14 (2017)

Reliable Mutual Node Evaluation for Trust-Based OLSR in Tactical MANETs

Ji-Hun Lim[1], Keun-Woo Lim[2], and Young-Bae Ko[1($\boxtimes$)]

[1] Ajou University, Suwon, Kyeonggi-do, South Korea
{limbee94,youngko}@ajou.ac.kr
[2] Telecom Paristech, INFRES, RMS, 75013 Paris, France
keunwoo.lim@telecom-paristech.fr

Abstract. This paper proposes a mutual node evaluation method in mobile ad hoc networks to recognize and reliably remove attacker nodes from deteriorating the network. We focus on a tactical networking environment, where the network is generally maintained in harsh and hostile areas while the applications require stringent service requirements. In these kinds of environments, it is desirable to utilize proactive routing methods such as Optimized Link State Routing (OLSR). However, OLSR have weaknesses against various security attacks. To solve this problem, we provide a trust-based evaluation approach where node evaluate each other based on the packet forwarding capabilities. We prove the performance of our proposed method through NS-3.

Keywords: Trust-based routing · Mobile ad hoc networks
Tactical networks · Optimized Link State Routing

1 Introduction

In a tactical Mobile Ad Hoc Networks (MANET), mobile nodes with wireless transmission capabilities, such as soldiers, vehicles, drones, and command centers are required to share and disseminate various tactical information. As the nature of the network tends to have high and frequently changing mobility, how to ensure reliability and connectivity of the network is of utmost priority in this area of research. To provide these capabilities, much research have been progressed in the area of wireless routing protocols, which allows multi-hop communication between tactical nodes on the battlefield.

One of the often considered wireless routing protocol for tactical MANETs is Optimized Link State Routing (OLSR) [1,2]. In the main procedure of OLSR, all nodes participating in the network periodically undergo a HELLO message broadcast and then a multipoint relay (MPR) selection process which structures a multi-hop routing table with the MPRs managing the link-state information. Then, a Topology Control (TC) message exchange is made by all MPRs to share

© ICST Institute for Computer Sciences, Social Informatics and Telecommunications Engineering 2018
L. Wang et al. (Eds.): QShine 2017, LNICST 234, pp. 114–119, 2018.
https://doi.org/10.1007/978-3-319-78078-8_12

each of their link information. This allows proactive creation and management of multi-hop routes to all nodes. Therefore, OLSR is considered to be beneficial for time-critical applications, such as tactical MANETs.

However, OLSR is also known to have risks and issues regarding security and trust, and reliability. These include link and identity spoofing attacks [3], wormhole attacks [4], HELLO and TC message tempering [2], and etc. In this paper, we focus on two specific categories of risks.

Denial-of-Service (DoS) Attacks: We specifically focus on nodes that may perform DoS attacks such as a blackhole attack [5] and node isolation attack [6]. Especially in OLSR, in the case of blackhole attack, a malicious node can prioritize itself to become a MPR and drop all packets instead of relaying them. In the case of a node isolation attack, the malicious node can advertise its TC message without the information of nodes that use itself as MPR which means that these nodes will become invisible to the entire network.

Mobility and Reliability Issues: Even if nodes are not attackers, specific nodes may not be reliable due to being located at or moving to unfavorable locations. It is important to be able to isolate these nodes from becoming MPRs. Li et al. [7] states that mobility affects the performance of MPR forwarding, and proposes a method of modeling the mobility of nodes and calculating the chances of a node becoming a MPR through this mobility model.

In this paper, we focus on mutual node evaluation to create a trust-based OLSR for tactical MANETs. To prevent the two risks mentioned above, we propose a trust-value based approach where each node evaluates all other nodes in the network using a trust-value. Based on these trust values during MPR selection, only nodes that are deemed trustworthy will be selected as MPRs. Successful data forwarding will award nodes into having a higher trust, while continuous failure in data transmission will degrade the trust of the node, eventually isolating the node from MPR selection.

2   Mutual Node Evaluation Method

The general procedure of our proposed mutual node evaluation method is progressed by adding and maintaining a *trusttable* to each node in the network. By sharing and referencing other nodes' trust values of all the other nodes, evaluation becomes mutual; henceforth the name of our method. There are four sequences of operations in the proposed scheme: (1) Creation and management of trust table, (2) Selection of MPR, (3) Recalculating the trust value, and (4) Extension of TC message for sharing trust value.

2.1   Creation and Management of Trust Table

In the initial phase of the OLSR, each node creates what we define as a *trust table*. The size of a trust table is defined as $m * m$, where m is the number of all nodes in the network. Each entry in the trust table is the *trust value*, which defines how much a node (in the row) trusts another node (in the column). From here onwards, we denote the trust value of node a to node b as $T_{a \to b}$. In the initial stage, the node will record a trust value of 100 to all other nodes, while keeping the evaluation of other nodes to $NULL$.

This table is updated whenever TC message is shared between all the nodes, where the trust table of each node is included in the TC message and exchanged. For example, if node b broadcasts its TC message, it includes $T_{b \to a}$, $T_{b \to b} = NULL$, $T_{b \to c}$, $T_{b \to d}$, and $T_{b \to e}$ values in the message. Once node a receives this message, it can update the trust table. The result of node a first generating its table and updating it can be observed in Table 1. A node will not send its trust value of itself as this value will not be used. Note that the values are all recorded in Table 1 are 100 or $NULL$ because it is an example of initial phase.

Table 1. Trust table of node a after receiving TC message from node b

	a	b	c	d	e
a	100	100	100	100	100
b	100	$NULL$	100	100	100
c	$NULL$	$NULL$	$NULL$	$NULL$	$NULL$
d	$NULL$	$NULL$	$NULL$	$NULL$	$NULL$
e	$NULL$	$NULL$	$NULL$	$NULL$	$NULL$

2.2 Trust-Based MPR Selection

Using the trust table, each node needs to select MPR nodes to forward its data. To do this, each node calculates the *aggregated* trust value of all 1-hop neighbors and chooses only the nodes with high aggregated trust values as MPRs. For example, if node a needs to calculate aggregated trust value $R_{a \to b}$ of a neighbor node b, Eq. 1 is used:

$$R_{a \to b} = (\sum_{x=1}^{n'} T_{x \to b})/n' \tag{1}$$

where n is the number of 1-hop neighbors and n' is the number of 1-hop neighbors with non $NULL$ value during the calculation of $R_{a \to b}$. After calculating aggregated trust values for all n, the node can select either the node with the highest value as MPR or even select multiple MPRs with satisfactory trust values if multiple MPRs are needed to maintain connectivity.

We elaborate on the calculation of aggregated trust values here with an example. Let us assume that node a maintains a trust table as shown in Table 2. When node a calculates the aggregated trust values, $R_{a \to b} = (100 + 80)/2 = 90$, $R_{a \to c} = 100 + 100/2 = 100$, $R_{a \to d} = 100 + 90 + 90/3 = 93.3$, and $R_{a \to e} = 100 + 90 + 75/3 = 83.3$. Therefore, for node a, node c will become its MPR. Note that all nodes, using its own trust table, will each make this calculation periodically to choose the MPR.

Table 2. Example of a trust table state of node a

	a	b	c	d	e
a	100	100	100	100	100
b	100	*NULL*	100	90	90
c	90	80	*NULL*	90	75
d	*NULL*	*NULL*	*NULL*	*NULL*	*NULL*
e	*NULL*	*NULL*	*NULL*	*NULL*	*NULL*

2.3   Recalculating the Trust Value

Once the MPR is selected for all nodes, the network will function with this configuration until the next period of new MPR selection. Before selecting a new MPR, each node will evaluate the performance of its MPR. To do this, we apply a cross-layer approach of deciding whether a data packet has been successfully transmitted on a end-to-end basis.

For transport protocol, if the transmission control protocol (TCP) [8] is used, the acknowledgment (ACK) can be used to check if a data transmission of a node has been successfully transmitted multi-hop to its destination. Using the ACK message, it is possible to calculate the current data rate of transmission and compare with the data rate requirements of the service application. If the data rate meets the requirements, then the MPR can be considered reliable and given an incentive to its trust value. On the other hand, if the requirements are not met, then the trust value will be given a penalty. If a protocol without ACK is used at the transport layer, it is possible to provide a simple ACK function on the application layer to calculate the data rate of a node's transmission.

Note that for our current implementation of the protocol, we have made some preliminary empirical analysis of the appropriate incentive and penalty values, and configure the settings to 5% and 10%. As an example, if node b was given a 5% incentive by node a, $T_{a \to b} = 95 * 1.05 = 99.75$. Through TC message sharing, this information will be shared to other nodes in the network. Therefore, malicious nodes, whether they are DoS attackers or under-performing nodes, can be naturally deteriorated and isolated from the network.

2.4   Extension of TC Message

The trust values of a node will be shared through periodical TC message exchange, which is already a default procedure in OLSR. However, to include this information, TC message needs to be extended. This can be simply done as TC messages are bound to change in size frequently due to the size of the topology that each node has to advertise. Therefore, it is convenient to add the information of a node's trust table (Only the information of its own trust values) on the end of the TC message. In our implementation we add the IPv4 address of each node, followed by the trust value in 4 bytes. Therefore, the induction of additional overhead in the TC message will be $(4bytes + 4bytes) * m$. We consider this much more acceptable than having to create another packet format exclusively to share trust table values.

3   Performance Evaluation

The performance of our mutual node evaluation method in OLSR is evaluated through NS-3 simulation. For our preliminary evaluation, we set our tactical environment as shown in Table 3.

Table 3. Simulation environment

Parameter	Value
PHY/MAC	IEEE 802.11a 54 Mbps
Routing	OLSR
Number of nodes	16
Data characteristics	64, 128, 192, 384 Kbps H.264 encoding
Mobility model	Random walk

The main performance parameter that we consider is number of dropped packets due to attack. As the main effect of black hole attacks and isolation attack both deteriorate the node data transmission, improving this factor was our foremost priority. We compare our method with the original OLSR, which is the most baseline performance. 16 nodes are deployed in a grid topology on a $200 * 200$ m space and each node moves randomly along a random walk mobility model. All nodes except the server node and the attacking node transmit multimedia data to the server node. The emulated data format is h.264 Mpeg-4 AVC video, with speeds differing based on screen resolution and frames per second. To receive acknowledgment of the data rate, we also implement a simple ACK mechanism on the application layer. The performance results are shown in

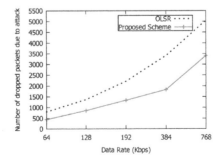

Fig. 1. Number of dropped packets comparison

Fig. 1. Our proposed scheme generally shows lower number of dropped packets than existing OLSR. This is mainly due to our method being able to successfully find and isolate an attacker node. Even though this may result in creation of longer routes because attacker nodes must be avoided, it is more reliable compared to the original OLSR which cannot avoid attacker nodes.

4 Conclusion

In tactical MANETs, security and reliable data delivery are the most important features that need to be guaranteed. To provide this, we propose a mutual node evaluation method based on OLSR protocol to exploit this problem. The performance evaluation shows that our method of detecting malicious nodes is effective in preventing them becoming MPRs in the OLSR algorithm. Note that the simulation results that we have presented are preliminary and we will continue to make more extensive simulation, as well as utilize testbeds to make a more practical environment. Finally, we will analyze methods to tune incentive and penalty values for a more intelligent calculation of the trust values.

Acknowledgement. This research was supported in part by the MIST (Ministry of Science and ICT), Korea, under the National Program for Excellence in SW supervised by the IITP (Institute for Information & communications Technology Promotion) (20150009080031001), and Basic Science Research Program through the National Research Foundation of Korea (NRF) funded by the Ministry of Education (NRF-2015R1D1A1A01059049).

References

1. Clausen, T., Jacquet, P., Laoiti, A., Minet, P., Muhlethaler, P., Qayyum, A., Viennot, L.: Optimized Link State Routing Protocol. IETF Internet Request For Comments RFC 3626 (2003)
2. Ronggong, S., Mason Peter, C.: ROLSR: a robust optimized link state routing protocol for military ad-hoc networks. In: IEEE MILCOM 2010 (2010)
3. Kannhavong, B., Nakayama, H., Nemoto, Y., Kato, N., Jamalipour, A.: SA-OLSR: security aware optimized link state routing for mobile ad hoc networks. In: IEEE ICC 2008 (2008)
4. Hu, Y.-C., Perrig, A., Johnson, D.: Wormhole attacks in wireless networks. IEEE J. Sel. Areas Commun. **24**(2), 370–380 (2006)
5. Gerhards-Padilla, E., Aschenbruck, N., Martini, P., Jahnke, M., Tolle, J.: Detecting black hole attacks in tactical MANETs using topology graphs. In: IEEE LCN 2007 (2007)
6. Schweitzer, N., Stulman, A., Shabtai, A., Margalit, R.D.: Mitigating denial of service attacks in OLSR protocol using fictitious nodes. IEEE Trans. Mobile Comput. **1**, 163–172 (2016)
7. Li, Z., Wu, Y.: Smooth mobility and link reliability based optimized link state routing scheme for MANETs. IEEE Commun. Lett. **21**(7), 1529–1532 (2017)
8. Postel, J.: Transmission Control Protocol. Internet Request For Comments RFC 793 (1981)

An Edge Caching Strategy for Minimizing User Download Delay

Tianhao Wu, Xi Li$^{(\boxtimes)}$, Hong Ji, and Heli Zhang

Key Laboratory of Universal Wireless Communications, Ministry of Education,
Beijing University of Posts and Telecommunications,
Beijing, People's Republic of China
{wutianhao,lixi,jihong,zhangheli}@bupt.edu.cn

Abstract. In the scenario with many small base stations (SBSs) deployed, edge caching technology could bring contents closer to users by caching files at SBSs. Considering these SBSs with limited storage capacity, how to effectively cache files is a difficult and interesting problem. Many factors should be considered, such as the popularity of files, user download delay and average hit rate. In this paper, we investigate this problem and propose a minimizing user download delay caching (MUDDC) algorithm. It decides which files should be cached and where to cache them for reducing download delay. There is a conflict between hit rate and download delay with the limited SBS storage capacity. We target the average user download delay and model an optimization problem with the constraint of average hit rate and find the optimal solution. The simulation results show that the system performance is improved.

Keywords: Edge caching network · Content distribution
Download delay · Hit rate

1 Introduction

As the explosive growth of smart devices and the advent of many new applications, traffic volume has been growing exponentially [1]. With the rapid growth of traffic demands in future cellular networks, one promising approach is to deploy more small base stations (SBSs) along with macro base stations (MBSs) [2]. In order to deal with the data requirements, the contents can be cached in SBSs, bringing the files closer to users [3]. It reduces the duplicate content transmissions and allows users to acquire files with less download delay. However, the storage capacity of these SBSs is limited. In this case, one SBS could not cache all the files that users may need. So some studies concentrate on a specific SBS storage mode in this circumstance. The cached files could be divided into two

T. Wu—This work is supported by National Natural Science Foundation of China under grant 61671088 and National Science and Technology Major Project of the Ministry of Science and Technology of China under grant 2016ZX03001017.

© ICST Institute for Computer Sciences, Social Informatics and Telecommunications Engineering 2018
L. Wang et al. (Eds.): QShine 2017, LNICST 234, pp. 120–130, 2018.
https://doi.org/10.1007/978-3-319-78078-8_13

parts. The first part has higher popularity and be stored by all the SBSs. The second part has lower popularity and are distributed in different SBSs. It is a kind of practical approach for edge caching.

There are many aspects should be considered when designing a caching scheme. With the limited storage, how to decide whether to store a file or not in a SBS connects with not only the file's popularity and hit rate, but also with users experience like transmission delay and personal preference. Moreover, spectrum resource, traffic offloading and throughput may also be taken into account.

In [4], the authors study the problem of content placement for caching at the wireless edge with the goal to maximize the energy efficiency (EE) of heterogeneous wireless networks. In [5], the authors introduce the optimal edge caching strategies to minimize the bandwidth consumption of fronthaul and storage costs in the fog radio access networks (F-RANs). In [6], the authors formulate an optimal redundancy caching problem to minimize the total transmission cost of the network, including cost within the radio access network (RAN) and cost incurred by transmission to the core network via backhaul links. In [7], the authors design the joint caching and association strategy to minimize the average download delay in a cache-enabled heterogeneous network. In [8], the authors propose a novel edge caching scheme to cache layered contents. The proposed method outperforms the exiting counterparts with a higher hit ratio and lower delay of delivering video contents.

Despite the previous work on edge caching network, it still needs further study that jointly consider the hit rate and user download delay. Because these two basic factors are significant indicators in evaluating network performance. Moreover, in the network scenario with limited storage, the growth of the hit rate may be conflict with the user average download delay. It is necessary to achieve a tradeoff between them.

In this paper, we study the edge caching scheme to minimize user average download delay under the premise of reaching a certain average hit rate and propose a minimizing user download delay caching (MUDDC) algorithm. The set of files stored in each SBS could be established according to a certain file placement strategy. All the files are sorted according to their popularity rank. A threshold value R is set to divide the stored files into two parts. The most popular R files are stored in every SBS to reduce average user download delay. While the rest files are distributed stored by different SBSs according to their storage capacity. This increases the diversity of stored files and improves the average hit rate to some extent. In this network scenario, the proposed algorithm establishes a connection state matrix for users and SBSs. In above conditions, the user average hit rate and download delay could be calculated. Eventually, we model the tradeoff between hit rate and delay into an optimization problem and find the optimal file placement strategy. Simulations are conducted which show that the proposed algorithm has a low average download delay and could achieve a good hit rate. Furthermore, the proposed algorithm could significantly improve the average hit rate with the similar download delay compared to that of the "most popular" placement scheme.

The remainder of the paper is organized as follows. Section 2 gives the system model and problem formulation. Section 3 indicates the whole process of MUDDC algorithm. Simulation results and discussions are given in Sect. 4. Finally, we conclude this paper in Sect. 5.

2   System Model and Problem Formulation

2.1   System Model

The edge caching network considered in this paper is shown in Fig. 1. The network is composed by one MBS and N SBSs with J mobile users in their coverage areas. Each SBS stores files according to the file placement strategy. For different files, the sizes of them are same. In Fig. 1, each colored square means one file and different colors denote different files.

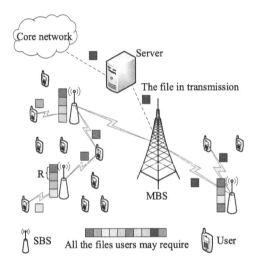

Fig. 1. Edge caching network (Color figure online)

The MBSs connect to the core network with wire links. The SBSs and MBSs are connected with wireless links. The users connect to SBSs via wireless links. The coverage areas of the SBSs may be sometimes overlapping, and therefore users can potentially be served by multiple SBSs. When a user wants to get a file from the network, the user requires contents from the storage of the SBSs they connecting to at first. When all the SBSs have this file, the user will control the SBSs it connects to cooperate with each other for getting a faster download speed. For example, the download speed could be nearly double with the user connecting to two SBSs. If only one SBS stores this file, the download speed is normal. In the circumstance that the file is not in the storage, one of the SBSs would require for the core network through the MBS and send to the user.

We assume that the set of N SBSs is $\mathbb{N} = \{1, 2, \cdots, n, \cdots, N\}$, where n is the nth SBS. We denote the set of J mobile users by $\mathbb{U} = \{U_1, U_2, \cdots, U_j, \cdots, U_J\}$, where U_j represents the jth user. For the jth user U_j, there is a matrix $\mathbb{A}_j$ which means the connectivity condition between U_j and the SBSs. The expression of $\mathbb{A}_j$ is $\mathbb{A}_j = [a_j^1, a_j^2, \cdots, a_j^n, \cdots, a_j^N]$, where a_j^n is a binary-state variable. Its value is either 0 or 1. When user j has connected to SBS n, the value of a_j^n is 1, otherwise the value is 0.

2.2   SBS Caching Model

The way that SBSs store files proposed here refers to [6] and is shown in Fig. 2. A SBS could store M files at most. We assume that the mobile users may request a file from Y ($Y \geq M \cdot N$) different popular files at a time. These files are predicted by the statistics of user information. All the Y files in the system are sorted according to their popularity rank. Each file corresponds to a serial number k, and the value of k is smaller means the file is more popular. As shown in Fig. 2, The first R files cached in all the SBSs are the most popular R files in the system. The remaining m ($m = M - R$) files cached in each SBS are different from others and are stored according to their serial numbers [6].

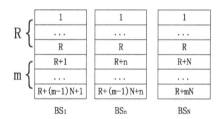

Fig. 2. The caching scheme

For the nth SBS, we could establish a set $\mathbb{K}_n$ to denote the files stored in this SBS. So $\mathbb{K}_n$ could be expressed as:

$$\begin{aligned} \mathbb{K}_n = \{1, 2, \cdots, R, R+n, R+N+n, \\ \cdots, R+(m-1)N+n\}. \end{aligned} \tag{1}$$

The contents of the collection are the serial numbers of the stored files in the nth SBS.

2.3   Average Hit Rate Model

From $\mathbb{K}_n$, we would know which files are stored in the nth SBS. So a matrix $\mathbb{H}_n$ could be established to reflect the relationship between the nth SBS and all the

Y files. The $\mathbb{H}_n$ would be denoted as:

$$\mathbb{H}_n = [h(1), h(2), \cdots, h(k), \cdots, h(Y)],$$

$$h(k) = \begin{cases} 1 & k \in \mathbb{K}_n \\ 0 & others \end{cases}. \tag{2}$$

The value of $h(k)$ is 1 means the kth file is stored in the nth SBS, otherwise the value is 0.

A user j could directly get files stored in the SBSs it connects to. So we would get a set $\mathbb{F}_j$ to express these files for the user. The expression of $\mathbb{F}_j$ is

$$\mathbb{F}_j = a_j^1 \cdot \mathbb{K}_1 \cup a_j^2 \cdot \mathbb{K}_2 \cup \cdots \cup a_j^N \cdot \mathbb{K}_N. \tag{3}$$

The elements of $\mathbb{F}_j$ are the serial numbers of the files user j could acquire from the SBSs directly.

According to the statistical result, a user has a probability P_k to require the kth file from the SBSs. From [6], we can get P_k through

$$P_k = \frac{1/k^\beta}{\sum\limits_{y=1}^{Y} (1/y^\beta)}. \tag{4}$$

In (4), β is a decay constant. So when the user j connecting to the SBSs, the expected hit rate is calculated as

$$q_j = \sum_{k \in \mathbb{F}_j} P_k. \tag{5}$$

After known q_j for every user, we could get the average hit rate Q of the network:

$$Q = \frac{\sum\limits_{j=1}^{J} q_j}{J}. \tag{6}$$

2.4   Average User Download Delay Model

The SBSs reuse the downlink resources of the MBS to serve the transmission to users [7]. As a result, there exists the interference by the MBS when users obtain files from SBSs. The neighboring SBSs could be allocated orthogonal frequency band to eliminate the in-layer interference. Each SBS divides its downlink bandwidth into many subchannels. All the subchannels have the same bandwidth w_n. Each user accesses only one subchannel at a slot. Similarly, each subchannel of the MBS has the bandwidth w_M.

Let P_n be the transmission power of the SBSs, and P_M is the transmission power of the MBS. Denote the noise power as σ^2. The channel gain between SBS n and user j could be $h_{n,j}$. Also $h_{M,n}$ means the channel gain between the MBS and SBS n. As in [9], we characterize the channel gain model as $h_{n,j} = L_0 d_{n,j}^{-\alpha}$ and $h_{M,n} = L_0 d_{M,n}^{-\alpha}$, where L_0 is a constant and α is the path loss exponent factor. $d_{n,j}$ and $d_{M,n}$ are the distance between SBS n and user j and the distance between MBS and SBS n respectively.

Therefore, the signal-to-interference-plus-noise ratio (SINR) $\gamma_{n,j}$ between SBS n and user j and the SINR $\gamma_{M,n}$ between MBS and SBS n could be denoted as $\gamma_{n,j} = \frac{P_n h_{n,j}}{\sigma^2 + P_M h_{M,n}}$ and $\gamma_{M,n} = \frac{P_M h_{M,n}}{\sigma^2}$. We assume that the size of all files is L. Thus we would know the delay $(D_{j,n})$ of SBS n sending a file to user j and the delay $(D_{n,M})$ of SBS n receiving a file from MBS. So $D_{j,n}$ could be represented as

$$D_{j,n} = \frac{L}{w_n \log_2(1 + \gamma_{n,j})}, \tag{7}$$

and $D_{n,M}$ is represented as

$$D_{n,M} = \frac{L}{w_M \log_2(1 + \gamma_{M,n})}. \tag{8}$$

2.5   Problem Formulation

In order to acquire the file download delay of every user, we would establish a file available degree matrix $\mathbb{T}_j$ for user j. The form of $\mathbb{T}_j$ could be $\mathbb{T}_j = [t_j(1), t_j(2), \cdots, t_j(k), \cdots, t_j(Y)]$, where $t_j(k)$ means the number of SBSs stored the kth file in connection with user j and $\mathbb{T}_j$ is calculated by

$$\mathbb{T}_j = \sum_{n=1}^{N} a_j^n \cdot \mathbb{H}_n. \tag{9}$$

The user download delay may be various with different files, so we should calculate the download delay of every file for user j. Thus, the download delay $D_j(k)$ of user j receiving file k is denoted as:

$$D_j(k) = \begin{cases} \frac{1}{t_j(k)} \cdot D_{j,n} & t_j(k) \geq 1 \\ D_{j,n} + D_{n,M} & t_j(k) = 0 \end{cases}. \tag{10}$$

Then the average file download delay D_j of user j would be calculated with

$$D_j = \sum_{k=1}^{Y} P_k \cdot D_j(k). \tag{11}$$

Therefore, the average user download delay $D(R)$ of the system could be known after calculating the delay of every user. The expression of $D(R)$ is

$$D(R) = \frac{\sum_{j=1}^{J} D_j}{J}. \tag{12}$$

From above analysis, we have expressed the average hit rate Q and the average user download delay $D(R)$. Our goal is to find an optimal file placement strategy for SBSs to minimize $D(R)$ under the premise of reaching a certain average hit rate Q_c. Considering that the value of R would not be bigger than the SBS storage capacity M, so the optimization problem could be modeled as

$$\min D(R)$$
$$\text{s.t.} \quad Q \geq Q_c$$
$$R \in \mathbb{Z} \tag{13}$$
$$0 \leq R \leq M$$

From (13), we know that R is an integer and $0 \leq R \leq M$. The traversal algorithm should be a useful way to find the optimum value of R.

3   The Proposed MUDDC Algorithm

The MUDDC algorithm proposed in this paper is divided into two parts. The first part is the process of SBS file distribution strategy. The second part is the process of user connection and requiring files.

For SBSs, the connectivity condition of all users should be determined. In the edge caching network, a user could connect to many SBSs. So the connectivity condition matrix for all the users and SBSs should be established firstly.

For users, the popular files that they may require should be predicted and ranked. The serial number is smaller means the file is more popular. Next each requiring probability of the files can be calculated by (4).

In order to find the optimal value of R conveniently, we should calculate $D_{j,n}$ and $D_{n,M}$ in advance by using (7)–(8).

When all the initial conditions are decided, the MUDDC algorithm will use (13) to model an optimization problem and use the traversal algorithm to solve the problem. After finding the appropriate strategy of file placement mode, the SBSs could be deployed with this strategy. All the SBSs should update their stored files simultaneously, and have the same way to store files. Then all the users begin the process of requiring files.

When the connected user wants to receive a file, it will firstly check whether this file has been stored in the SBSs. If this file is stored in all SBSs, the user will let connected SBSs collaborate with each other to shorten download delay. When only one connected SBS has this file exactly, this SBS sends the required file to the user. The download delay is normal. If this file is not stored in any connected SBSs, one of the SBSs would require the file from MBS and then send to the user. This would add delay of MBS sending the file to SBS to download delay. The process of the MUDDC algorithm is summarized in Algorithm 1.

4   Simulation Results and Discussions

In this section, we evaluate the performance of the MUDDC algorithm and analyze the influence of important parameters by simulation. For comparison,

Algorithm 1. The MUDDC Algorithm

1: The users connect to the SBSs.
2: Initialization:
   a)Set $\mathbb{N}$, $\mathbb{U}$, and matrix $\mathbb{A}_j$;
   b)SBS storage capacity M, the number of all files Y, the size of the files L, and the threshold value of hit rate Q_c;
   c)SBS transmission power P_n, transmission power P_M, noise power σ^2, channel gain h_n and h_M.
3: Model the optimization problem by (1)–(13).
4: Use traversal algorithm to find the value of R which minimizes the delay $D(R)$.
5: SBSs execute the file placement strategy shown in Fig. 2 according to R.
6: Users begin to require files.
7: **for all** $U_j \in \mathbb{U}$ **do**
8:    User U_j requires a file.
9:    **if** this file is stored in all SBSs **then**
10:       The connected SBSs would cooperate to send this file to U_j.
11:    **else**
12:       **if** this file is stored in only one SBS **then**
13:          The stored SBS sends the file to U_j.
14:       **else**
15:          One of the connected SBS require the file from MBS and then send to U_j.
16:       **end if**
17:    **end if**
18: **end for**

we emulate the "most popular" placement (MPP) scheme mentioned in [4]. In MPP scheme, each SBS stores the M most popular files.

In the simulation, we let the size of each file $L = 10$ Mbits, $\beta = 0.8$, $Y = 600$, $M = 50$, $J = 50$, and $\alpha = 4$. In [4], we know that the MBS coverage area radius is 500 m, and the SBS coverage area radius is 45–60 m. For simplicity, we assume $d_{n,j} = 30$ m for all SBSs and users and $d_{M,n} = 200$ m for all SBSs and the MBS. The values of P_n and P_M are 100 mW and 20 W respectively, and $L_0 = -30$ dB [9]. The value of σ^2 is -100 dBm [10]. We assume that $\omega_M = \omega_n = 1$ MHz.

Figure 3 shows the relationship between average user download delay and R on the condition of different value of Q_c. The value of the threshold Q_c is related to the system performance and has a certain randomness. In Fig. 3, from 28 to 46 the value of R, the value of Q_c is $0.525, 0.520, 0.515, 0.510, 0.505, 0.500, 0.495$ respectively. The number of SBSs is 4. From Fig. 3, we know that reducing the value of R is conducive to improving user hit rate. And this would increase the download delay. The larger the value of R is, the more files there are stored in all the SBSs. Therefore the download delay of these most popular files is shortened, and then decreases the average download delay. However, the file diversity would be lower. Thus the poor average hit rate appears. This is the reason of the conflict between these two factors.

Figure 4 indicates the changes of R with different number of total SBSs. We set the value of Q_c according to the system performance. In Fig. 4, from 4 to 10 the total number of SBSs, the value of Q_c is $0.525, 0.53, 0.51, 0.51, 0.505, 0.5, 0.46$ respectively. It is the same with Figs. 5 and 6. When the total number of SBSs is increasing, the files would be placed more dispersedly. The hit rate decreases with the reduced value of R. Moreover, the download delay may be increased. So the files stored in all SBSs is more with the number of total SBSs to improve the system performance.

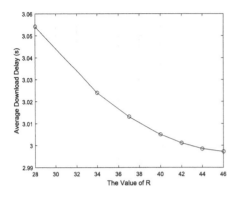
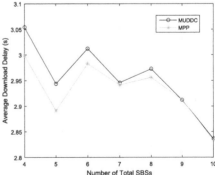

Fig. 3. Average download delay with different value of R

Fig. 4. The value of R with different number of total SBSs

In Fig. 5, we compare the performance of average hit rate between the MUDDC algorithm and the MPP algorithm. From Fig. 5, the network performance of the MUDDC algorithm is obviously better than the MPP algorithm in the matter of average hit rate. That is because the MPP algorithm let all the SBSs store M most popular files. So no matter how many SBSs a user connects

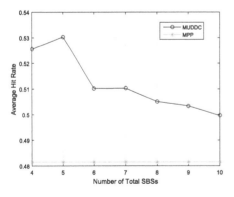
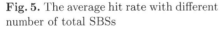

Fig. 5. The average hit rate with different number of total SBSs

Fig. 6. The average download delay with different number of total SBSs

to, only M files could be acquired directly from SBSs. The average hit rate is not changed. However, all the SBSs store R files and $R \leq M$. This may make a user get more than M files from the connected SBSs directly. As a result, the average hit rate in MUDDC algorithm is higher than that in MPP algorithm.

Figure 6 illustrates the relationship between the average download delay and the number of total SBSs in above two algorithms. In general, the download delay decreases as the increasing number of SBSs. This is because the value of R has a rising trend. Figure 6 clearly shows that there is little difference on average download delay between MUDDC and MPP algorithm. However, the average hit rate in MUDDC algorithm is higher than MPP compared with Fig. 5. This illustrates the proposed MUDDC algorithm successfully minimizes the download delay under the condition of achieving an average hit rate Q_c to some extent.

5 Conclusion

In this paper, the MUDDC algorithm, a file placement algorithm for limited SBSs storage has been proposed. On the premise of meeting a certain average hit rate, the MUDDC algorithm could minimize the download delay. In this algorithm, an optimization model is established and a traversal algorithm is used to find the optimal solution. The simulation results show that compared to the existing algorithm, the MUDDC algorithm could reach a higher hit rate with the similar download delay. For future work, to improve the system performance, we would consider the MUDDC algorithm with social features and derive the optimal solution for the problem.

References

1. Wang, S., Zhang, X., Zhang, Y., Wang, L., Yang, J., Wang, W.: A survey on mobile edge networks: convergence of computing, caching and communications. IEEE Access **5**, 6757–6779 (2017)
2. Ghosh, A., Mangalvedhe, N., Ratasuk, R., Mondal, B., Cudak, M., Visotsky, E., Thomas, T.A., Andrews, J.G., Xia, P., Jo, H.S., Dhillon, H.S., Novlan, T.D.: Heterogeneous cellular networks: from theory to practice. IEEE Commun. Mag. **50**(6), 54–64 (2012)
3. Yang, C., Yao, Y., Chen, Z., Xia, B.: Analysis on cache-enabled wireless heterogeneous networks. IEEE Trans. Wirel. Commun. **15**(1), 131–145 (2016)
4. Gabry, F., Bioglio, V., Land, I.: On energy-efficient edge caching in heterogeneous networks. IEEE J. Sel. Areas Commun. **34**(12), 3288–3298 (2016)
5. Wang, X., Leng, S., Yang, K.: Social-aware edge caching in fog radio access networks. IEEE Access **5**, 8492–8501 (2017)
6. Wang, S., Zhang, X., Yang, K., Wang, L., Wang, W.: Distributed edge caching scheme considering the tradeoff between the diversity and redundancy of cached content. In: 2015 IEEE/CIC International Conference on Communications in China (ICCC), pp. 1–5, November 2015
7. Wang, Y., Tao, X., Zhang, X., Mao, G.: Joint caching placement and user association for minimizing user download delay. IEEE Access **4**, 8625–8633 (2016)

8. Su, Z., Xu, Q., Hou, F., Yang, Q., Qi, Q.: Edge caching for layered video contents in mobile social networks. IEEE Trans. Multimedia **19**(10), 2210–2221 (2017)
9. Jia, C., Lim, T.J.: Resource partitioning and user association with sleep-mode base stations in heterogeneous cellular networks. IEEE Trans. Wirel. Commun. **14**(7), 3780–3793 (2015)
10. Zhang, H., Wang, Y., Ji, H.: Resource optimization-based interference management for hybrid self-organized small-cell network. IEEE Trans. Veh. Technol. **65**(2), 936–946 (2016)

Performance Analysis for Content Distribution in Crowdsourced Content-Centric Mobile Networking

Chengming Li[1](✉), Xiaojie Wang[2], Shimin Gong[1], Zhi-Hui Wang[2], and Qingshan Jiang[1]

[1] Shenzhen Institutes of Advanced Technology,
Chinese Academy of Science, Shenzhen, China
cm.li@siat.ac.cn
[2] School of Software, Dalian University of Technology, Dalian, China

Abstract. Content-Centric Networking emerges as a promising paradigm which has a better content distribution efficiency and mobility via named data and in-network caching compared with the IP-based network. However, providing a high quality of experience in content distribution of Content-Centric Mobile Networking (CCMN) is challenging due to the heterogeneous networks, varying wireless channel conditions and incentive strategies to mobile users. In this work, we propose a novel crowdsourced content distribution framework for CCMN. This framework enables the nearby mobile users to crowdsource their caching resources and radio links for cooperative content distribution. We formulate the problem as the maximization of the payoff of all users which considers content retrieve time and energy cost. Further, we analysis the upper bound and lower bound of the proposed system in term of user payoff, which can be a benchmark for the future scheduling algorithms and incentive mechanisms design.

Keywords: Information-Centric Networks
Content-Centric Networking · Mobile crowdsourcing
In-network caching

1 Introduction

The exponentially growing mobile cellular network traffic is evolving from the steady increase in demand for conventional host-centric communications, such as phone calls and text messages, to the explosion of content-centric communications, such as social networks, video streaming and content sharing [1–3]. The mobile cellular network model of today is still IP-based Internet which is originally designed as a communication model, e.g., a conversation between exactly two machines. However, according to the Cisco Visual Networking Index [4], mobile video will increase 9-fold between 2016 and 2021, accounting for 78

© ICST Institute for Computer Sciences, Social Informatics and Telecommunications Engineering 2018
L. Wang et al. (Eds.): QShine 2017, LNICST 234, pp. 131–141, 2018.
https://doi.org/10.1007/978-3-319-78078-8_14

percent of total mobile data traffic. We can see that one of the main applications of the mobile cellular networks today is the content distribution and retrieval, especially for multimedia content.

To better support global information publication, dissemination and retrieval, Content-Centric Networking (CCN) [5] (or Named-Data Networking) has been proposed. CCN is one of the promising clean-slate Information-Centric Network (ICN) architectures which try to establish a new network architecture to adapt to the characteristics of current Internet. CCN names content directly and concerns the security of naming content rather than transmission path. In-network caching is a fundamental property of CCN, and it is the key to reduce redundant transmission and improve bandwidth utilization.

It is a challenging issue in Content-Centric Mobile Networking (CCMN) that how to effectively utilize these existing capabilities for massive content distribution in mobile networks. In today's mobile networks, caching and computing capabilities are already ubiquitous, both at base stations and user devices. However, providing high quality of experience for content distribution in CCMN is challenging due to the heterogeneous networks and varying wireless channel conditions [6,7]. Moreover, for mobile users, not all users are willing to share their cache and radio resources because of 3G/4G communication expense and battery power consumption.

Some of the existing work on CCMN focus on video streaming. ICN enabled Peer to Peer applications are proposed for live adaptive video streaming in cellular networks [8–10]. These applications enable a small set of neighbouring devices with cellular/Wi-Fi connections to increase the quality of video playback by using the Wi-Fi to share the portion of the live stream downloaded by each peer via the cellular network. However, these work focus on a single video streaming for multiple users, rather than multiple content for multiple users. Moreover, none of them consider whether or not the cooperative users are willing to share their cache and radio resources.

To improve the efficiency of content distribution in CCMN, we propose a crowdsourced content distribution framework for CCMN inspired by adaptive video streaming technologies [11,12]. This framework enables the nearby mobile users forming a cooperative group (via WiFi or Bluetooth) to crowdsource their caching resources and radio links for cooperative content distribution. We formulate the problem as the maximization of all users' payoff and analysis the upper bound and lower bound of proposed system. The performance analysis results can serve as a benchmark for the future scheduling algorithm and incentive mechanism design.

2   Network Architecture

Due to named data and in-networking caching, CCN achieves better efficiency and mobility on data distribution than traditional IP based networks. In order to make full use of CCN features, we propose a crowdsourced mobile content distribution framework for CCMN, called Crowdsourced Content-Centric Mobile

Networking (CCCMN). As illustrated in Fig. 1, the network scenario of CCCMN consists of a small set of neighbouring mobile users (mobile cellular devices), Base Stations installed CCN protocol stack, backbone of CCN network and Content Providers (CPs).

We consider a set I of mobile users, and each mobile device of users has several interfaces (e.g., Cellular, WiFi, Bluetooth) available for simultaneous communications. All mobile devices will be equipped with name-based routing and content caching. Users move randomly in a certain area, and nearby users can form a cooperative group (via WiFi) and crowdsource their radio connections and cache resources for cooperative content distribution. Each user connects to Base Station (BS) by cellular network (3G/4G) with varying link capacity. Although incentive mechanism is a key issue which motivates all users to be willing to participate in CCCMN system to improve the performance of whole network, here we firstly focus on the CCCMN framework.

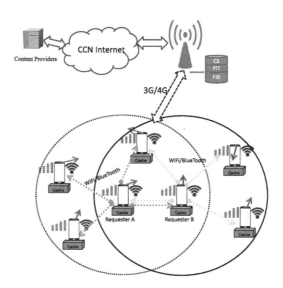

Fig. 1. An example of CCCMN network scenario

We consider the operation in a period of continuous time $T \triangleq [0, T]$, where $t = 0$ is the initial time and $t = T$ is the ending time. The cellular link capacity of user i is denoted by $r_i^c(t)$, where $t \in [0, T]$. BSs are equipped with CCN protocol stack in network layer and have large cache capacity. Requests and data are transmitted between BSs and CPs via the backbone of CCN. BSs calculate the popularity of each content and cache the popular content to avoid the retransmission of popular data.

We use a set F to denote all content files requested by users I, and f is a single content file, $f \in F$. $|F|$ and $|f|$ represent the whole catalog size and the size of content f, respectively. We consider a typical CCN standard, where a single content file f is partitioned into multiple chunks by CPs, $f = \{f^1, f^2, ..., f^K\}$. Let $|f^k|$ signify the k-th chunk size of content file f. Users request a content by the sequence of chunks. Requested chunks are cached in the devices it passed by and if there's no enough cache space, stale chunks will be replaced by fresh chunks based on the cache replacement schemes.

3   Problem Formulation

The system model of CCCMN consists of three procedures: the first step is to aggregate requests and recruit participants; the aim of second step is to assign the task to each participant rationally base on some scheduling policies and each participant download the uncached chunks by cellular link; the last step is to transmit the downloaded chunks and/or cached chunks to each requester by the D2D connections (WiFi/BlueTooth). There are two kinds of users, to distinguish them we call **requesters** as the users who send the original request for the chunks, and we call **participants** as the users who help the requesters by the cached chunks or to download the chunks by cellular connections. No doubt that the requesters can also to be the participants and help themselves to download the chunks by cellular network.

3.1   Content Retrieve

In time $[0, T]$, all requested content files are represented by a set $S^\dagger = \{f_j | f \in F, j \in I\}$, where f_j denotes the content file requested by requester user j. The task of $S^\dagger$ is assigned to participants by chunks for the cooperative content distribution. After receiving the task, each participant user i firstly checks the CS, then decides the downloading operation via cellular which can be characterized by a sequence:

$$S_i = \{S_i^m(f_j^k) | m = 1, 2, ..., |S_i|; k \in \{1, 2, ..., |f|\}\}, \tag{1}$$

where m is the downloading sequence number, f_j^k is the k-th chunk of f requested by requester user j and $S_i^m(f_j^k)$ denotes the participant user i will download f_j^k in m-th order for requester user j while f_j^k is not cached. $S_i^m(f_j^k)$ includes the associated information of f_j^k, and we can rewrite $S_i^m(f_j^k)$ as a tuple: $S_i^m(f_j^k) = (f_{S_i^m}^k, r_{S_i^m}^c, t_{S_i^m}^s, t_{S_i^m}^e)$, where $f_{S_i^m}^k$ is the m-th downloaded the k-th chunk of f by participant user i, $r_{S_i^m}^c$ is downloading link rate of participant user i via cellular link, $t_{S_i^m}^s$ is downloading start time and $t_{S_i^m}^e$ is downloading end time.

To make sure $S_i^m(f_j^k)$ can be completely downloaded, namely, the chunk f_j^k is to be downloaded by participant user i in the m-th order with the time interval $[t_{S_i^m}^s, t_{S_i^m}^e]$, there is a cellular link capacity constraint:

$$\int_{t_{S_i^m}^s}^{t_{S_i^m}^e} r_i^c(t)dt \geq |f_j^k|, \quad m \in \{1, 2, ..., |S_i|\}. \tag{2}$$

Let $\overline{S}_j$ denote the sequence of receiving chunks in requester user j. As the downloading sequences of all users $S_i, \forall i \in I$, $\overline{S}_j$ can be derived as following:

$$\overline{S}_j = \{S_i^m(f_{j'}^k)|\forall i \in I, j' = j, i \neq j\} \cup C_i = \{C_i(f_{j''}^k)|\forall i \in I, j'' = j, i \neq j\}, \quad (3)$$

where $C_i(f_{j''}^k)$ represents the chunk $f_{j''}^k$ cached by user i. Similarly, the receiving operation of user j can be characterized by a sequence:

$$\overline{S}_j = \{\overline{S}_j^n(f_j^k)|n = 1, 2, ..., |\overline{S}_j|\}, \quad (4)$$

where $\overline{S}_j^n(f_j^k)$ represents the n-th receiving chunk f_j^k by the requester user j from participant user i with the WiFi link rate $r_j^w(t)$. We can also write the $\overline{S}_j^n(f_j^k)$ as a tuple includes the receiving information: $\overline{S}_j^n(f_j^k) = (f_{\overline{S}_j^n}^k, r_{\overline{S}_j^n}^w, t_{\overline{S}_j^n}^s, t_{\overline{S}_j^n}^e)$.

We assume that each request user j receives the chunks of a content by the chunk sequence number. In other words, the requester is to receive the $(k+1)$-th chunk of f after received the k-th chunk of f. It can not improve the Quality of Experience to requesters that receiving the $(k+1)$-th chunk of f is done before receiving the k-th chunk of f. Hence, for the different chunks of same content, f_j^k and f_j^{k+1}, the time constraint can be denoted as follows:

$$t_{\overline{S}_j^{n'}(f_j^k)}^e \leq t_{\overline{S}_j^n(f_j^{k+1})}^s, \forall k \in \{1, ..., |\overline{S}_j| - 1\}; n, n' \in \{1, ..., |\overline{S}_j|\}, n' < n; \quad (5)$$

3.2   User Payoff

The payoff of a mobile user mainly consists of two parts: a utility function capturing Quality of Service (QoS) and Quality-of-Experience (QoE) for data retrieve; and a cost function capturing the user's energy consumption for both data downloading and data transport by D2D.

User Utility. We firstly focus on QoS by the data retrieve time for the requesters and a shorter data retrieve time brings a higher QoS for users. Let $S_j^{\dagger}$ denote the set of requested content by user j and $S_j^{\dagger}$ is a subset of $S^{\dagger}$. Let $t_j(f^1)$ denote the sending time of the request for the first chunk of f by user j. Then we define the $\tau_j(f)$ as the content f retrieve time by requester j:

$$\tau_j(f) = t_{\overline{S}_j^n}^e(f^K) - t_j(f^1), \quad K = |f|, f \in S_j^{\dagger}. \quad (6)$$

We adopt average content retrieve rate, represented by ξ_j, to express the QoS of requester j. The average content retrieve rate ξ_j is calculated by the Eq. 7.

$$\xi_j = \frac{\sum_{f \in S_j^{\dagger}} |f|}{\sum_{f \in S_j^{\dagger}} \tau_j(f)}, \quad (7)$$

A higher content retrieve rate brings a higher QoE for users. Let $U_j(\xi_j)$ represent the utility function of user j, which is formulated as follows [13]:

$$U_j(\xi_j) = log(1 + \theta_j \xi_j), \quad (8)$$

where $\theta_j > 0$ is a user-specific evaluation factor capturing user j's desire for a short content retrieve time. Obviously, $U_j(.)$ is a monotonically increasing function and meets diminishing marginal returns.

Energy Cost. In the CCCMN, energy is a precious resource for mobile users because usually mobile devices are powered by batteries. Such energy cost mainly includes the energy consumption for data downloading by cellular links and data exchange over D2D links (WiFi). In this paper, we consider the energy consumption of requester j for requesting f_j as the total energy consumption of retrieving f_j by participants and requester. Then the total energy consumption of requester user j can be formulated as: $E_j = E_j^c + E_j^w$, where E_j^c and E_j^w denote the energy consumption of requester j and participants by cellular links and by WiFi links, respectively.

When mobile users download the content by cellular networks, the energy consumption is determined by the transmission energy and Radio Resource Control (RRC). The transmission energy is proportional to the length of a transmission; and the RRC protocol is responsible for channel allocation and scaling the power consumed by the radio based on inactivity timers [14].

$$E_j^c = \varepsilon_{tran}^c \sum_{f_j \in S_j^\dagger} \sum_{i \in I} \sum_{f_j^k \notin C_i} \varepsilon_{pow,i}^c |S_i^m(f_j^k)|, \tag{9}$$

where ε_{tran}^c (J/B) denotes the transfer and control energy factor to get data by cellular, $\varepsilon_{pow,i}^c$ indicates the transmit power level of participant i by cellular link.

WiFi on phones typically uses the Power Save Mode (PSM), the cost of maintaining the association is small. When associated, the energy consumed by a data transfer is proportional to the size of the data transfer and the transmit power level [14]. In this paper, we consider the same transmit power level of WiFi for all users.

$$E_j^w = \varepsilon_{tran}^w \sum_{f_j \in S_j^\dagger} \sum_{i \in I} (\sum_{f_j^k \notin C_i} |S_i^m(f_j^k)| + \sum_{f_j^k \in C_i} |C_i(f_j^{k'})|), \tag{10}$$

where ε_{tran}^w (J/B) denotes the transfer energy factor to get data by WiFi. Let η_j denote the energy consumption per unit data, QoE of user j for energy cost can be formulated as follows:

$$Cost_j(\eta_j) = log(1 + \phi_j \eta_j) = log(1 + \phi_j \frac{\sum_{f \in S_j^\dagger} |f|}{E_j}), \tag{11}$$

where $\phi_j > 0$ is a user-specific evaluation factor capturing user j's desire for energy cost. Similar to user utility, $Cost_j(.)$ is a monotonically increasing function and meets diminishing marginal returns.

Problem Formulation. According to the above, we formulate the payoff function of requester j as $W_j = U_j - Cost_j$. We consider an ideal scenario with complete network information in this work, the problem of task assignment in CCCMN system can be formulated as the maximization of all users' payoff:

$$\mathbf{W} = \max_{S_i, \overline{S}_j, i, j \in I} \sum_{j=1}^{|I|} (U_j - Cost_j), \quad s.t. \quad \text{Eqs. 2 and 5.} \tag{12}$$

4   Performance Bound Analysis

4.1   Cached Data

In a period of continuous time $[0, T]$, the proposed crowdsourced system includes $|I|$ users (requesters and participants) and system mobility is considered by the dynamic of I (users increase or decrease). Let P^I, $0 \leq P^I < 1$, denote the probability of users dynamic, and the number of users in the time interval $[0, T]$ can be bounded as $|I|(1 - P^I) \leq |I| \leq |I|(1 + P^I)$. Furthermore, the total cache size of all users, denoted by $|\hat{C}|$, is bounded as following:

$$|\hat{C}^\dagger| = \sum_{i=1}^{|I|(1-P^I)} |\hat{C}_i| \leq |\hat{C}| \leq |\hat{C}^\ddagger| = \sum_{i=1}^{|I|(1+P^I)} |\hat{C}_i|, \tag{13}$$

where $\hat{C}_i$ represent the cache resource of user i, $|\hat{C}_i|$ indicates the size of $\hat{C}_i$, $\hat{C}^\dagger$ is the lower bound of $\hat{C}_i$, and $\hat{C}^\ddagger$ is the upper bound of $\hat{C}_i$.

We assume that the content popularity complies the Mandelbrot-Zipf distribution [15]. Accordingly, the probability of request of each file f, P_f^F, can be calculated as following:

$$P_f^F = \frac{(f + q)^{-\alpha}}{\sum_{f'=1}^{|F|} (f' + q)^{-\alpha}}, \tag{14}$$

where α and q are the parameters of the distribution, and f is the rank of the content file.

Let $|S^\dagger|\beta$, β is proportion rate and $\beta \in [0, 1]$, represent the portion of requested files which are satisfied by the cached data. We consider two extreme cases of caching data of all users: (1) all users cache the most popular files of the catalog F, accordingly there are $|S^\dagger|\beta^\ddagger$ files that can be satisfied by cached data; (2) on the contrary, all users cache the least popular files of F, moreover $|S^\dagger|\beta^\dagger$ files can be retrieved by cached data. $\beta^\dagger$ and $\beta^\ddagger$ are constraint by the $\hat{C}^\dagger$ and $\hat{C}^\ddagger$, respectively. Therefore, we formulate the bound of β as following:

$$\beta^\dagger = \sum_{f=L^\dagger}^{|F|} P_f^F \leq \beta \leq \beta^\ddagger = \sum_{f=1}^{L^\ddagger} P_f^F,$$

$$P^r \sum_{f=L^\dagger}^{|F|} |f| \leq \hat{C}^\dagger \leq P^r \sum_{f=L^\dagger-1}^{|F|} |f|, \quad P^r \sum_{f=1}^{L^\ddagger-1} |f| \leq \hat{C}^\ddagger \leq P^r \sum_{f=1}^{L^\ddagger} |f|, \tag{15}$$

where $\beta^\dagger$ and $\beta^\ddagger$ are the lower bound and upper bound of β, respectively. P^r is the parameter of cache non-redundant proportion, $P^r \in (0, 1]$.

Proposition 1. *In a period of continuous time* $[0, T]$, $S^{\ddagger}$, $S^{\ddagger} \subseteq S^{\dagger}$, *is the set of files satisfied by the cached data in the system, κ is a constant real number, then the theoretical performance bound of the proportion of $S^{\ddagger}$ is bounded by*

$$\kappa \sum_{f=L^{\dagger}}^{|F|} (f+q)^{-\alpha} \leq \frac{|S^{\ddagger}|}{|S^{\dagger}|} \leq \kappa \sum_{f=1}^{L^{\ddagger}} (f+q)^{-\alpha}$$

Proof: Let $\kappa = \sum_{f'=1}^{|F|} (f' + q)^{-\alpha}$, then the proposition can be proved as mentioned above by Eqs. 13, 14 and 15.

4.2   Downloaded Data

The objective of this crowdsourced system is to maximize the system's payoff, in other words, to reduce the completion time of system tasks and minimise the system energy cost. Let T_d denote the data downloading time by cellular links. Since both the total amount of files to be downloaded and the link resources of all users are determined, we may formulate the system completion time, $T_d^{\ddagger}$, in ideal case as following:

$$T_d^{\ddagger} = \frac{\sum_{i=1}^{|I|} \sum_{m=1}^{|S_i|} |S_i^m(f_j^k)|}{\sum_{i=1}^{|I|} \hat{r}_i^c},$$

where the $\hat{r}_i^c$ represents the average cellular link rate of participant i and $T_d^{\ddagger} < T$.

Actually, it is hard to complete all the downloading task in time $T_d^{\ddagger}$ in practice because that the smallest download unit is chunk and $|S_i|, \forall i \in I$, is an integer for each user. Let γ_f represent the chunk size of file f which is decided by content providers.

Proposition 2. *If $\forall f \in F, \gamma_f \to 0$, then we have $T_d = T_d^{\ddagger}$. Let $T_d^{\dagger}$ be the completely downloading time for all chunks $S_i^m(f_j^k)$, $\forall i \in I$, with chunk size $Z\gamma_f, \forall f \in F$, Z is an integer, then $T_d \geq T_d^{\dagger}$.*

This proposition can be proved by showing that with infinitely small chunk sizes $\gamma_f \to 0$ in proposed the crowdsourced system, we can assign the downloading task to each participant based on her/his cellular link rate $\hat{r}_i^c$ and guarantee that all users complete downloading task at the same time $T_d^{\ddagger}$. Any downloading operation under chunk sizes $Z\gamma_f, \forall f \in F$, can be equivalently achieved under chunk sizes $\gamma_f, \forall f \in F$, by the multiple same operations.

4.3   User Payoff Bound

Given a requested content files set $S_j^{\dagger}$ of requester j in a period of continuous time $[0, T]$, there are $|S_j^{\dagger}|\beta_i$ content files can be satisfied by cached data, and $|S_j^{\dagger}|(1 - \beta_i)$ content files need to be downloaded by cellular links. Compared to cellular networks, the WiFi transmission bandwidth is larger and more stable via Point to Point communication in short distance, then we assume that all users have the same WiFi link rate r^w and $r^w > r_i^c, \forall i \in I$. Due to $|S_j^\dagger|(1 - \beta_i)$ content files also need to be transmitted to requester user j^1, then ξ_j can be reformulated as following:

$$\xi_j = \sum_{f \in S_j^\dagger} |f| \div (T_{c,j} + T_{d,j}) = \sum_{f \in S_j^\dagger} |f| \div (\frac{\sum_{f \in S_j^\dagger}}{r^w} + T_{d,j}), \tag{16}$$

where $T_{c,j}$ and $T_{d,j}$ denote the data retrieving time of requester j by WiFi and cellular, respectively. According to Eq. 16, we know that ξ is can be a function of parameter β and T_d. Therefore, ξ can be bounded by:

$$\xi(\beta^\dagger, T_d^\dagger) \leq \xi(\beta, T_d) \leq \xi(\beta^\ddagger, T_d^\ddagger) \tag{17}$$

Transmission of the same size of the data, energy consumption of WiFi is much smaller than that of cellular network [14]. Energy cost includes the energy consumption for data downloading on cellular links and energy consumption for data exchange via WiFi. According to Eq. 10, given a $S_j^\dagger$ for requester user j, the energy consumption of WiFi is almost constant. Furthermore, E_j is mainly decided by the energy consumption on cellular links. Hence, the energy consumption of all requesters is bounded by:

$$E(\beta^\ddagger, T_d^\ddagger) \leq E(\beta, T_d) \leq E(\beta^\dagger, T_d^\dagger) \tag{18}$$

Based on the above, we have the following theorem.

Theorem 1. *Given a proportion rate of cached data β and a set of chunk sizes $\gamma_f, \forall f \in F$, the theoretical performance bound $\mathbf{W}$ is bounded by:*

$$\mathbf{W}(\beta^\dagger, T_d^\dagger) \leq \mathbf{W}(\beta, T_d) \leq \mathbf{W}(\beta^\ddagger, T_d^\ddagger) \tag{19}$$

The bound of proposed crowdsourced system is mainly influenced by the proportion rate of cached data β and the chunk sizes $\gamma_f, \forall f \in F$. In future work, we should consider the proportion rate of cached data and the chunk sizes for practical implementation of the proposed crowdsourced content distribution system.

5 Conclusion

In this work, we proposed a CCCMN framework for content distribution, and analyzed the theoretical performance bound of proposed system. The bound of proposed crowdsourced system is mainly influenced by the proportion rate of cached data and the chunk size of each file. Our performance bound analysis is an

---

[1] Here we ignore the data retrieved by user j herself/himself via the cellular link.

important first step towards the future practical implementation of the proposed crowdsourced content distribution system. It can be a benchmark to study the practical scheduling algorithms and incentive mechanisms for the CCCMN in the scenario without complete network information. Improving the popular data caching ratio and setting a reasonable chunk size are the key factors to enhance the proposed crowdsourced system performance.

Acknowledgment. This work is supported in part by National Nature Science Foundation of China under grant No. 61602462 and No. 61601449, and supported in part by Shenzhen Science and Technology Foundation under grant No. JCYJ20150630114942277 and No. JSGG20160229123657040.

References

1. Jiang, X., Jun, B.I., Nan, G., Zhaogeng, L.I.: A survey on information-centric networking:rationales, designs and debates. China Commun. **12**(7), 1–12 (2015)
2. Ning, Z., Hu, X., Chen, Z., Zhou, M., Hu, B., Cheng, J., Obaidat, M.: A cooperative quality-aware service access system for social internet of vehicles. IEEE Internet Things J. (2017). https://doi.org/10.1109/JIOT.2017.2764259
3. Ning, Z., Xia, F., Ullah, N., Kong, X., Hu, X.: Vehicular social networks: enabling smart mobility. IEEE Commun. Mag. **55**(5), 49–55 (2017)
4. Cisco: Cisco visual networking index: global mobile data traffic forecast update, 2016–2021. CISCO White Paper (2017)
5. Jacobson, V., Smetters, D., Thornton, J., Plass, M., Briggs, N., Braynard, R.: Networking named content. In: Proceedings of the 5th International Conference on Emerging Networking Experiments and Technologies, pp. 1–12. ACM (2009)
6. Su, Z., Xu, Q.: Content distribution over content centric mobile social networks in 5G. IEEE Commun. Mag. **53**(6), 66–72 (2015)
7. Tourani, R., Misra, S., Mick, T.: IC-MCN: an architecture for an information-centric mobile converged network. IEEE Commun. Mag. **54**(9), 43–49 (2016)
8. Lee, J., Jeon, S.: Low overhead smooth mobile content sharing using content centric networking (CCN). IEICE Trans. Commun. **94**(10), 2751–2754 (2011)
9. Han, B., Wang, X., Choi, N., Kwon, T., Choi, Y.: AMVS-NDN: adaptive mobile video streaming and sharing in wireless named data networking. In: 2013 IEEE Conference on Computer Communications Workshops (INFOCOM WKSHPS), pp. 375–380. IEEE (2013)
10. Detti, A., Ricci, B., Blefari-Melazzi, N.: Mobile peer-to-peer video streaming over information-centric networks. Comput. Netw. **81**, 272–288 (2015)
11. Gao, L., Tang, M., Pang, H., Huang, J.: Performance bound analysis for crowd-sourced mobile video streaming. In: Conference on Information Science and Systems, pp. 366–371 (2016)
12. Tang, M., Wang, S., Gao, L., Huang, J., Sun, L.: MOMD: a multi-object multi-dimensional auction for crowdsourced mobile video streaming. In: IEEE INFO-COM 2017 - IEEE Conference on Computer Communications (2017)
13. Joseph, V., de Veciana, G.: NOVA: QoE-driven optimization of dash-based video delivery in networks. In: 2014 Proceedings of INFOCOM, pp. 82–90. IEEE (2014)

14. Balasubramanian, N., Balasubramanian, A., Venkataramani, A.: Energy consumption in mobile phones: a measurement study and implications for network applications. In: Proceedings of the 9th ACM SIGCOMM Conference on Internet Measurement Conference, pp. 280–293. ACM (2009)

15. Manaris, B., Vaughan, D., Wagner, C., Romero, J., Davis, R.B.: Evolutionary music and the Zipf-Mandelbrot law: developing fitness functions for pleasant music. In: Cagnoni, S., Johnson, C.G., Cardalda, J.J.R., Marchiori, E., Corne, D.W., Meyer, J.-A., Gottlieb, J., Middendorf, M., Guillot, A., Raidl, G.R., Hart, E. (eds.) EvoWorkshops 2003. LNCS, vol. 2611, pp. 522–534. Springer, Heidelberg (2003). https://doi.org/10.1007/3-540-36605-9_48

An Interference Management Strategy for Dynamic TDD in Ultra-dense Networks

Shuming Seng, Xi Li[✉], Hong Ji, and Heli Zhang

Key Laboratory of Universal Wireless Communications, Ministry of Education,
Beijing University of Posts and Telecommunications,
Beijing, People's Republic of China
{seng,lixi,jihong,zhangheli}@bupt.edu.cn

Abstract. Ultra-dense networks (UDNs) are considered to meet demands for fast increasing throughput requirements per unit area in hotspots. Along with the dynamic variation of the throughput for the uplink/downlink (UL/DL), flexible resource allocation schemes become very important in UDNs based on time division duplex (TDD) for densely deployed access points (APs) and user equipments (UEs). In this paper, we propose a strategy to resolve the interference problem brought by dynamic TDD in UDNs. Firstly, we design a clustering method based on the Chameleon algorithm to reduce the inter-cluster interference. With the clustering results, the throughput requirements of each cluster become similar. Then we adopt a dynamic UL/DL resource allocation (DRA) for small cells in each cluster, with fewer adopted frame structures reaching more users' throughput requirements adequately. At last, in each cluster, we adopt multi-cell beamforming (MBF) in small cells with the same frame structure to further mitigate inter-cell interference (ICI). Simulation results show that our proposed strategy could achieve satisfactory performance in UL/DL throughput.

Keywords: UDNs · TDD · Clustering · ICI · MBF

1 Introduction

Cisco Visual Networking Index (VNI) in 2017 forecasts that by 2021, the global mobile data traffic will reach up to 49 EBs/month and the average mobile transmission rate will exceed 20 Mbps [1]. Ultra-dense networks (UDNs) could improve the throughput per unit area by densely deploying low-power and small-coverage access points (APs) in hotspots. The density of APs λ_a and the density of user equipments (UEs) λ_u are in the same order of magnitude [2]. It is considered as an inspiring research field in the fifth generation (5G) mobile communication system [3].

Many new network applications have high demands for uplink (UL) traffic, which achieve or even exceed demands for downlink (DL) traffic. And in hotspots,

© ICST Institute for Computer Sciences, Social Informatics and Telecommunications Engineering 2018
L. Wang et al. (Eds.): QShine 2017, LNICST 234, pp. 142–152, 2018.
https://doi.org/10.1007/978-3-319-78078-8_15

throughput requirements for UL/DL of UEs per unit area have a significant dynamic variation due to the densification of UEs [4]. The cases drive UDNs design to consider dynamic time division duplex (TDD) schemes as one of the feasible solutions. Dynamic TDD schemes, in which DL and UL subframes can be dynamically allocated to APs due to real-time UL/DL throughput requirements of small cells, were proposed to allow APs to effectively adapt the quick variation of UL/DL throughput requirements. Still, the scenario considering both UDNs and TDD schemes causes severe inter-cell interference (ICI) [5], which contains ordinary inter-cell interference (OICI) and cross-subframe inter-cell interference (CICI). The CICI is caused by adjacent cells in different transmission directions.

Various technologies were proposed to mitigate ICI in TDD networks. [6] offers a dynamic resource allocation scheme which reduces interference with lower complexity for dynamic TDD-based heterogeneous cloud radio access networks. [7] proposes a distributed user-centric clustering algorithm which focuses on DL interference. But these technologies may not work well in TDD-based UDNs because algorithms of them do not need to process high density and dynamic data reflecting information about APs like that in UDNs. And they often only focus on the interference in DL, because the interference in UL caused by low-power UEs without a high density is often ignored in considered scenarios. However, the interference in UL is also severe in UDNs because of the shorter distance between UEs.

The authors in [8] prove a beneficial performance of the traffic adaptation to the service time and energy efficiency in UDNs with dynamic TDD schemes. But an effective dynamic UL/DL resource allocation (DRA) and an interference management (IM) method of the TDD scheme require a dynamic inter-cell coordination, which could be hard to implement in high-density, high-dynamism and low-cost UDNs. That impels TDD-based UDNs to perform a flexible and real-time IM strategy whose algorithm can process large data dynamically. Considering the above problems, we propose an IM strategy jointly using the Chameleon clustering (CC) algorithm, a DRA and the multi-cell beamforming (MBF) in dynamic TDD-based UDNs.

In this paper, we consider that adopting TDD schemes in UDNs could bring high throughputs per unit area and high UL/DL resource utilization efficiency in time domain by utilizing appropriate technologies. We use the CC algorithm considering dynamic locations of small cells and dynamic throughput requirements of UEs as two significant parameters. Besides, the CC algorithm can process large and dynamic data to adapt to high-density and complex UDNs. The clustering result reduces inter-cluster ICI and makes the throughput requirement of each cluster similar. And the similar throughput requirement ensures fewer UL/DL frame structures can meet more users' throughput requirements in each cluster. Then we jointly adopt the DRA in time domain and the MBF in spatial domain in each cluster to mitigate intra-cluster interference and ensure users could get on-demand throughputs of UL/DL.

2   System Model

We consider a typical TDD-based UDN consisting of N densely and randomly deployed single-antenna APs, M densely and randomly distributed single-antenna UEs and one central controller. The density of APs and UEs is respectively λ_a and λ_u. Also, we assume the central controller knows the perfect channel state information (CSI) and one UE accesses only one AP in each small cell, so there are corresponding M small cells to be clustered. The network deployment is shown in Fig. 1, where B_0 and B_1 are orthogonal, and the icon U (UL) or D (DL) expresses a real-time transmission mode of small cells. Figure 1 shows that by using the proposed strategy, the ICI remains between small cells with the same bandwidth B_1 in adjacent clusters.

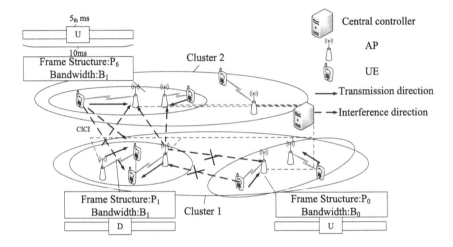

Fig. 1. A typical TDD-based UDN deployment

Subframe	UL/DL Frame Structure										Proportion of
Number	0ms	1ms	2ms	3ms	4ms	5ms	6ms	7ms	8ms	9ms	UL Subframe t_u
P_0	D	S	U	U	U	D	S	U	U	U	0.6
P_1	D	S	U	U	D	D	S	U	U	D	0.4
P_2	D	S	U	D	D	D	S	U	D	D	0.2
P_3	D	S	U	U	U	D	D	D	D	D	0.3
P_4	D	S	U	U	D	D	D	D	D	D	0.2
P_5	D	S	U	D	D	D	D	D	D	D	0.1
P_6	D	S	U	U	U	D	S	U	U	D	0.5

D	DL Subframe		S	Special Subframe		U	UL Subframe

Fig. 2. Dynamic TDD frame structures of TD-LTE

We adopt the frame structures defined in TD-LTE, which is shown in Fig. 2. Based on the proposed clustering algorithm, M small cells will be divided into

K clusters, denoted by $\mathbb{CL} = \{CL_1, CL_2, \ldots, CL_K\}$. For CL_k, the sum of the throughput requirements is denoted by TR_k, where $k = \{1, \ldots, K\}$. And the throughput requirement of each cluster is similar after the proposed clustering algorithm. If TR_k is too large without being controlled, it will be difficult to effectively satisfy users' requirements with the finite number of UL/DL frame structures. In the CL_k, by comparing throughput requirements of the given small cells in the same cluster with one threshold value β, the central controller will reconfigure frame structures for each AP into the matched configuration to constitute the secondary cluster. Each secondary cluster uses one matched configuration. At the same time, in each cluster, the system spectrum will be divided into different secondary clusters to eliminate the ICI in the same cluster. After that, the central controller will transmit the precoding matrix to APs for using the MBF to eliminate the ICI further.

We denote $\mathbf{P_x} = \{p_{t1}, p_{t2}, \ldots, p_{t10}\}$, where $\mathrm{x} = \{0, \ldots, 6\}$ to express one of the standard frame structures (SFS) defined in TD-LTE, where $p_t = 0$ (UL subframe) or 1 (DL subframe). When the transmission mode of the transceiver switches from DL to UL, a special subframe is required. For the sake of simplicity, a special subframe is used as a DL subframe in this paper. For example, the SFS of number "0" can be denoted by $\mathbf{P_0} = \{1, 1, 0, 0, 0, 1, 1, 0, 0, 0\}$.

3   DRA and MBF Based on CC Algorithm (DRA-MBFCC)

In TDD-based UDNs, the clustering algorithm should adapt to many new challenges as mentioned above. So the CC algorithm has to process large dynamic data and mitigate the severe ICI caused by the high densification of active APs and UEs. Besides, to reduce intra-cluster ICI and ensure the on-demand throughput requirement of each user, we jointly adopt DRA and MBF. The details are described in the following.

3.1   Chameleon Clustering

The most obvious advantage of the CC algorithm is considering both interconnectivity and closeness between adjacent clusters at the same time [9]. We regard the coordinates of active APs in TDD-based UDNs as coordinates of data set during the clustering process. Firstly, we need several sub-clusters as a data set of the clustering algorithm, and each sub-cluster should contain at least two small cells. We get required sub-clusters by using the k-nearest algorithm by setting a proper k in this paper, which is related to the number of small cells. Then we merge sub-clusters by the Chameleon algorithm. The interconnectivity called relative interconnection (RI) is associated with the geographical position of the given small cells (denoted as the coordinates of active APs). The closeness called relative closeness (RC) is subjected to both geographical position and throughput requirements of clusters. The two values, RI and RC co-determine if adjacent sub-clusters can be merged. $RI(sCL_p, sCL_q)$ is calculated to measure the ICI between adjacent sub-clusters, sCL_p and sCL_q, which is expressed as:

$$RI(sCL_p, sCL_q) = \frac{2|EW(sCL_p, sCL_q)|}{|EW(sCL_p)| + |EW(sCL_q)|} \tag{1}$$

where $|EW(sCL_p)|$ indicates the sum of edge weights between APs in the sub-cluster sCL_p. It is the same for $|EW(sCL_q)|$. $|EW(sCL_p, sCL_q)|$ is the weight of edges that connect APs between sCL_p and sCL_q. The weighted value is the reciprocal of the corresponding edge length, and the above defined parameters can be calculated as: $|EW(sCL_p)| = \sum_i \frac{1}{l_p^i}$ and $|EW(sCL_p, sCL_q)| = \sum_i \frac{1}{l_{p,q}^i}$, where l_p^i, $l_{p,q}^i$ is respectively the length of the corresponding weighted edge, and i is the index of corresponding small cells.

In each cluster, adopting more frame structures means more CICI exists, which is hard to mitigate. On the other hand, with the constraint of the throughput requirement of each cluster, fewer frame structures can efficiently satisfy the throughput requirement of each UE as required, so it is necessary to restrict the sum of the throughput requirement of each cluster. $RC(sCL_p, sCL_q)$ is calculated to measure the closeness between adjacent sub-clusters sCL_p, sCL_q, and the threshold γ restricts the sum of the throughput requirements in each cluster. $RC(sCL_p, sCL_q)$ is calculated as:

$$\begin{cases} 0, & TR_{p,q} > \gamma \\ \dfrac{(|n_p| + |n_q|)|\overline{EW}(sCL_p, sCL_q)|}{|n_q||\overline{EW}(sCL_p)| + |n_p||\overline{EW}(sCL_q)|}, & TR_{p,q} \leq \gamma \end{cases} \tag{2}$$

where $|\overline{EW}(sCL_p, sCL_q)|$ is the mean of edge weights that connect vertices between sCL_p and sCL_q. It is the same to $|\overline{EW}(sCL_p)|$, $|\overline{EW}(sCL_q)|$. $|n_p|$, $|n_q|$ is respectively the number of small cells in sCL_p, sCL_q. γ is a threshold value set according to both the whole throughput requirement of the network, TR, and the expected number of clusters, K ($\gamma \geq TR/K$). $TR_{p,q}$ can be calculated as: $TR_{p,q} = TR_p + TR_q$, where TR_p, TR_q is respectively the throughput requirements of sCL_p, sCL_q. Besides, $RIC(sCL_p, sCL_q)$ determines if sub-clusters can be merged, which is calculated as:

$$RIC(sCL_p, sCL_q) = RI(sCL_p, sCL_q) \times RC(sCL_p, sCL_q) \tag{3}$$

If $RIC(sCL_p, sCL_q)$ arrives at a preset threshold δ, the sCL_p and sCL_q can be merged. The pseudo-code of the proposed clustering algorithm is shown in Algorithm 1. The greater the value of $RIC(sCL_p, sCL_q)$ is, the possibility of merging sCL_p and sCL_q is higher, which means that the adjacent sub-clusters could merge when the distance between them becomes far enough. That reduces the inter-cluster ICI. On the other hand, the set of γ makes the sum of the throughput requirement of each merged cluster similar. After the above, the intra-cluster ICI has not been mitigated. Therefore, we should mitigate intra-cluster ICI further in the next steps.

Algorithm 1. CC algorithm

1: Input: update the coordinates of L sub-clusters, $s\mathbb{CL}_l$ consisting of small cells, which are expected to be clustered after the k-nearest algorithm as coordinates of initial data set, and uniformly choose K sub-clusters, $s\mathbb{CL}_m$ from the initial data set, $s\mathbb{CL}_l$.

2: Initialization:
   a) γ: the threshold in (2); b) δ: the threshold compared with RIC; c) K: the number of clusters expected; d) TR_p: the throughput requirement of the p_{th} cell; e) $p=1$, variable $q = 1, \cdots, L$.

3: Output: K expected clusters.

4: Step1:

5: **while** $(s\mathbb{CL}_l\{q\} \neq \emptyset) \bigcap (p \leq K)$ **do**

6:    **if** there existing adjacent $s\mathbb{CL}_m\{p\}$, $s\mathbb{CL}_l\{q\}$ for $q = 1, \cdots, L$, and $(TR_p + TR_q) \leq \gamma$ **then**

7:       calculate corresponding $RIC(s\mathbb{CL}_m\{p\}, s\mathbb{CL}_l\{q\})=\mathbb{C}\{q\}$, put the value $\mathbb{C}\{q\}$ in $\mathbb{C}$, and carry out the step 2

8:    **else**

9:       $p = p + 1$, and carry out the step 1

10:   **end if**

11:   Step2:

12:   **if** $\max(\mathbb{C}) = \mathbb{C}\{r\} \geq \delta$ **then**

13:      merge $s\mathbb{CL}_m\{p\}$ and $s\mathbb{CL}_l\{q\}$ as a new sub-cluster, $s\mathbb{CL}_m\{p\}$, let $s\mathbb{CL}_l\{r\}=\emptyset$, $\mathbb{C}=\emptyset$, and carry out the step 1

14:   **else**

15:      $p = p + 1$, and carry out the step 1

16:   **end if**

17: **end while**

3.2 DRA-MBF Based on CC in Each Cluster

After the clustering algorithm is finished, intra-cluster ICI should be mitigated further. Firstly, we adopt the dynamic UL/DL frame structure allocation depending on the throughput requirement of UL. Then we adopt dynamic spectrum allocation according to the result of the above to mitigate ICI between small cells with different UL/DL frame structures in adjacent clusters. Finally, we adopt MBF to mitigate ICI further. The details are described as following. As mentioned in Sect. 2, we adopt the SFSs defined in TD-LTE, which are listed in Fig. 2. The proportions of UL subframe in each frame structure are different. We set 5 thresholds to partition them, denoted as $\{\beta_1,\ldots,\beta_5\} = \{0.15, 0.25, 0.35, 0.45, 0.55\}$. These thresholds partition $0-1$ into 6 parts $\{0-0.15, 0.15-0.25, \ldots, 0.45-0.55, 0.55-1\}$, corresponding to frame structures $\{P_5, P_4, P_3, P_1, P_6, P_0\}$. The central controller can obtain the UL/DL throughput requirement of each small cell, TR^U/TR^D. And the ratio of UL throughput requirements can be calculated as $R^u = TR^u/(TR^u + TR^d)$. Small cells will be allocated the corresponding spectrum due to R^u. We choose 6 mentioned frame structures above as candidate frame structures. Small cells which be allocated different frame structures will be uniformly allocated 2 different sizes of the bandwidth in each cluster. Assuming the k_{th} cluster consists n_k small cells, the UL/DL throughput requirement of which is respectively $TR_{i,k}^u/TR_{i,k}^d$ ($i = 1, 2, \ldots, n_k$), and the ratio of UL throughput requirements can be calculated as: $R_{i,k}^u = \frac{TR_{i,k}^u}{TR_{i,k}^u + TR_{i,k}^d}$.

Then the central controller collects and sorts $R_{i,k}^u$ in ascending order and respectively calculates the mean of top $n_k/2$ or $(n_k + 1)/2$ and last $n_k/2$ or $(n_k - 1)/2$ values, denoted as $\overline{R_{Tk}^u}$ and $\overline{R_{Lk}^u}$. By comparing $\overline{R_{Tk}^u}$ and $\overline{R_{Lk}^u}$ with $\{\beta_1, \beta_2 \ldots, \beta_5\}$, two sets of small cells adopt matching frame structures. The detailed algorithm is listed in Algorithm 2. To mitigate the ICI between small cells with the same frame structure, we adopt space division multiplexing (SDM). The central controller which knows CSI can calculate the matrix of precoding and detection. In this paper, we use zero forcing (ZF) algorithm to get the precoding and detection matrix, which can mitigate the interference among transmitting or receiving antennas in the view of SDM. In [10], the normalised precoding matrix W and detection matrix V based on ZF algorithm are presented to realise SDM, which can be calculated as: $W = \frac{H(HH^H)}{\|H(HH^H)^{-1}\|}$ and $V = (HH^H)^{-1}H$, where H is the DL channel matrix.

$$SINR_{i,t_0}^D = \frac{\|H_{k,k}W_k\|^2 P_i^a}{\underbrace{\|\sum_{l \in \mathbb{CL}, l \neq k}\sum_{j \in \mathbb{CL}_k} I_{i,j}J_{i,j}H_{k,l}W_l\|^2 P_j^a + N_0}_{OICI}}$$

$$+ \frac{\|H_{k,k}W_k\|^2 P_i^a}{\underbrace{\|\sum_{l \in \mathbb{CL}, l \neq k}\sum_{j \in \mathbb{CL}_k} I_{i,j}\overline{J_{i,j}}V_k H_{k,l}^2 W_l\|^2 P_j^u + N_0}_{CICI}} \quad (4)$$

$$SINR_{i,t_0}^U = \frac{\|V_k H_{k,k}^H\|^2 P_i^u}{\underbrace{\|\sum_{l \in \mathbb{CL}, l \neq k}\sum_{j \in \mathbb{CL}_k} I_{i,j}J_{i,j}V_k H_{k,l}^2 W_l\|^2 P_j^u + N_0}_{OICI}}$$

$$+ \frac{\|V_k H_{k,k}^H\|^2 P_i^u}{\underbrace{\|\sum_{l \in \mathbb{CL}, l \neq k}\sum_{j \in \mathbb{CL}_k} I_{i,j}\overline{J_{i,j}}H_{k,l}W_l\|^2 P_j^a + N_0}_{CICI}} \quad (5)$$

The above process is one kind of MBF, where the number of transmitting antennas N_t is equal to N_r, assuming that APs not serving UEs is in idle mode. The intra-cluster ICI between the small cells with different frame structures is eliminated because of the allocation of different sizes of the bandwidth. Assuming that the TDD network is strictly synchronous, the OICI refers to AP-to-UE/UE-to-AP interference, and the CICI refers to AP-to-AP/UE-to-UE interference. By adopting MBF, the interference only remains in inter-cluster ICI between small cells with the same frequency spectrum. In the k_{th} cluster CL_k, UL and DL signal-to-interference-plus-noise ratios (SINR) at time t_0 can be calculated as (4), (5) where i, j is the index of AP/UE corresponding to the i_{th}/j_{th} small cell. $\mathbb{CL}$ and $\mathbb{CL}_k$ is respectively the set of all clusters and the k_{th} cluster. $r_{i,j}$ is the distance between AP_i/UE_i and AP_j/UE_j. $I_{i,j}$ is equal to 0 or 1 depending on the frequency spectrum of AP_i/UE_i and AP_j/UE_j at t_0. $J_{i,j}$ is equal to 0 or 1 depending on the subframe types of AP_i/UE_i and AP_j/UE_j at t_0 (0 means they are in the same subframe). $H_{k,k}$, $H_{k,l}$ is respectively DL channel matrix in the k_{th} and k_{th}-to-l_{th} cluster. P_i^a, P_i^u, N_0 is respectively the power of an AP, a UE and the noise per unit.

4 Simulation and Result

In this section, we show the simulation results of the proposed strategy by matlab-based Monte Carlo method. We consider a TDD-based UDN consisting of N APs, M UEs and one central controller in two-dimensional scenes. The detailed values of simulation parameters are listed in Table 1. The distribution of APs follows a Poisson point process and UEs are distributed randomly. The channel fading model is Rayleigh fading. Assuming that the central controller can transmit the precoding and detection matrix to active APs. Besides, we

---

Algorithm 2. The proposed DRA algorithm

1: Input: K known clusters after CC algorithm, denoted as $\mathbb{CL}$, where there are n_k small cells in $\mathbb{CL}_k$ respectively, $k = \{1, \cdots, K\}$, and $R_{i,k}^u$

2: Initialization:
   a) B_0: available bandwidth; b) $\mathbb{P} = \{P_5, P_4, P_3, P_1, P_6, P_0\}$: selectable configurations;
   c) $\beta = \{\beta_1, \beta_2, \ldots, \beta_5\}$: thresholds which influence the choices of adopted frame structures.

3: Output: small cells allocated frame structures and expected bandwidth

4: Step1:

5: **for** $k = 1, \cdots, K$ **do**

6:   **for** $i = 1, \cdots, n_k$ **do**

7:     Step2: calculate each $R_{i,k}^u$ and sort values in $\mathbb{CL}_k$ in ascending order

8:     divide n_k small cells in CL_k into 2 sets with the equal cell number according to sorting results

9:     Step3: calculate the mean values $\overline{R_{Tk}^u}$ and $\overline{R_{Lk}^u}$, and adopts matched the frame structure according to the comparison result between $\overline{R^u}$ and each threshold β

10:     Step4: evenly allocate B_0 to 2 sets of small cells in CL_k independently

11:   **end for**

12: **end for**

Table 1. Network design parameters

Parameters	Value	Parameters	Value
System bandwidth, B_0	20 MHz	Noise power density	-174 dBm/Hz
AP number, N	150	UE density, λ_u	$200, 400, 600$ UEs/km^2
Cluster number, K	$3, 6, 9$	AP density, λ_a	1000 APs/km^2
UE number, M	$30, 60, 90$	Transmit power of AP	25 dBm
Area	300 m × 500 m	Transmit power of UE	20 dBm

consider x different subcarriers with the bandwidth, B_0/x. In each cluster, x subcarriers will be divided into two equally between two to be allocated in two specific sets of small cells. Each set of small cells refers to the set of small cells allocated the same frame structure.

Figure 3 shows the result of clustering using the proposed clustering algorithm, where 60 small cells are divided into 6 clusters with an area of 300 m × 500 m. λ_u and λ_a is respectively 400 active UEs/km^2 and 1000 APs/km^2. The marked points are the central point of each small cell, and different markers, colors respectively mean different clusters and sizes of the bandwidth. As a consequence, the proposed clustering algorithm controls the distances between adjacent clusters and makes the throughput requirement of each cluster similar.

Figure 4 shows the result that comparing the proportion of achievable UL throughput per UE with the throughput requirement of each UE, where the cluster number $K = 9$, λ_u and λ_a is respectively 400 active UEs/km^2 and 1000 APs/km^2. The horizontal axis expresses the x_{th} user in the considered network. For each UE, the UL-to-DL ratio of achievable throughput (AT) R_{u_d} and required throughput (RT) R'_{u_d} are calculated as: $R_{u\_d} = \dfrac{T_u}{T_d}$ and $R'_{u\_d} = \dfrac{TR_u}{TR_d}$, where T_u/T_d and TR_u/TR_d respectively denote UL/DL achieved throughput and required UL/DL throughput of each UE. By adopting the proposed strategy, achievable UL/DL throughput of each UE will be dynamically adjusted with the variation of the UL/DL throughput requirement. In another word, that also improves resource utilization efficiency by allocating time slot for UL/DL.

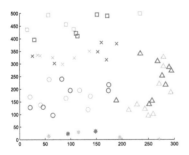

Fig. 3. The result of proposed clustering algorithm

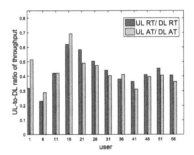

Fig. 4. The performance of the proposed strategy in UL/DL throughput adaptation

Figure 5 shows how the average AT of each UE changes with increasing cluster number and user density by using the proposed strategy. As a result, the throughput of each UE will reduce with the increase of user density, but the cluster number has a little effect. The value of achievable average throughput is calculated as: $T_a = T_u \times t_u + T_d \times (1 - t_u)$, where t_u is the proportion of UL subframes in one frame structure listed in Fig. 2. The result proves the proposed

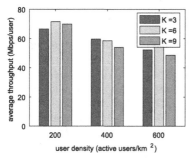
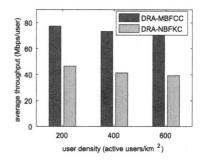

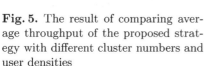

Fig. 5. The result of comparing average throughput of the proposed strategy with different cluster numbers and user densities

Fig. 6. The result of comparing average throughput of the proposed strategy and DRA-NBFKC

strategy can bring a high throughput gain. In Fig. 6, we compare the average throughput each user gets based on the proposed strategy DRA-MBFCC where $K = 6$ with a conventional interference management strategy: the DRA without MBF using k-means clustering (DRA-NBFKC). The result shows that the former has a $68\% - 72\%$ gain over the latter in the average throughput of each UE because MBF can mitigate ICI further after clustering.

5 Conclusion

In this work, we studied an IM method in based-TDD UDNs by using the proposed DRA-MBFCC algorithm. The proposed clustering algorithm will mitigate inter-cluster interference and make the sum of the required throughput TR of each cluster similar. The dynamic UL/DL frame structure allocation is based on TR of each cluster. If TR is too large, it will be difficult to meet users' requirements with the finite number of UL/DL frame structures. Then we adopt DRA and MBF to meet users' throughput requirements for UL/DL and mitigate ICI between small cells with the same UL/DL frame structure in each cluster. And simulation results prove that the UL/DL resource could be dynamically allocated as required by the proposed algorithm. Furthermore, in each cluster, MBF is adopted between the small cells with the same bandwidth to mitigate intra-cluster ICI between adjacent small cells in the same bandwidth. And simulation results also prove the proposed algorithm can bring a high throughput gain.

Acknowledgments. This work is supported by the National Science and Technology Major Project of the Ministry of Science and Technology of China (2016ZX03001017) and the National Natural Science Foundation of China (61671088).

References

1. Cisco: Cisco visual networking index: global mobile data traffic forecast update, white paper, 2016-2021. Cisco Mobile VNI (2017)
2. Ding, M., Lopez-Perez, D., Mao, G., Wang, P., Lin, Z.: Will the area spectral efficiency monotonically grow as small cells go dense. In: 2015 IEEE Global Communications Conference (GLOBECOM), pp. 1–7, December 2015
3. Bhushan, N., Li, J., Malladi, D., Gilmore, R., Brenner, D., Damnjanovic, A., Sukhavasi, R.T., Patel, C., Geirhofer, S.: Network densification: the dominant theme for wireless evolution into 5G. IEEE Commun. Mag. **52**(2), 82–89 (2014)
4. 3GPP: Further enhancements to LTE time division duplex (TDD) for downlink-uplink (DL-UL) interference management and traffic adaptation. In: 3GPP TR 36.828 (Vll.0.0) (2012)
5. Levanen, T., Venalainen, J., Valkama, M.: Interference analysis and performance evaluation of 5G flexible-TDD based dense small-cell system. In: 2015 IEEE 82nd Vehicular Technology Conference (VTC2015-Fall), pp. 1–7 (2015)
6. Yu, Z., Wang, K., Ji, H., Li, X., Zhang, H.: Dynamic resource allocation in TDD-based heterogeneous cloud radio access networks. China Commun. **13**(6), 1–11 (2016)
7. Lagen, S., Agustin, A., Vidal, J., Soret, B., Pedersen, K.I.: Distributed user-centric clustering and precoding design for comp joint transmission. In: 2015 IEEE Global Communications Conference (GLOBECOM), pp. 1–7 (2015)
8. Sun, H., Sheng, M., Wildemeersch, M., Quek, T.Q.S., Li, J.: Traffic adaptation for small cell networks with dynamic TDD. In: 2016 IEEE Global Communications Conference (GLOBECOM), pp. 1–7 (2016)
9. Karypis, G., Han, E.-H., Kumar, V.: Chameleon: hierarchical clustering using dynamic modeling. Computer **32**(8), 68–75 (1999)
10. van Zelst, A.: Space division multiplexing algorithms. In: Proceedings of the 2000 10th Mediterranean Electrotechnical Conference. Information Technology and Electrotechnology for the Mediterranean Countries, MeleCon 2000 (Cat. No.00CH37099), vol. 3, pp. 1218–1221, May 2000

Key Technologies of MEC Towards 5G-Enabled Vehicular Networks

Xiaoting Ma[1,2], Junhui Zhao[1,2(✉)], Yi Gong[3], and Yijie Wang[1]

[1] School of Information Engineering, East China Jiaotong University,
Nanchang 330013, China
eeejhzhao@163.com, wangyijie0528@163.com
[2] School of Electronic and Information Engineering,
Beijing Jiaotong University, Beijing 100044, China
16111030@bjtu.edu.cn
[3] Department of Electrical and Electronic Engineering,
Southern University of Science and Technology, Shenzhen 518055, China
gongy@sustc.edu.cn

Abstract. Mobile edge computing (MEC) can satisfy the communication requirements of ultra-high reliability and ultra-low latency in 5G-enabled vehicular networks, since it provides Internet service environment and cloud computing capability for wireless access network. In this paper, the architecture and characteristics of MEC for unmanned driving are explored. Meanwhile, the key technologies of MEC are discussed. With the assist of clustering, we propose the scheme of mobile vehicle cloud (MVC)-aided communication, and examine the network performance including computing resource allocation by MEC and link performance. The numerical results show that the network performance is improved effectively.

Keywords: 5G vehicular networks · MEC · MVC-aided communication
Clustering · Network performance

1 Introduction

With the advanced technologies, unmanned driving has been widely concerned by mainstream carmakers and internet firms, such as Mercedes Benz, Ford, TOYOTA, Volvo, and Google. Unmanned driving requires more thorough awareness, more comprehensive ability of interconnection and deeper wisdom in vehicular networks so as to build a new mobile wisdom space. Up to data, vehicular networks are mainly facing the challenge of integration of computing, communication, network and application, which has greatly restricted the development of complete automation of intelligent transportation system (ITS). At present, it is generally believed that mobile edge computing (MEC) technology is expected to break through the bottleneck of communication in unmanned systems, and catalyze the deployment of unmanned vehicles. For instance, in 2017, a vehicular network prototype was demonstrated built on top of the virtualized MEC platform at Mobile World Congress.

© ICST Institute for Computer Sciences, Social Informatics and Telecommunications Engineering 2018
L. Wang et al. (Eds.): QShine 2017, LNICST 234, pp. 153–159, 2018.
https://doi.org/10.1007/978-3-319-78078-8_16

The network architecture of 5G vehicular networks is about to transform from connection-centeric to content-centeric, with the aid of emerging MEC technology. As shown in Fig. 1, the traditional cloud architecture is divided into three parts: mobile vehicle cloud (MVC), mobile edge cloud (MEC) and remote central cloud (RCC). MVC is formed to improve routing utility in ad hoc networks through the communication between vehicles with on-board units. The edge cloud nodes include base stations and roadside units, which can communicate through backhaul with each other, in MEC. As a variant of RCC, MEC integrates infrastructure with Internet business. The content-centeric architecture relaxes the traffic pressure in wireless networks, which facilitates system to evolve towards Software Defined Network (SDN), Network Function Virtualization (NFV) and network open capability [1].

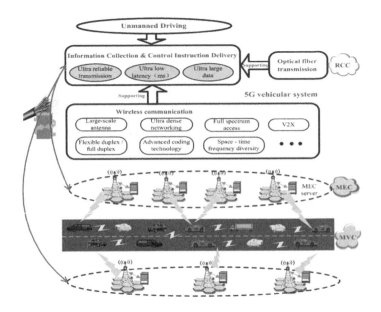

Fig. 1. MEC-based 5G vehicular network system architecture

In this paper, we first look into the architecture in MEC-based 5G vehicular networks. MEC is beneficial to realize the flattening of vehicular network architecture. Thereafter, we attempt to find the characteristics of MEC in the context of vehicular networks, and then the related key technologies are analyzed. On basis of the above research, we propose a MVC-aided communication scheme, where the communication capability of MVC is fully exploited according to the clustering of vehicles. With the scheme, the communication performance is improved significantly.

The remainder of this paper is organized as follows. Section 2 introduces the architecture, characteristics and technologies key of MEC in 5G-enabled vehicular networks. The scheme of MVC-aided communication is presented and verified in Sect. 3. Finally, we conclude the paper in Sect. 4.

2   MEC in Vehicular Networks

With the development of a variety of communication modes, such as vehicle-to-vehicle (V2V), vehicle-to-roadside unit (V2R), vehicle-to-pedestrian (V2P), and so on, big data analysis and sharing are getting more and more important. MEC technology is expected to realize the big data analysis and sharing among vehicles, infrastructures and pedestrians.

2.1   Architecture of Distributed MEC

MEC is mainly located near the management layer in the terminal-management-cloud framework [2], and sinks to the wireless access network. As shown in Fig. 2, the information transmission process includes four parts: wireless access network layer, data sensing and forwarding layer, MEC layer and cloud computing layer.

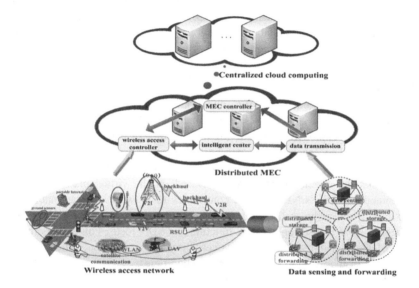

Fig. 2. Distributed information transmission scheme of MEC

In MEC layer, the decision-making center, MEC controller is mainly responsible for network source scheduling and computing task offload. The wireless network access and data transmission are completed by wireless access controller, which can realize the seamless connection of various heterogeneous resources and the cross layer cooperation between communication resources and computing resources. The data filtering and preliminary analysis are completed by the intelligent center, while the control and storage of data delivery are completed in the data transmission controller. The safety of unmanned vehicles depends on the period of the information update, i.e., with the faster information update, the driving will be safer. The deployment of MEC can accelerate the data update cycle in the network and alleviate the congestion of packets.

In vehicular networks, MEC servers are often deployed near RSUs, so that the deployment and performance of MEC will be limited by RSUs. Due to the unique nature of MEC towards vehicular networks, the characteristics of MEC deserve to be noticed. The first is the finiteness. Since the data in the MEC server is derived from RSUs, the service scope of the MEC server is limited. Meanwhile, the computing ability of MEC will also be reduced to a certain degree. Another important property is heterogeneity. Because of the different network environments and communication technologies, MEC should support a variety of hardware and software devices to satisfy the demand of safety. In addition, the transmission management and server selection of MEC must adapt to the mobility of the vehicle, in order to achieve low latency and security in high-speed mobile environments.

2.2   Key Technologies of MEC

MEC provides three functions: data storage, computing and wireless access. Based on this, there are three main key features in 5G-enabled vehicular networks: network functional virtualization, the collaboration among MVC, MEC and RCC, and multi-layer heterogeneous network. Therefore, the key technologies of MEC are divided into the following three aspects.

(a) MEC networking

There are three schemes of MEC networking: independent deployment as an element, integration in RSU, MEC combination with SDN/NFV. When MEC is independently deployed, there are some difficulties in deployment, maintenance and update. The scheme of integration shortens the physical communication distance, whereas the complexity of proprietary hardware integration and operation limits the development of MEC. Based on the virtual platform, MEC is combined with SDN/NFV, which contributes to network programmability and flexibility, and reduces the running time of business maturity. In the virtual platform, NFV focuses on network function and SDN focuses on the separation of control plane and user plane. However, there are still some difficulties to be overcame in the integration of multiple technologies.

(b) Collaborative management of resources

In order to realize the cooperation among vehicles, roads and people, resource managements have to combine MVC, MEC and RCC. However, vehicle mobility requires major changes to collaborative management of resource to ensure real time. Therefore, the rapid and reasonable scheduling is the key of resource collaboration.

(c) Heterogeneous network

With the increasing of applications in ITS, mobile heterogeneous computing and seamless connection are the significant challenges for MEC in heterogeneous network. In heterogeneous networks, we can take RCC as the root node, MEC as the intermediate node, and MVC as the leaf node. Generally speaking, at the network layer the separation of user plane and control plane can satisfy the requirement of fast data transmission in mobile scene. Due to the high-speed mobility of vehicles, the link layer protocol is changed to adapt the constant change of topology at the link layer.

3   MVC-Aided Communication

As a technology to achieve the integration of computing and communication, MEC plays a pivotal role in the wireless access network. Up to now, the researches about MEC especially focus on the offloading with the optimization of minimum energy consumption or maximum service efficiency within the maximum tolerable delay range [3–5]. However, these studies didn't consider the ability of MVC. It is well known that platoon model based on the clustering of vehicles can achieve ultra-low latency in vehicular networks [6]. Consequently, we especially examine the action of MVC on study of MVC-aided communication. Due to the clustering of vehicles, the vehicles that can communicate directly with each other by one hop are divided into one platoon, which is a MVC.

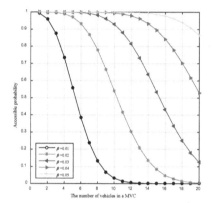
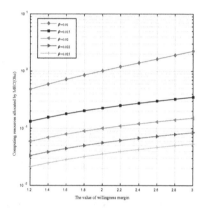

Fig. 3. The number of vehicles in a MVC   **Fig. 4.** Resource allocation of MEC

The process of MEC-aided communication is divided into the following phases:

(1) The target vehicle node which attempts to run an application becomes the leader of MVC and recruits members. The target vehicle establishes a MVC member list with members' IDs, position information and corresponding task assignment information.

(2) The adjacent vehicle willing to share resource sends hello packets including the geo-information and computing capability to the leader. Then adjacent vehicle is labeled as member of MVC and recorded in the leader's list. In MVC, every member can communicate with each other, which guarantees the link performance of MVC ad hoc network.

(3) According to the communication ability and the computing resource block quantity of every node, the application is split into several task blocks, and the target vehicle offloads the task blocks to MVC members.

(4) Due to the mobility, the MVC list is updated in real time and maintains the corresponding entries. When there is member joining or leaving the MVC, some task blocks need to be reallocated according step 3.

(5) Judging whether the resources of the MVC satisfy the needs of the running application. If yes, jump to step 7. Otherwise, jump to step 6.
(6) The leader of MVC offloads the rest of the task blocks to MEC, according to the projected consumption of time and energy.
(7) The output results of MVC members and MEC are transmitted to the target node.
(8) The target node processes the collected results to obtain the output content, and saves/publishes it.
(9) When target vehicle no longer uses the resource of MVC or is unable to connect with members, MVC is dismissed.

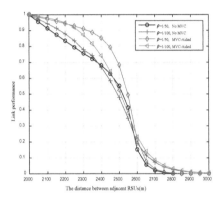

Fig. 5. Link performance based on MVC

Assuming the transmission radius of vehicles is 500 m and ρ represents the vehicle density measured in vehicles per meter. As shown in Fig. 3, the number of vehicles in a MVC under different densities is obtained according to [7]. Figure 3 reflects the relationship between the node number within the MVC and the network access probability under different vehicle densities. According to [8], the willingness margin value is introduced to study the significance of MVC for offloading in the paper. As shown in Fig. 4, the vehicle computing resources within the MVC can be fully utilized and the computational power of MVC is enhanced as the increasing of vehicle density. Thanks to MEC, it is not necessary to access Internet through the core network when the vehicle requests the network service, which greatly reduces the transmission delay. It means that there is a large channel competition in the network, with the vehicle density increasing. MVC can effectively manage the transmission in the network, and consequently, the channel contention between vehicle and RSU is reduced. In this article, the communication between two adjacent RSUs is considered as a network, where the transmission range of RSU is 1000 m. As shown in Fig. 5, the link performance based on MVC is improved because of the reduction of data collisions probability. MVC plays a significant role especially in computing tasks and network performance. In conclusion, with the increase of vehicles number, there are more available resources in a MVC. Therefore, the leasing of resources of MEC is reduced. And under the management of MVC, the link performance is improved.

4 Conclusion

MEC provides an effective integration solution of computing, storage and Internet. Up to now, with the development of technological advancement, the challenges of MEC in vehicular networks focus on mobility management and resource scheduling in heterogeneous networks. Based on the study of MEC, we look into the MEC-aid communication, considering the traffic load, computing and storage capacity, energy consumption and delay. In this paper, we prove that the resource leasing of MEC is reduced and the network communication is effectively managed, while the capability of MVC is fully taken advantage of. Under the research background of new generation communication technology, this paper provides the direction and ideas for the research of MEC in vehicular networks.

Acknowledgments. This work was supported in part by the National Natural Science Foundation of China (61471031, 61661021), the State Key Laboratory of Rail Traffic Control and Safety (Contract No. RCS2017K009), the Key Technology Research and Development Program of Jiangxi Province under Grant No. 20171BBE50057, the Open Research Fund of National Mobile Communications Research Laboratory, Southeast University (No. 2017D14), Science and technology project of Jiangxi Provincial Transport Bureau (No. 2016D0037), Training Plan for the Main Subject of Academic Leaders of Jiangxi Province (No. 20172BCB22016), and Natural Science Foundation of Guangdong Province under Grant No. 2015A030313844.

References

1. Hu, Y.C., Patel, M., Sabella, D.: Mobile edge computing: a key technology towards 5G. ETSI White Paper **11**(11), 1–16 (2015)
2. Zhao, J.H., Chen, Y., Huang, D.C.: Study on key technology of VANET sin terminal management cloud model. Telecommun. Sci. **32**(8), 2–9 (2016)
3. Zhang, K., Mao, Y., Leng, S., Maharjan, S., Zhang, Y.: Optimal delay constrained offloading for vehicular edge computing networks. In: IEEE International Conference on Communications (ICC), pp. 1–6. IEEE Press, Paris (2017)
4. Zhang, K., Mao, Y., Leng, S.: Predictive offloading in cloud-driven vehicles: using mobile-edge computing for a promising network paradigm. IEEE Veh. Technol. Mag. **12**, 36–44 (2017)
5. Hou, X., Li, Y., Chen, M., Wu, D., Jin, D., Chen, S.: Vehicular fog computing: a viewpoint of vehicles as the infrastructures. IEEE Trans. Veh. Technol. **65**, 3860–3873 (2016)
6. Campolo, C., Molinaro, A., Araniti, G., Berthet, A.O.: Better platooning control toward autonomous driving: an LTE device-to-device communications strategy that meets ultralow latency requirements. IEEE Veh. Technol. Mag. **12**, 30–38 (2017)
7. Zhao, J.H., Chen, Y., Gong, Y.: Study of connectivity probability based on cluster in vehicular ad hoc networks. In: 8th International Conference on Wireless Communications & Signal Processing (WCSP), pp. 1–5. IEEE Press, Yangzhou (2016)
8. Reputation-Based Approach for Computation Offloading in Vehicular Edge Computing. http://www.arocmag.com/article/02-2018-09-002.html

Wireless Networking Algorithms
and Protocols

PySNS3: A Real-Time Communication Interface and Protocol for Vehicular Ad-Hoc Networks

Tong Wang⬭ and Azhar Hussain(✉)⬭

College of Information and Communication Engineering,
Harbin Engineering University, Harbin 150001, China
wangtong@hrbeu.edu.cn, engrazr@gmail.com

Abstract. Vehicular Ad-hoc Network (VANET) being a key part of
Intelligent Transportation Systems (ITS), is gaining interest among road
authorities, automotive industry, network operators, and public for its
numerous solutions related to road safety, comfort, and traffic efficiency.
The prohibitive cost of deploying large-scale Testbeds for these solutions has attracted VANET's research community towards cooperative
ITS simulation platforms. SUMO is a widely adopted microscopic traffic
simulator with a Traffic Control Interface (TraCI) in various programming languages. Recently, Python has become the first priority programming language (used by many companies such as Google, Yahoo!, CERN,
NASA, etc.) for data science, web development, embedded applications,
artificial intelligence, information security and computation-driven scientific research. Moreover, only Python-based SUMO's TraCI has full
support for the up-to-date set of commands. The lack of a Python-
based cooperative ITS simulation platform, capable to communicate
SUMO's TraCI with a widely adopted network simulator NS3, has led us
to develop PySNS3 (a Python-based communication model for SUMO
and NS3). We have tested the robustness and reliability of PySNS3 for
VANET's experimentation, and compared its mobility as well as communication related simulation results with state-of-the-art NS2-mobility-
model. The results have proved the reliability and robustness of the proposed PySNS3.

Keywords: Vehicular Ad-Hoc Networks
Intelligent transport system · Automobile industry · SUMO · NS3
Traffic Control Interface

1 Introduction

The traditional transportation system is becoming increasingly unable to adapt
to the challenges of road safety, traffic congestion, fuel efficiency, infotainment
and eco-system offered by worldwide society development and unprecedented
demands for transportation. Recently, the advancement in wireless communications and automobile industry has brought many vehicular applications that

© ICST Institute for Computer Sciences, Social Informatics and Telecommunications Engineering 2018
L. Wang et al. (Eds.): QShine 2017, LNICST 234, pp. 163–171, 2018.
https://doi.org/10.1007/978-3-319-78078-8_17

can meet these challenges by deploying VANET strategies for cooperative ITS. However, the cost of deploying large-scale VANET's test beds (from Physical layer to the Application layer) in real traffic environment is prohibitively huge. Therefore VANET's research community mostly rely on cooperative ITS simulation platforms for the analysis of various protocols and interfaces before their actual deployment in road traffic. In ITS simulation study, vehicular mobility and communication modeling for VANET has some distinctive aspects. Traditionally, car manufacturers have deployed safety features such as, safety belts for seats, airbags, bumpers, and anti-lock systems for vehicles. Moreover, in recent years, automobile industry has introduced massive vehicular active safety systems based on sensors (such as radars, lasers and cameras, etc.). VANET has the potential to improve the usage of these new active safety systems [1], which will aid safety factor. It can also help the traffic department to directly manage traffic lights through the knowledge of real-time traffic situations [2]. Bidirectional interaction between network simulator and traffic simulator plays a major role in VANETs simulations [3]. For both safety and non-safety related cases, there is a demand for strong interaction between the network protocol and vehicular mobility. For example, the road traffic information can support efficient routing [4] of vehicles. Hence, there is a unique relationship between mobility and communications in VANET.

Unfortunately, for many years, the traffic simulators have never been created to communicate with network simulators and are designed to be controlled separately, with almost no interaction. However, VANET community has worked in the past few years to define efficient interfaces [5–16] between the two simulators. A communication interface of network and traffic simulator is usually categorized as Isolated, Federated, and Embedded. SUMO is a microscopic traffic simulator [17]. It is one of the most widely adopted traffic simulator for cooperative ITS simulation platforms. SUMO's TraCI support is available in various programming languages such as, Python, Java, C++ and .Net etc. During the past decade, Python has become a de-facto standard for exploratory, interactive, and computation-driven scientific research. The lack of a Python based platform, capable to communicate SUMO's TraCI with a widely adopted network simulator NS3 [18] for VANET simulations has led us to develop PySNS3.

The main contributions of this paper are as follows:

(1) The proposed PySNS3 can test VANET routing protocols (programmed in NS3 either through C++ or Python) by coupling SUMO with NS3 for cooperative ITS solutions.
(2) The proposed model supports up-do-date versions of SUMO and NS3 platforms. Which has made possible the evaluation and usage of various new features in these platforms. On the other hand, recent couplings [11,12,14,15] were not based on Python language. However, only the Python-based TraCI supports all traffic mobility related commands and maintained on daily basis [19].
(3) NS3 has a set of communication protocols for vehicular mobility as well as propagation loss models. A MAC layer model in WAVE [20] (Wireless Access

in Vehicular Environment) adapts MAC changes according to mobility of vehicles. However, as per best of our knowledge, online dynamic mobility for nodes in WAVE project was not studied and tested before. Moreover, PySNS3, supports transformation between network-coordinates and geo-coordinates, and vice versa especially in the case of Geographic Routing Protocols as described in [21] for VANET. We have compared VANET's simulation results of PySNS3 with the state-of-the-art NS2-mobility-model [22] in NS3. For this purpose, firstly, we generated an offline-trace-file of urban traffic environment of Harbin City in China. Secondly, we used this offline-trace-file by NS2-mobility-model for performance analysis of WAVE architecture along with GPSR routing protocol to get important network statistics, such as WAVE Packet Delivery Ratio (PDR), MAC-PHY Over-Head, and average routing GoodPut. Thirdly, we deployed PySNS3 to man-age the dynamic communication between SUMO and NS3 for the same experiment to get one to one comparison of stated statistics in offline and online approaches. Finally, we have compared the effect of varying maximum speed limitation on the vehicular statistics such as WAVE PDR, CO_2 emissions and Fuel consumption as well. The simulation results proved that the proposed PySNS3 communication model can offer online coupling between SUMO and NS3 for cooperative ITS simulations in a much reliable and robust way. Figure 1(a) shows architecture block diagram of PySNS3. The rest of the paper is organized as follows. Section 2 briefly describes the archi-tecture of PySNS3 and simulation approach, Sect. 3 presents the procedure for performance evaluation of PySNS3. Section 4 illustrates the simulation results of the performance evaluation procedure discussed in Sect. 3. Finally, Sect. 5 draws the main conclusions derived from this work.

2   Description of Proposed PySNS3

PySNS3 works cooperatively with PyViz to handle the communication between NS3 and SUMO as shown in Fig. 1(a). In NS3, PyViz is a live simulation visu-alizer, which means that it uses no trace files. It is the most useful tool for debugging purposes, i.e. to figure out if the mobility models are same as expected, where packets are being dropped, etc. PySNS3 exploits the power of Python lan-guage to offer robustness as well ease in developing VANET simulations. PySNS3 communication model has made SUMO an optional feature in PyViz GUI as shown in Fig. 1(b). The main idea behind proposed model is the integration of PySNS3 with NS3 to get access to its simulation state and offer dynamic vehic-ular mobility coupling with SUMO. It provides simulation as well as synchro-nization control. The performance evaluation of different routing protocols as well as traffic efficiency applications can also be incorporated in PySNS3. It also provides cross layer interaction support, since it has complete access to various layers of network nodes of NS3. The simulation scenario scene from SUMO can be brought inside the PyViz GUI for better understanding and development of dif-ferent ITS applications. The routing statistics access can offer efficient solutions to the vehicular rerouting. In other words, it can dynamically give the analysis of the relation between Road traffic routing and Network protocol routing.

In order to start SUMO TraCI from PyViz GUI, an optional PySNS3's SUMO launch button (SUMO (F4)) is shown in Fig. 1(b). Moreover, the vehicles are represented by traditional nodes of NS3 and green arrows portraying the in-simulation communications. The process flow of PySNS3 starts by providing the visualizer implementation option to the main NS3 simulation program. At start, the visualizer-thread acquires main simulation lock and the main NS3 topology is scanned for each node and the canvas is created. All nodes are placed on the canvas. The mobility of nodes is provided by an initial-trace-file without movements (for one to one comparison with NS2-mobility-model). Another thread called Simulation-thread waits for the Simulation_GO signal, so that it can acquire the simulation lock. At this point if the SUMO launch support is enabled, then a separate thread is created, we call it SUMO-thread. A flag called SUMO_enable is set to True from its initial state (False). Python based TraCI server then starts listening at a specified port in SUMO. And then the loading of .net.xml, .rou.xml and any other additional file, starts as described in SUMO configuration file. After this, the connection to TraCI server is established. The next step sets the SUMO simulation step to 0 s. At this point the PySNS3 communication control plane waits for another global flag called SUMO_FLAG_GO to be set to True (initial is set to False). The SUMO_FLAG_GO can only be set to True by the simulation-thread. Once this flag is set to True, the SUMO-thread acquires the simulation lock and performs the simulation step. Then the retrieval or assignments of vehicular values, such as position, speed, angle, emission, fuel consumption and traffic lights control, etc. is carried out. At the same time assignment of these values to the NS3 nodes is also performed using python based NS3 getters and setters. The simulation step is incremented and the SUMO_FLAG_GO is set to False and the simulation lock is also released by SUMO-thread. If there is any car inside the SUMO platform, this thread also waits for SUMO_FLAG_GO to be set to True to perform another TraCI simulation step. Otherwise, the TraCI connection is closed and flushed.

The visualizer-thread waits for the simulation start button to initiate the cooperative simulation between NS3 and SUMO. At this instant SIMULATION_GO flag is enabled. This flag sets the Simulation-thread to acquire the simulation lock. The NS3 simulation events are performed for the specified simulation period. After that the simulation-thread releases simulation lock. Meanwhile the visualizer-thread updates the GTK events. The release of simulation lock from Simulation-thread enables the SUMO_FLAG_GO to True only if the SUMO_ENABLE is already in True state. Simulation-thread then waits for the Simulation_GO signal from visualizer to again perform the operations. As SUMO-thread gets the SUMO_FLAG_GO flag to True, it acquires the simulation lock and performs the respective tasks for the same time period. Later on, SUMO-thread releases the simulation lock and sets the SUMO_FLAG_GO to False. And then the visualizer update model lock is acquired and if the SUMO_FLAG_GO is already set to False, then it performs the periodic updates,

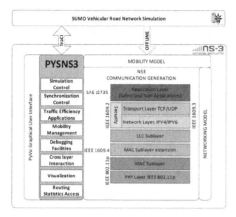

(a) The basic architecture of PySNS3   (b) Embedding SUMO's mobility option in PyViz

Fig. 1. The basic architecture of PySNS3 and its SUMO-NS3 mobility coupling (Color figure online)

otherwise the update model lock is released and the visualizer lock is acquired to update the nodes on the canvas for their respective positions, taken from NS3. Traditional PyViz's arrows drawing and flow bitrates are also performed. The visualizer plugin is then called upon and the lock is released and then again the Simulation-thread acquires simulation lock. The whole process in this way gets synchronized, which not only enables the robustness of the coupling process between SUMO and NS3, but it also makes the debugging of the mobility related handling much convenient for VANET simulations.

3 Performance Evaluation of PySNS3

The reliability and validity of the proposed scheme is tested by comparing the results obtained by online-mobility of PySNS3 and offline-mobility of state-of-the-art NS2-mobility-model of NS3. The first step is related to the comparison of simulation results of WAVE PDR, MAC-PHY overhead, and average routing GoodPut due to the mobility inputs to NS3 simulator from SUMO through; (i) PySNS3 and (ii) NS2-mobility-model. The purpose of this step is to validate the performance of WAVE architecture in NS3 along with GPSR routing protocol under a City mobility scenario ($5369 \times 4092\,\mathrm{m}^2$ area of Harbin, China). The scenario consists of 93 vehicles traversing random trips on Harbin road network (as shown in Fig. 1(b)) having state-of-the-art Krauss car following model implemented in SUMO. The simulation time is set to 576 s. In performance evaluation scenario, we have considered a Dedicated Short Range Communications (DSRC) broadcast network where each DSRC node has a continuous access to a 10 MHz control channel (CH) for all traffic. All vehicles transmit a 200-byte safety message at 10 Hz with data rate of 6 Mbps. All vehicles also attempt to route additional 64-byte packets at an application rate of 2.048 Kbps to one of 10 other vehicles, selected as sink vehicles. The routing protocol is GPSR. The antenna height of each vehicle is 1.5 m. Transmit power is set to 10 dBm. Regarding the radio propagation models, a combination of the Nakagami probabilistic model (in order to model Multi-Path Fading), and the Two Ray Ground Reflection Model (representing the exponential decay of signal power over distance) is used. The calculation of parameters like WAVE PDR, MAC-PHY OverHead and average routing GoodPut is performed as described in [20]. And finally, in the second step the vehicular statistics like CO_2 emissions and Fuel consumption during each simulation time along with a combination of Friss fading model and Two Ray Ground Reflection loss model are also acquired from SUMO during the NS3 simulation. Moreover, in this step the effect on WAVE PDR by varying maximum speed limits in SUMO through PySNS3 is also evaluated.

4   Simulation Results

The mobility input can be either given offline through various mobility models in NS3, or by direct coupling NS3 with SUMO. In both cases the output should cor-

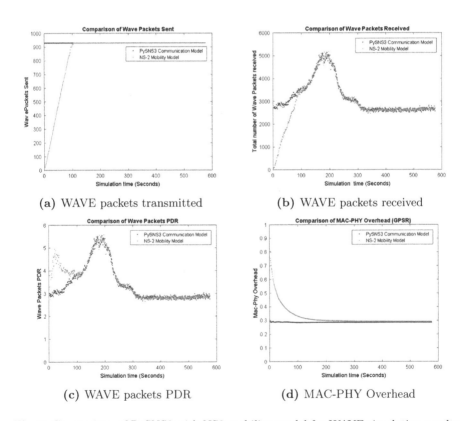

(a) WAVE packets transmitted

(b) WAVE packets received

(c) WAVE packets PDR

(d) MAC-PHY Overhead

Fig. 2. Comparison of PySNS3 with NS2-mobility-model for WAVE simulation results

respond to the input mobility. In order to evaluate and validate the performance of PySNS3 with that of NS2-mobility-model, we have performed experiment with specification described in Sect. 3. Basic Safety Message (BSM) packets are sent at regular intervals. BSMs are transmitted assuming the WAVE Short Message Protocol (WSMP), whereas non-BSM data packets are relayed by using GPSR (IP-based routing) protocol. Additionally, to validate the comparison, we have setup the number of WAVE packets for the first 103 s differently for both models as shown in Fig. 2(a). It is also clear that in the case of PySNS3 Communication model each vehicle starts sending WAVE packets with an interval of 0.1 s, right at the start of simulation (i-e. from 0th seconds). Which means each vehicle will send 10 WAVE packets every second and since the number of vehicles is 93, so a total of 930 WAVE packets are sent each second throughout the simulation time (576 s). Comparatively, in NS2-mobility-model the WAVE packets are generated until 103 s as shown in Fig. 2(a). The Fig. 2(b) shows corresponding number of WAVE packets successfully received. The WAVE PDR is shown in Fig. 2(c). It is clear from Fig. 2(c) that the WAVE PDR in both models follows the same pattern after 103 s. Since the vehicles are moving in both models so the respective

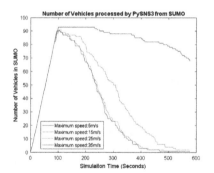

(a) Number of vehicles that have not reached destination

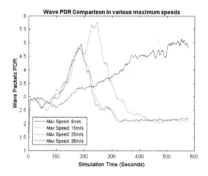

(b) Wave packets PDR for various speeds

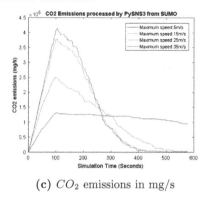

(c) CO_2 emissions in mg/s

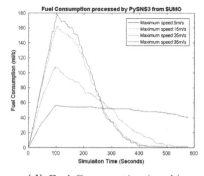

(d) Fuel Consumption in ml/s

Fig. 3. Performance evaluation results of PySNS3 for SUMO's vehicular and NS3's WAVE PDR statistics

PDR at each simulation second depends on the position and velocity values of vehicles. The respective MAC-PHY OverHead with GPSR protocol is shown in Fig. 2(d). The average routing GoodPut for NS2-mobility-model and PySNS3 is 0.4791 Kbps and 0.4898 Kbps respectively. Figure 3(a) shows the effect on number of vehicles that have not reached their destinations by setting the maximum speed of each vehicle to 5 m/s, 15 m/s, 25 m/s and 35 m/s through PySNS3.

It is clear that for slow speed (5 m/s) the number of vehicles in simulation that have not reached their destinations, at the end of simulation time (576 s) is more than that of 15 m/s to 35 m/s. The Fig. 3(b) shows corresponding effect on WAVE PDR with various speeds under a combination of Friss fading model and Two Ray Ground Reflection loss model. In the 5 m/s scenario, most of the vehicles (about 75%) are still traveling at time 576 s, which roughly corresponds to the situation at 220 s for 15 m/s speed case. The maximum speed limitations corresponding to 25 m/s and 35 m/s have not shown much difference in terms of WAVE packets PDR. Finally, Fig. 3(c) shows the effect of varying max speed on the average vehicular CO_2 emissions. Average fuel consumption (with every vehicle having emission class HBEFA3/PC-G-EU4) during each simulation time is displayed in Fig. 3(d). It is revealed that the fuel consumption increases as the maximum allowable speed for each vehicle is increased.

5   Conclusion

The proposed communication model PySNS3 is a python based platform and it can provide dynamic coupling between SUMO and NS3 in a much reliable and robust way. The proposed scheme has opened a new way towards better understanding and simulation of cooperative ITS applications and it can also be seen as a capability enhancement in the live visualization support of NS3. The performance of proposed model is tested and analyzed for both mobility and communication scenarios. In future, we will use PySNS3 for vehicular real-time rerouting under different VANET routing protocols and traffic congestion scenarios to analyze the impact of traffic congestion on the performance of routing protocols.

Acknowledgment. This paper was supported by the National Natural Science Foundation (61102105), the Engineering and Physical Sciences Research Council of UK (EPSRC) (Funding number EP/N01300X/1), the Harbin Science Fund for Young Reserve Talents (No. 2015RAQXJ008), Key Program for International S&T Cooperation Projects of China No. 2015DFG12150.

References

1. Tong, W., Jiyi, W., He, X., Jinghua, Z., Charles, M.: A cross unequal clustering routing algorithm for sensor network. Measur. Sci. **13**(4), 200–205 (2013)
2. Younes, M.B., Boukerche, A.: An efficient dynamic traffic light scheduling algorithm considering emergency vehicles for intelligent transportation systems. Wirel. Netw. J. Mobile Commun. Comput. Inf. (2017). Springer, New York. https://doi.org/10.1007/s11276-017-1482-5

3. Rondinone, M., Maneros, J., Krajewicz, D., Bauza, R., Cataldi, P., Hrizi, F., Gozalvez, J., Kumar, V., Rockl, M., Lin, L., Lazaro, O., Leguay, J., Harri, J., Vaz, S., Lopez, Y., Sepulcre, M., Wetterwald, M., Blokpoel, R., Cartolano, F.: iTETRIS: a modular simulation platform for the large scale evaluation of cooperative ITS applications. Simul. Model. Pract. Theory **34**, 99–125 (2013)

4. Tian, R., Zhang, B., Zheng, J., et al.: A new distributed routing protocol using partial traffic information for vehicular ad hoc networks. Wireless Netw. **20**, 1627–1637 (2014). https://doi.org/10.1007/s11276-014-0699-9

5. Bononi, L., Di Felice, M., D'Angelo, G., Bracuto, M., Donatiello, L.: MoVES: a framework for parallel and distributed simulation of wireless vehicular ad hoc networks. Elsevier Comput. Netw. **52**(1), 155–179 (2008)

6. Gorgorin, C., Gradinescu, V., Diaconescu, R., Cristea, V., Iftode, L.: An integrated vehicular and network simulator for vehicular ad-hoc networks. In: Proceedings of the European Simulation and Modelling Conference (ESM), pp. 1–8 (2006)

7. Wang, S.Y., Chou, C.L.: NCTUns tool for wireless vehicular communication network researches. Elsevier Simul. Model. Pract. Theory **17**(7), 1211–1226 (2009)

8. Killat, M., Hartenstein, H.: An empirical model for probability of packet reception in vehicular ad hoc networks. EURASIP J. Wireless Commun. Netw. **2009**, 721301 (2009)

9. Multiple Simulator Interlinking Environment (MSIE) for C2CC in VANETs. http://www.cn.uni-duesseldorf.de/projects/MSIE

10. Mangharam, R., et al.: GrooveSim: a topography-accurate simulator for geographic routing in vehicular networks. In: Proceedings of the 2nd ACM International Workshop on Vehicular Ad hoc Networks (VANET 2005), September 2005

11. Piorkowski, M., Raya, M., Lugo, A.L., Papadimitratos, P., Grossglauser, M., Hubaux, J.-P.: TraNS: realistic joint traffic and network simulator for VANETs. In: Proceedings of the ACM SIGMOBILE Mobile Computing and Communications Review, January 2008

12. Pigne, Y., Danoy, G., Bouvry, P.: A platform for realistic online vehicular network management. In: Proceedings of IEEE GLOBECOM Workshops, pp. 595–599 (2010)

13. Sommer, C., German, R., Dressler, F.: Bidirectionally coupled network and road traffic simulation for improved IVC analysis. IEEE Trans. Mobile Comput. **10**(1), 3–15 (2011)

14. The iTETRIS project. http://www.ict-itetris.eu/10-10-10-community/

15. VSimRTI. https://www.dcaiti.tu-berlin.de/research/simulation/

16. Wu, H., Lee, J., Hunter, M., Fujimoto, R., Guensler, R.L., Ko, J.: Efficiency of simulated vehicle-to-vehicle message propagation on Atlantas I-75 corridor, transportation research record. J. Transp. Res. Board **1910**, 82–89 (2005)

17. Behrisch, M., Bieker, L., Erdmann, J., Krajzewicz, D.: SUMO: simulation of urban mobility: an overview. In: Proceedings of the Third International Conference on Advances in System Simulation (SIMUL 2011), pp. 63–68 (2011)

18. NS3, The network simulator NS-3. http://www.nsnam.org/

19. Interfaces by Programming Languages. http://sumo.dlr.de/wiki/TraCI

20. NS3 WAVE Model. https://www.nsnam.org/docs/models/html/wave.html

21. Wang, T., Cao, Y., Zhou, Y., Li, P.: A survey on geographic routing protocols in delay/disruption tolerant networks. Int. J. Distrib. Sensor Netw. **2016**, 1–12 (2016). Article ID 3174670

22. NS2 mobility Helper. https://www.nsnam.org/docs/models/html/mobility.html

A Pseudo Random Sequence Based Multichannel MAC Protocol for Directional Ad Hoc Networks

Hang Zhang[1,2], Bo Li[1], Zhongjiang Yan[1(✉)], Mao Yang[1], and Xiaofei Jiang[2]

[1] School of Electronics and Information, Northwestern Polytechnical University,
Xi'an 710072, China
80090385@qq.com, {libo.npu,zhjyan,yangmao}@nwpu.edu.cn
[2] Science and Technology on Communication Networks Laboratory,
Shijiazhuang 053200, China

Abstract. In directional ad hoc networks, the character of directional transmission and directional reception of the links makes it difficult to let one directional link aware of the other concurrent transmission links, so that the collision probability of the concurrent transmission links need to be reduced. In this paper, a pseudo random sequence (PRS) based multi-channel multiple access control (MAC) protocol is proposed to reduce the collision probability of the concurrent transmission links. The proposed PRS MAC protocol is based on the time division multiple access (TDMA) frame structures. After the neighbour discovering sub-frame, the proposed PRS MAC protocol works in the reservation sub-frame, and in each time slot it works in a three-way handshake method to reserve the data slots in the data transmission sub-frame. On one hand, with the introduction of multiple channels, the concurrent transmission links can be distributed to different channels such that the collision probability of each channel can be reduced. On the other hand, with the introduction of the pseudo random sequence, each of the concurrent transmission links may take different PRS such that the collisions of the concurrent trans-mission links are randomized. Simulation results show that the proposed PRS MAC protocol outperforms the existing DTRA protocol in terms of lower collision probability and higher aggregated throughput.

Keywords: Directional ad hoc networks · Pseudo random sequence
Multi-channel · Medium access control

1 Introduction

Directional ad hoc network is characterised as a distributed, easy-deployed, and self-organized network, composed of a set of wireless nodes equipped with direc-tional antennas. It finds widely applications in search-and-rescue, battle scenario, and other emergency scenarios. Therefore, it has attracted many research inter-ests from the academic and industrial areas [1,2].

© ICST Institute for Computer Sciences, Social Informatics and Telecommunications Engineering 2018
L. Wang et al. (Eds.): QShine 2017, LNICST 234, pp. 172–182, 2018.
https://doi.org/10.1007/978-3-319-78078-8_18

In directional ad hoc networks, each node is communicating with its neighbours through directional antennas, where the wireless signals are concentrated only in one direction instead of over all directions. Thus, directional transmitting and directional receiving (DTDR) has many advantages in terms of long transmission distances, small interference ranges and low collision probability between concurrent transmission links. However, at the same time DTDR also brings many challenges to the multiple assess control (MAC) protocols. For example, it is difficult for a directional communication link to discover the other concurrent transmission links such that the collisions between the concurrent transmission links are difficult to be avoided. Reference [3] studies the collision tolerant transmission with directional antennas, which finds that the transmission success probability is quite high when the antenna beamwidth is quite narrow. However, when the beamwidth is wide the collisions between the concurrent transmission can not be ignored. When the density of the network is high the collisions of the concurrent links become serious, which cause low throughput and even network meltdown. Thus, it is significant to design a high efficient MAC protocol which can reduce the collision probabilities of the concurrent links and increase the network throughput.

The conventional MAC protocols for directional ad hoc networks can be classified into two categories, i.e., the random access based and the synchronized, which is time division multiple access (TDMA) based [1]. It has been shown that the synchronized MAC protocols outperform the random access based ones in terms of the network throughput [4,5]. Reference [6] proposes a novel MAC protocol based on the DTRA algorithms in Ref. [4] to allocate the data transmission slots to the concurrent transmission links.

In this paper we also mainly focus on the synchronized ones. Reference [4,5] are the pioneers of the synchronized protocols for directional antennas, in which the time is divided into time frames and each frame is further divided into three sub-frames, i.e., the neighbour discovery sub-frame, the reservation sub-frame and the data transmission sub-frame. In the neighbour discovery sub-frame, each node discovers its neighbours with the neighbour discovery algorithms [7–12] and the discovered neighbours, or the node pairs, reserve a specified slot in the reservation sub-frame. The nodes pairs exchange information in the specified slot of the reservation sub-frame, and coordinate the data slots resources of the data transmission sub-frame. Although the synchronized protocols are better, the data slots coordination are distributed, i.e., the resource allocation between the concurrent links. Therefore, the collision problem of the concurrent links is also serious in the synchronized protocols.

Reference [13] has studied the capacity of the directional ad hoc netowrk with multiple channels. The analysis results have shown that there exists a large improvement space when the multi-channel technology is introduced into the directional ad hoc networks. Reference [14] shows that there exists a upper bound on the number of channels to ensure collision free communication in multi-channel directional ad hoc network, when the total number of nodes is given. Particularly, the channel assignment problem is studied and is formulated as a graph colouring problem. Such that the number of the colors can represent the number of the channels. Thus it can be concluded that multiple channel technologies can be employed to reduce the collision probability of the concurrent transmission links. However, to the best knowledge of the authors, there are no synchronized multiple channel protocols proposed to assignment the channels to the concurrent links, which motivates our work.

In this paper, we propose a pseudo random sequence (PRS) based multichannel MAC protocol for directional ad hoc networks, with the aim of reducing the collision probability of multiple concurrent transmission links. On one hand, with the introduction of multiple channels, the concurrent transmission links can be distributed to different channels such that the collision probability of each channel can be reduced. On the other hand, with the introduction of the pseudo random sequence, each of the concurrent transmission links may take different PRSs such that the collisions of the concurrent transmission links are randomized. Furthermore, with the introduction of PRSs, the anti-interference capability and the security of the concurrent links also can be enhanced.

The main contributions of this paper are three-folds and listed as follows:

- Firstly, to reduce the collision probabilities of the concurrent links a multiple channel TDMA frame structure is proposed.
- Secondly, a pseudo random sequence based method is proposed to organize the time-frequency blocks which not only can help to randomize the collisions but also help to improve the efficiency of the proposed MAC protocol when the PRSs are non-orthogonal.
- Thirdly, two algorithms are proposed which are used to generate the PRS mask for a selected PRS, and used to confirm the PRS mask respectively.

Simulation results show the advantage of the proposed PRS MAC protocol in terms of low collision of concurrent transmission links and high aggregated throughput.

The following sections are organized as follows. Section 2 presents the system model of the proposed PRS MAC protocol, and illustrates the proposed TDMA frame structures. The operation procedures of the PRS MAC protocol are illustrated in Sect. 3. Section 4 evaluates the performance of the PRS MAC protocol. And Sect. 5 concludes this paper.

2   System Model

2.1   Directional Antenna and TDMA Frame Structures

Suppose that there are several wireless nodes equipped with switched directional antennas randomly distributed in the directional ad hoc networks. Let B denote the number of the directional antennas. Each node also equips with a GPS chip, which can provide second pulse such that all of the nodes can operate in a synchronization mode. The system operates in time division multiple access (TDMA) mode, where each TDMA frame consists of three sub-frames, i.e., the neighbour discovery sub-frame, the reservation sub-frame and the data transmission sub-frame.

Assume that there are $(n + 1), n \geq 0$, channels in the network, one of which is the control channel and the remaining n channels are the data channels. The control channel is responsible for neighbour discovering, reservation and data transmissions, while the data channels are responsible only for reservation and data transmissions. Among these $(n + 1)$ multiple channels, in each timeslot of the reservation and data transmission sub-frames, any node can work on at most N_c, $1 \leq N_c \leq (n + 1)$, channels. The TDMA frame structure of the proposed PRS MAC protocol is given in Fig. 1.

In the neighbour discovery sub-frame all nodes switch to the control channel to discover each other, and the neighbours make an agreement that when (in which time slot) and where (in which channel) to do the reservation and who will be the sender and receiver. Next in the reservation sub-frame the node pairs switch to the coordinated data channels to reserve the following data transmission slots, and the reservation result is stored in the *reserved link state table*. Finally in the data transmission sub-frame the nodes transmit or receive packets with their neighbours according to the reserved link state table. The proposed PRS MAC protocol mainly works in the reservation sub-frame, and details how the reservation result is produced with the PRS based method.

In the reservation sub-frame, each slot consists of 3 mini-slots, and the neighbours reserve the data slots in the data transmission sub-frame in a 3-way handshake process, i.e., the HELLO-RESPONSE-CONF packet exchanging process. In each mini-slot, one packet is sent. Let N_d denote the numbers of slots in the data transmission sub-frame. Then the *reserved link state table* can be denoted as $\mathbf{A} = [a_{i,b,c}]_{N_d \times B \times (n+1)}$, where $a_{i,b,c} = (u, v)$ denotes that node u will send data to node v at slot i, beam b, in channel c. Let $\mathbb{I}(a_{i,b,c}) = 0$ if $a_{i,b,c} = (-1, -1)$ and $\mathbb{I}(a_{i,b,c}) = 1$ otherwise.

In directional ad hoc networks, with the switched directional antenna constraint, at any timeslot i only one beam can be activated and thus we have $B_i = \sum_b \sum_c \mathbb{I}(a_{i,b,c}) \leq 1$. And if one beam b is activated the N_c multiple

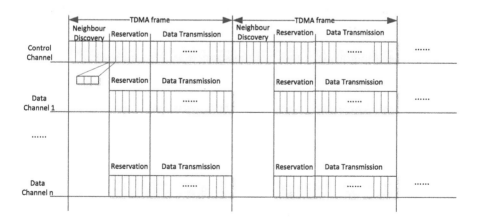

Fig. 1. TDMA frame structures of the proposed PRS MAC protocol

channels can only be used within this beam, which means $C_{i,b} = \sum_c \mathbb{I}(a_{i,b,c}) \le N_c$. We note that this is the main distinguish of directional ad hoc networks from the traditional wireless ad hoc networks.

2.2 Pseudo Random Sequence

Let $\mathbf{P} = [p_{m,i}]_{M \times N_d}$ be a pseudo random sequence (PRS) pattern held by all of the nodes in the network, where M is the total number of PRSs listed in the pattern. Let P_m denote the mth PRS with size of N_d. In other words, the PRS is a sequence of channel numbers corresponding to each time slot. Thus, $p_{m,i}$ denotes the channel index at slot i in channel $p_{m,i}$, where $1 \le p_{m,i} \le (n+1)$. Figure 2 shows an example of PRS pattern, and the shaded area is the first PRS in pattern $\mathbf{P}$, which means that at time slot 1 to slot 4 the channels $\{1, 2, 3, 4\}$ are employed.

We note that there may exist several PRS pattern generation methods, and each different PRS pattern may have different attributes. For example, any two PRSs in a given PRS pattern may be orthogonal, i.e., no overlapped time-frequency blocks, or non-orthogonal, i.e., having one or multiple overlapped time-frequency blocks. Therefore, when different concurrent transmission links employ different PRSs the collisions can be controlled. In other words, when the PRSs are orthogonal and different links choose different PRSs then there are no collisions between the concurrent links. While when the PRSs are non-orthogonal and different links choose different PRSs then the collisions can be controlled smaller than the number of overlapped time-frequency blocks.

Note that given the number of the data slots N_d and the number of channels $(n+1)$, the more overlapped time-frequency blocks of any two PRSs, the more collisions may occur. However, there always exist a trade-off between the aggregated throughput and the collision. Thus, to improve the efficiency of the proposed PRS protocol, the relationships between the number of the concurrent transmission links and the level of the non-orthogonal of the PRSs should be studied. In this paper, we only focus on the procedures how to use PRS in the proposed MAC protocol, and omit the studies of the relationships, and the discussions of the PRS pattern generation method and the attributes of the PRSs due to the space limitation, which will be studied as a future work.

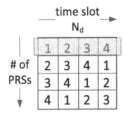

Fig. 2. An example of PRS pattern

3   PRS Based Multi-channel MAC Protocol

In this section, we detail how the proposed PRS MAC protocol works. The proposed PRS MAC protocol mainly works in the reservation and data transmission sub-frames, and the neighbour discovering is assumed completed in the neighbour discovery sub-frame. Then for each slot in the reservation sub-frame, a three way handshakes is completed to reserve the data slots in the data transmission sub-frame.

At each time slot of the reservation sub-frame, let node S be the sender and let node D be the corresponding receiver. Figure 3 shows an overview of the proposed PRS based method working process. Next we detail how each step works.

Step 1: Node S sends HELLO. At the beginning of each time slot, node S will select m available PRSs which have not been used by node S's neighbours as far as node S knows. Then these m PRSs will be packed into the HELLO packet. After HELLO is sent out, node S will wait for the response packet REP from node D.

The formats of the HELLO, REP and CONF packets are given in Fig. 4, where TYPE is the packet type, and SA and DA are the source address and destination address of the packets. PRSnum is the number of PRSs packed in the HELLO packet, i.e., m. PRS1, $\cdots$, PRSm are the m PRSs. A2Breq is the data transmission requests from node S to node D. PRSsel in REP is the selected PRS by node D from the m PRSs listed in HELLO. PRS mask is generated by node D with the data transmission request B2Areq by using the selected PRS PRSsel.

Step 2: Node D receives HELLO and responds REP. After node D receives the HELLO packet from node S, it will check each PRS listed in the HELLO packet whether available or not from its view. In other words, there may exist some PRS which is available from node S's view but is not available from node D's view. If no available PRS is found it will ignore this HELLO packet.

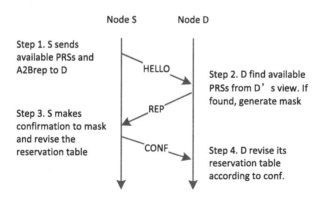

Fig. 3. An overview of PRS working process

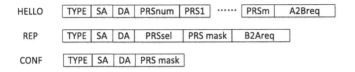

Fig. 4. The formats of the HELLO, REP and CONF packets

Otherwise if at least one available PRS is found the PRSsel can be selected. For example, with the consideration of the number of available time-frequency blocks, the one with the maximum of available time-frequency blocks can be selected out as the PRSsel, which will be packed into the REP. Then node D will generate the PRS mask with the inputs of PRSsel, A2Breq, B2Areq and node D's reserved link state table $\mathbb{A}^D$.

Let $P_m = [p_{m,i}]_{1 \times N_d}$ denote the selected PRS, and we recall that $p_{m,i}$ denote the time-frequency block at slot i in channel $p_{m,i}$. Let $K_m = [k_{m,i}]_{1 \times N_d}$ denote the PRS mask of P_m, and $k_{m,i}$ denote the mask of $p_{m,i}$, where $k_{m,i}$ is a two bits variable. Assume that $k_{m,i} = B'00$ means $p_{m,i}$ is not available for the communication link $S \leftarrow D$ or $S \rightarrow D$, and $k_{m,i} = B'11$ means $p_{m,i}$ is available for the communication link $S \leftarrow D$, and $k_{m,i} = B'10$ means $p_{m,i}$ is available for the communication link $S \rightarrow D$. The basic idea of generating the PRS mask is to check whether each time-frequency block available or not. Then the available time-frequency blocks will be allocated to link $S \leftarrow D$ or $S \rightarrow D$, according to the comparisons of the values of A2Breq and B2Areq. The pseudo code of the PRS mask generating algorithm is given in Algorithm 1. After the PRS is selected and the PRS mask is generated, they will be packed into the REP packet and then sent back to node S.

Step 3. Node S receives REP and responds CONF. If node S receives REP, the PRSsel and PRS mask will be extracted, which will be used by node S to confirm the reservation of data slots. Let P_m denote the PRSsel, and K_m denote the PRS mask, and K'_m denote the final confirmation information. After the confirmation, the link state table of node S, $\mathbf{A}^S$, will be revised and the confirmation information K'_m will be packed into the CONF packet by node S. Finally, the CONF packet will be sent to node D.

The basic idea of confirmation to REP is as follows. For each time-frequency block in the selected PRS of node D, i.e., PRSsel, it will be checked whether it is available or not in $\mathbf{A}^S$. If it is available then the corresponding element in $\mathbf{A}^S$ will be set as a reservation for transmission from node S to D or from node D to S. The pseudo code of the confirmation to REP algorithm is given in Algorithm 2.

Step 4: Node D receives CONF. After node D receives CONF, it will extract the confirmation information, i.e., PRS mask. Let K'_m denote the confirmation information, i.e., PRS mask. Then node D will check each two bits in K'_m and revise the corresponding element in node D's link state table, i.e., $\mathbf{A}^D$. For the ith two bits in K'_m, if $k_{m,i} = B'11$ then revise $a_{i,p_{m,i}} = (S, D)$, otherwise if $k_{m,i} = B'11$ then revise $a_{i,p_{m,i}} = (D, S)$.

Algorithm 1. PRS Mask Generating Algorithm

Require: P_m, A2Breq, B2Areq and $\mathbf{A}^D$.
Ensure: K_m.

1: **for** $i = 1 \rightarrow N_d$ **do**
2:     **if** $B_i \neq 0$ and $\{(S$ is not in D's b_i area) or (S is in D's b_i area but the number
       of used multiple channel is larger than $N_c)\}$ **then**
3:         $k_{m,i} = B'00$, continue;
4:     $j = p_{m,i}$;
5:     **if** $a_{i,j} = (-1, -1)$ **then**
6:         **if** $A2Breq > 0$ and $A2Breq > B2Areq$ **then**
7:             $k_{m,i} = B'11$, $A2Breq = A2Breq - 1$;
8:         **else if** $B2Areq > 0$ and $A2Breq \leq B2Areq$ **then**
9:             $k_{m,i} = B'10$, $B2Areq = B2Areq - 1$;
10:    **else**
11:        $k_{m,i} = B'00$;

Algorithm 2. Confirmation to REP Algorithm

Require: P_m, K_m and $\mathbf{A}^S$.
Ensure: $\mathbb{A}^S$ and K'_m.

1: **for** $i = 1 \rightarrow N_d$ **do**
2:     **if** $k_{m,i} \neq B'00$ and $a_{i,p_{m,i}} = (-1, -1)$ **then**
3:         **if** $k_{m,i} = B'11$ **then**
4:             $a_{i,p_{m,i}} = (S, D)$, $k'_{m,i} = B'11$;
5:         **else if** $k_{m,i} = B'10$ **then**
6:             $a_{i,p_{m,i}} = (D, S)$, $k'_{m,i} = B'10$;
7:         **else**
8:             $k'_{m,i} = B'00$;
9:     **else**
10:        $k'_{m,i} = B'00$;

---

4   Performance Evaluation

Extensive simulations are done in *NS2* to evaluate the performance of the proposed PRS MAC protocol. The simulations parameters are set as follows.

There are N nodes deployed in a 200 m × 2000 m area, where N is increased from 10 to 50. The total number of channel is set from 1 to 4. The traffic load for each discovered neighbours is increased from 5 to 30, with a step of 5.

Figure 5 shows that with the increase of the number of nodes N, i.e., from 10 to 50 with a step of 5, the total number of the successful transmitted packets increases. And when the number of nodes is 10, PRS and multichannels do not provide much improvements since there are few collisions between the concurrent transmission links. In other words, the collisions when there are 10 nodes is not so seriously, such that the multi-channel do not provide much performance enhancement. However when there are more nodes, e.g., 50 nodes, with the number of the multi-channel increase, the total number of successful transmitted packets increases. That is because when there are more nodes the number of concurrent transmission links is large, thus there are more collisions when there is only one channel.

It also can be found that the gap of successful transmitted packets between 1 channel and 2 channels, is smaller than that between 2 channels and 3 channels. This implies that the collisions are reduced from high collision probability when there are 2 channels to a low level, and so when one more channel is added not so much improvement is obtained.

Figure 6 shows that when the traffic load between each discovered neighbours, i.e., a directional link, is increased, how the total number of successful transmitted packets varies with the number of channels. It can be seen that with the increase of the traffic load, the number of successful transmitted packets first increase and then also saturate when the traffic load is large. The gaps between different nodes number, i.e., $N = 10, 20, 50$, with different channel numbers are different, and the the gaps for $N = 50$ is largest. This is because the collisions are more serious when the nodes number is large, from which it can also be seen the gain of the proposed PRS MAC.

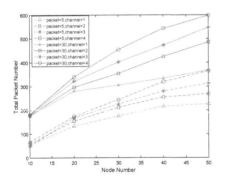

Fig. 5. The total number of the successful transmitted packets with variable nodes numbers when the traffic load is fixed.

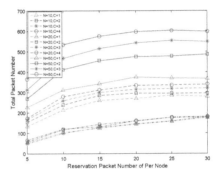

Fig. 6. The total number of the successful transmitted packets with variable traffic load when the number of nodes is fixed.

5   Conclusion

Directional transmission and directional reception brings many advantages comparing with the omni-directional transmission, in terms of longer transmission distance, smaller interference range and lower collision probability between concurrent transmission links. However, it also challenges the MAC protocol since the existence of the other concurrent transmission links may not be aware by one specified link which is reserving the data slots. If one data slot is reserved by more than one directional links, they may collide with each other.

To reduce the collision probability of the concurrent transmission links, a pseudo random sequence (PRS) based multi-channel MAC protocol is proposed, which is based on the TDMA frame structures. With the introduction of multiple channels, the concurrent transmission links may be scattered to different channels such that the collisions may be scattered. With the pseudo random sequence, the time-frequency block, i.e., a frequency resource within a slot, is organized in a random sequence, such that when different concurrent links select different PRSs the collisions may be randomized and the collision probability is reduced. The detailed three-way handshake process to fulfil the proposed PRS based method is given in a step by step way. Extensive simulations are carried to evaluate the performance of the proposed PRS MAC protocol.

As future works, the generation method of the PRSs and PRS patterns, the relationship between the level of non-orthogonal PRSs and the collision probability will be studied.

Acknowledgments. This work was supported in part by the National Natural Science Foundations of CHINA (Grant No. 61771392, No. 61771390, No. 61501373, and No. 61271279), the Science and Technology on Communication Networks Laboratory Open Projects (Grant No. KX162600031, KX172600027), the National Science and Technology Major Project (Grant No. 2016ZX03001018-004), and the Fundamental Research Funds for the Central Universities (Grant No. 3102017ZY018).

References

1. Bazan, O., Jaseemuddin, M.: A survey on MAC protocols for wireless adhoc networks with beamforming antennas. IEEE Commun. Surv. Tutor. **14**(2), 216–239 (2012)
2. Wong, D.T.C., Chen, Q., Chin, F.: Directional medium access control (MAC) protocols in wireless ad hoc and sensor networks: a survey. J. Sens. Actuat. Netw. **4**(2), 67–153 (2015)
3. Dai, H.N., Ng, K.W., Wu, M.Y.: On collision-tolerant transmission with directional antennas. In: Wireless Communications and Networking Conference, WCNC 2008, pp. 1968–1973 (2008)
4. Zhang, Z.: DTRA: directional transmission and reception algorithms in WLANs with directional antennas for QoS support. IEEE Netw. Mag. Global Internetwork. **19**(3), 27–32 (2005)
5. Zhang, Z.: Pure directional transmission and reception algorithms in wireless ad hoc networks with directional antennas. In: IEEE International Conference on Communications, vol. 5, pp. 3386–3390 (2005)
6. Tu, Y., Zhang, Y., Zhang, H.: A novel MAC protocol for wireless ad hoc networks with directional antennas. In: IEEE International Conference on Communication Technology, pp. 494–499 (2014)
7. Tian, F., Liu, B., Cai, H., Zhou, H., Gui, L.: Practical asynchronous neighbor discovery in ad hoc networks with directional antennas. IEEE Trans. Veh. Technol. **65**(5), 3614–3627 (2016)
8. Zhang, W., Peng, L., Xu, R., Zhang, L., Zhu, J.: Neighbor discovery in three-dimensional mobile ad hoc networks with directional antennas. In: Wireless and Optical Communication Conference, pp. 1–5 (2016)

9. Mir, Z.H., Jung, W.S., Ko, Y.B.: Continuous neighbor discovery protocol in wireless ad hoc networks with sectored-antennas. In: IEEE International Conference on Advanced Information Networking and Applications, pp. 54–61 (2015)
10. Tian, F., Hu, R.Q., Qian, Y., Rong, B., Liu B., Gui, L.: Pure asynchronous neighbor discovery algorithms in ad hoc networks using directional antennas. In: Global Communications Conference, pp. 498–503 (2014)
11. Liu, B., Rong, B., Hu, R.Q., Qian, Y.: Neighbor discovery algorithms in directional antenna based synchronous and asynchronous wireless ad hoc networks. IEEE Wireless Commun. **20**(6), 106–112 (2013)
12. Zhang, Z., Li, B.: Neighbor discovery in mobile ad hoc self-configuring networks with directional antennas: algorithms and comparisons. IEEE Trans. Wireless Commun. **7**(5), 1540–1549 (2008)
13. Wang, J., Kong, L., Wu, M.Y.: Capacity of wireless ad hoc networks using practical directional antennas. In: Wireless Communications and Networking Conference, pp. 1–6 (2010)
14. Dai, H.N., Ng, K.W., Wu, M.Y.: Upper bounds on the number of channels to ensure collision-free communications in multi-channel wireless networks using directional antennas **29**(16), 1–6 (2010)

Collision Scattering Through Multichannel in Synchronous Directional Ad Hoc Networks

Yusheng Liang[1,2], Bo Li[1], Zhongjiang Yan[1(✉)], Mao Yang[1], Xiaofei Jiang[2], and Hang Zhang[2]

[1] School of Electronics and Information, Northwestern Polytechnical University, Xi'an 710072, China
liangys@mail.nwpu.edu.cn, {libo.npu,zhjyan,yangmao}@nwpu.edu.cn
[2] Science and Technology on Communication Networks Laboratory, Shijiazhuang 053200, China

Abstract. Unique advantages of directional antennas have attracted much interest of the researchers, such as longer transmission distance, large transmission antenna gains and large spatial reuse gains. However, the feature of directional transmission and reception (DTR) also brings challenges to the media access control (MAC) protocols, which means the nodes can only sense the wireless channel in a given direction and thus the interference or collision between the concurrent transmission links is difficult to be avoided. To address this problem, in this paper a novel collision scattering method is proposed to decrease the collision probabilities of the concurrent transmission links. The basic idea is to distribute the concurrent transmission links to different channels, which are divided in the wireless spectrum, such that multiple transmission links can be ongoing concurrently. A time division multiple access (TDMA) based multichannel MAC protocol is proposed based on the collision scattering method. Extensive simulations are carried out to evaluate the performance of the proposed protocol and the gain of the collision scattering. The simulation results show that the aggregation throughput of the proposed protocol outperforms the existing protocols and the collision scattering gain is achieved.

Keywords: Directional ad hoc networks · Collision scattering
Multi-channel · Medium access control

1 Introduction

Directional ad hoc networks [1,2] are composed of many nodes equipped with directional antennas, which are self-organized and coordinated. Directional antennas have many advantages comparing to omnidirectional antennas, such as large transmission or reception antenna gains, longer transmission distance, less interference and large spatial reuse gains [3,4]. However, directional transmission and reception (DTR) also brings a significant challenge to the media

© ICST Institute for Computer Sciences, Social Informatics and Telecommunications Engineering 2018
L. Wang et al. (Eds.): QShine 2017, LNICST 234, pp. 183–193, 2018.
https://doi.org/10.1007/978-3-319-78078-8_19

access control (MAC) protocols, which is that the receiver can only sense the wireless channel in a given direction and thus the interference or collision between the concurrent transmission links is difficult to be avoided. Therefore, the collision between the concurrent transmission links becomes the main concern of the directional MAC (DMAC) protocol designs.

Academic researchers devote extensive works to solve the concurrent transmission collision problems [1,2]. The existing works can be divided into two categories based on the main method to decrease the probability of collisions. The first one is following the carrier sense multiple access with collision avoidance (CSMA/CA) method, the basic idea of which is to use the physical and virtual carrier sensing to avoid the collision. And the second one is the synchronous, i.e., time division multiple access (TDMA), the basic idea of which is to synchronize the network and the time is divided into slots such that the collision only occurs within each slot. These two categories are named as CSMA/CA based one and the TDMA based one in this paper.

The CSMA/CA based multichannel DMACs can be divided into four types, i.e., tone based, control-channel based, no-control-channel based and power-control based.

– *Tone Based*: Ref. [5] proposed a dual-busy-tone DBTMA/DA. The channel is divided into a data channel and a control channel, the data channel is used to transmit ORTS/DCTS/DDATA/DACK frames, while the control channel is used to transmit two busy tones. These two busy tones (transmit busy tone and receive busy tone) which are turned on only when transmitting frames can be heard by all nodes within their directional transmission ranges. The main idea of the protocol is using tones to notify the surrounding nodes and guarantee the current transmission.

– *Control-Channel Based*: Ref. [6] proposed a deafness-aware MAC (DA-MAC) protocol. The channel is divided into two channels: a control channel and a data channel. The sending node sends the DRTS on the control channel and the data channel, and the receiving node makes the corresponding reply according to whether the two channels receive the DRTS. DCTS will be transmitted on both channels if the DRTS is received on both channels. Likewise, data will be transmitted on data channel if the DCTS is received on both channels. The main idea of the protocols is using two channels to ensure the current transmission and to let other nodes quickly occupy the channel.

– *No-Control-Channel Based*: Ref. [7] proposed a multi-channel MAC protocol for directional antennas (MCMDA) protocol. A pair of nodes transmit data in chosen free data channel. When a node receives a DRTS, it replies a DCTS and immediately sends a VCTS in the opposite direction to defer the nodes that can receive the VCTS transmit over this data channel until the current transmission is over in this same free data channel. The main idea of MCMDA is multiple pairs of transmissions can be ongoing in multiple data channels with spatial reuse and multi-channel diversity.

– *Power-Control Based*: Ref. [8] proposed a multi-channel power-controlled DMAC (MPCD-MAC) protocol. The nodes transmit RTS and CTS at full power on the control channel in each direction, and Data and ACK are transmitted in one of available data channel in the selected direction.

- *Hybrid-Contention Based*: Ref. [9] is a hybrid-contention-based multi-channel MAC protocol with directional antennas (MMAC-DA). A frame is divided into two windows: ATIM window and Data window. Channel access and data transfer reservations are done through random contention in the ATIM window, and the data transfer is done by synchronous mode in the Data window. *The simulation result indicates MMAC-DA has higher aggregate throughput than the Random DMAC in IEEE 802.11.*

Most of the TDMA-based DMACs are based on single channel. Ref. [10] proposed a direction of arrival (DOA) MAC which is based on the slotted ALOHA with each slot broken into three mini-slots. In the first mini-slot, all transmitters transmit a simple tone towards their receivers. The receivers then run a DOA algorithm to identify the direction of the transmitters. Each receiver forms its directed beam towards the direction that has the maximum power. The packet is transmitted in second mini-slots. After receiving the packet correctly, the receiver responds with an ACK in the last mini-slot. The simulation results show that DOA-MAC achieves higher throughput than the Basic Random DMAC. Ref. [11] proposed a Reservation Directional MAC (RDMAC) for multi-hop wireless networks with directional antennas. The RDMAC protocol is divided into a reservation period and a transmission period similar to [9]. Reservations are done in the reservation period and data is transmitted in transmission period. Ref. [12] proposed a Neighbor-Discovery/Reservation/Data-Transmission single-channel MAC protocol (DTRA). Neighbour-Discovery aims to find the neighbour nodes, the purpose of the Reservation is to make data transmission for node pairs and Data-Transmission is for the data transmission.

In summary, the TDMA-based works may outperform the CSMA/CA based works [1,9,10,12]. However, with the using of multichannel the CSMA/CA based multichannel DMACs may outperform the TDMA-based works, since the collision between the concurrent transmission links may be scattered. Furthermore, most of the TDMA-based DMACs are single channel based. Thus, how does it perform if the TDMA-based multichannel DMAC is proposed? Will the collision scattering still gain? To answer these two questions, in this paper a TDMA based multichannel DMAC is proposed and the performance of it and the collision scattering gain is evaluated. The main contributions of this paper are listed as follows.

- A collision scattering method is proposed for the synchronous directional ad hoc networks. The basic idea is to distribute the collisions between concurrent transmission links to different channels such that the collision probability of the concurrent transmission links can be reduced.
- A collision scattering based multichannel TDMA DMAC procol is proposed, and the detailed working procedures are described.
- Extensive simulations are carried out and the performance of the proposed DMAC and the gain of the collision scattering are evaluated.

The rest of the paper is organized as follows. The system model and the frameworks of the proposed protocol are given in Sect. 2. In Sect. 3, the proposed DMAC protocol is vividly illustrated in details. Performance evaluation is presented in Sect. 4. The conclusion and future work are given in Sect. 5.

2   System Models and Frameworks of the Proposed Protocol

2.1   System Models

In directional ad hoc networks, N wireless nodes are randomly deployed, each of which is equipped with directional antennas to communicate with its neighbours. The switched directional antennas are assumed, and at any time instant only one of directional antennas can be activated. Let B denote the number of directional antennas. The angle range of a directional antenna is assumed as ω, $\omega = 2\pi/B$. The switching time from one direction to another direction of the directional antennas is omitted.

Each node is also equipped with a synchronous device, e.g., GPS. Such that the network is synchronized, and the time line is slotted. In each time slot, the node works in a half-duplex mode, i.e., the node can transmit or receive but not both. And in each time slot, only one directional antenna can be activated. The number of the available channels in the network is denoted as E, $E \geq 1$. In each time slot, each node can only work on one assigned channel and the channel switching time is also omitted.

2.2   Frameworks of the Proposed Protocol

Figure 1 shows the framework of the proposed protocol. Firstly the time line is divided into super frames. Each super frame is composed of three phases, i.e., the scanning phase, the reservation phase and the data transmission phase. The main functions of each phase are illustrated as follows.

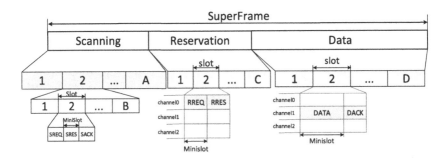

Fig. 1. The framework of the proposed protocol

- In the scanning phase, each node executes the neighbour discovery algorithm to discover its neighbours, and makes reservations with its neighbours that they communicate the data transmission requests in the reservation phase. Particularly, in the scanning phase all nodes work in the same channel, but they can reserve different time slots in different channels in the reservation phase. Suppose that there are $A \times B$ slots in the scanning phase, and each slot can be divided into 3 mini-slots. Note that A is the neighbour discovering number of rounds, and B is the number of directional antennas.
- In the reservation phase, the neighbours which make reservation communicate the transmission requests and then reserve the data slots in the data transmission phase. Same with the scanning phase, the neighbours can reserve different time slots in different channels in the data transmission phase. Suppose that there are C slots in the reservation phase, and each slot can be divided into 2 mini-slots.
- In the data transmission phase, the neighbours transmit their traffic in the reserved data slots and the reserved channels. Suppose that there are D slots in the data transmission phase, and each slot can be divided into 2 mini-slots.

To facilitate the programming the proposed DMAC, we define the data structures of the proposed DMAC as follows. After the scanning phase, each node can obtain the neighbour node table X and the slot reservation table Y, where $X = [x_i]_{1 \times B}$ and x_i is the set of neighbours of the ith direction, and $Y = [y_i]_{1 \times C}$ and $y_i = (s, r, e)$ is a three tuple meaning that node s will transmit a request packet to node r in the ith slot at channel e. Then in the reservation phase, the nodes communicates with their neighbours according to the slot reservation table Y. And after reservation phase, the data slot reservation table Z in the data transmission phase can be obtained, where $Z = [z_i]_{1 \times D}$ and $z_i = (s, r, e)$ is also a three tuple, with the similar meaning of y_i, i.e., node s will transmit a data packet to node r in the ith slot at channel e.

3   Description of the Proposed DMAC Protocol

The whole working procedures are described in this section, particularly the collision scattering method is detailed. We note that the frameworks of the proposed DMAC protocol is based on [12]. Before introducing the proposed DMAC protocol we illustrate the basic idea of collision scattering.

3.1   The Basic Idea of Collision Scattering

We take the scanning phase as an example to illustrate the basic idea of collision scattering. And the disadvantages of [12] is illustrated first and then we illustrate the collision scattering method.

The collision problem between the concurrent transmission links in the reservation phase in [12] may exhibit a phenomenon, where after the scanning phase the node can discover its neighbours and make reservation with its neighbours in the reservation phase, but the communication in the reserved slot fails. The main reasons which cause failure in [12] in the reservation phase, i.e., collisions between the concurrent transmission links, may include the following two terms. The first is that there is only one channel and the second is that there are no coordination between the concurrent transmission links. For example, link $\mathcal{L}_1$ communicates its request in slot i_1 in the reservation phase, while link $\mathcal{L}_2$ communicates its request in slot i_2 in the reservation phase. Although $i_1 \neq i_2$, link $\mathcal{L}_1$ and link $\mathcal{L}_2$ may reserve the same slot i_d in the data transmission phase. Such that a collision may occur between the concurrent transmission links $\mathcal{L}_1$ and $\mathcal{L}_2$ at time slot i_d when these two links transmit data, since there is only one channel.

However, after the collision scattering through multichannel method is employed, although link $\mathcal{L}_1$ and link $\mathcal{L}_2$ may reserve the same slot i_d, they can choose different channels since there are totally E, $E \geq 1$, channels. Such that the collisions between the concurrent transmission links can be scattered.

3.2 Collision Scattering Method in Scanning Phase

In the scanning phase, the scan based neighbour discovering algorithm [12] is employed in this paper. The basic idea is to let the master neighbour discovering nodes switch their directional antennas *clockwise*, while let the slave neighbour discovering nodes switch their directional antennas *counter clockwise*. The directional antennas will be switched at the beginning of the time slot. Note that each slot in the scanning phase is divided into 3 mini-slots, and the SREQ-SRES-SACK (Scanning REQuest packet, Scanning RESult packet, Scanning ACKnowledgement packet) packets exchanging process is defined in [12] with one packet sending in one mini-slot. Therefore, the master neighbour discovering nodes is the nodes who send the SREQ and the SACK packets, while the slaves is the nodes who send SRES packet.

However, we would like to point out the changes when we employ the scan based neighbour discovering algorithm proposed in [12].

- Firstly, we note that in [12] there is only one channel while in the proposed DMAC there are totally E, $E \geq 1$, channels. Thus the main difference of the outcome in the scanning phase is the slot reservation table Y in the reservation phase.
- Secondly, we would like to note that the collision scattering method is employed in this phase with the employment of the multichannel. That is to say when the neighbours make reservation in the reservation phase after they choose a common free slot, they can randomly choose one common available channel, such that the collisions between concurrent transmission links can be scattered.

The detailed working steps are given as follows. Each node is acting as a master node in probability of p_s, while acting as a slave node in probability of $1 - p_s$. The initial direction of the mater node is the 12 o'clock direction while the initial direction of the slave node is 6 o'clock. The switching direction of the master node during scanning is clockwise as the time slot increases. While the switching direction of the slave node during scanning is counter clockwise as the time slot increases. The scanning process is divided into three-way handshake that is similar to [12].

Handshake Step 1-At $Minislot$ 0, the master nodes send SREQ packet, meanwhile, the slave nodes are ready to receive SREQ. SREQ contains the source node address, i.e., the mater node's ID, the destination node address, i.e., broadcast ID, and the beam index, i.e., current beam index.

Handshake Step 2-At $Minislot$ 1, the nodes received the SREQ will reply a SRES (Scanning Response) packet containing RISI (Reservation Idle Slot Indication) with the probability of p_r, meanwhile, the master nodes are ready to receive SRES. RISI $= [d_i]_{1 \times C}$, where $d_i = 0$ denotes the slot i is idle while $d_i = 1$ means the slot i is busy. After receiving the SRES, the master nodes make comparison of RISI that SRES contained with its own and allocates a reservation slot which is randomly selected from the common free slots. Finally, the free slot, a random channel, a random reservation launching state are wrapped to be RRRA (Result of the Reservation Resource Allocation). SRES contains the source node address, i.e., the slave node's ID, the destination node address, i.e., the master node's ID, the reservation idle slot indication, i.e., RISI, and the beam index, i.e., current beam index.

Handshake Step 3-At $Minislot$ 2, when the master node received the SRES correctly, it firstly update its X and Y table, and then replies a SACK (Scanning Acknowledgement) packet carrying the RRRA. Likewise, the X and Y table will be updated when the SACK is correctly received at the slave node. SACK contains the source node address, i.e., the request node's ID, the destination node address, i.e., the response node's ID, the result of the reservation resource allocation, i.e., RRRA, and the beam index, i.e., current beam index.

After several rounds of scanning, i.e., A, most of the neighbour nodes are scanned. Each node will generate a X table and a Y table at the end of the scanning phase.

3.3   Collision Scattering Method in Reservation Phase

As described in the previous subsection, during the neighbour discovery process, two nodes detect each other and agree on a common time slot at which the two nodes would see if they can make any reservations. When the time slot arrives, each node only needs to extract its own X table and Y table to prepare for reservation. Next we take the ith slot where $y_i = (s, r, e)$ as an example to illustrate the detailed working steps in the reservation phase.

At $Minislot$ 0, the sender s sends RREQ (Reservation Request) to the receiver r in the ith slot (or beam) in channel e. For example, firstly, node 0 extracts $y_0 = (0, 1, 2)$ from its Y table while node 1 extracts $y_0 = (1, 0, 2)$ from its Y table at slot 0. That means node 0 will send a packet to node 1 at slot 0 in channel 2. Secondly, node 0 extracts $x_0 = \{1\}$ from its X table while node 1 extracts $x_3 = \{0, 2\}$ from its X table. That means node 0 will send on beam

0 and node 1 will receive on beam 3. Finally, node 0 sends RREQ on beam 0 while node 1 are receiving on beam 3 at slot 0 in channel 2. RREQ contains the source node address, i.e., the launching node's ID, the destination node address, i.e., the falling node's ID, the traffic demand of the launching node address, i.e., the launching node's demand and the data transmission resource idle indication of launching node, i.e., DRII (Data Resource Idle Indication).

The sender's demand specifically refers to the total packet number to the receiver and each packet will be transmitted in one slot. Let DRII $= [e_i]_{1 \times D}$, where $e_i = 0$ denotes the slot i is idle while $e_i = 1$ means the slot i is busy. The receiver executes the reservation procedure to allocate the data resource block and update its DRII table and Z table after receiving RREQ.

At $Minislot$ 1, the receiver node replies RRES (Reservation Response) carrying the reservation result to the launching node, the launching node prepares to receive RRES, respectively. The reservation result table of the launching node is renewed when it receives RRES. RRES contains the source node address, i.e., the falling node's ID, the destination node address, i.e., the launching node's ID and the reservation result, i.e., RDRA (Result of the Data Resource Allocation).

Let RDRA $= [f_i]_{1 \times D}$, where $f_i = 0$ denotes the slot i is not allocated while $f_i = 1$ means the slot i is allocated to the pair nodes. Each node will generate a Z table when the reservation phase ends. A different reservation procedure determines different data allocation result but the overall performance difference is not large. We are more concern about the gain that the multichannel can bring than the single channel, so we proposed a heuristic reservation method that is allocating resources according to traffic demand to illustrate the advantages of our protocol. The heuristic reservation method is divided into two part, the first part is getting the common free data slots by comparing the DRIIs of the two nodes, and the second part is randomly selecting the slots as more as possible according to traffic demand.

3.4 Data Transmission Phase

In the data transmission phase, each node sends packets according to Z table similar to reservation phase. DATA is transmitted at $Minislot$ 0 while DACK (Directional ACK) is replied at $Minislot$ 1 if the DATA is correctly received. With the density of node increased, even if there will be more than one pairs of node are transmitting DATA in the same mini-slot, the probability of collision will be not increase because the collision will be scattered by multichannel.

4 Performance Evaluation

4.1 Simulation Parameters Setting

To evaluate its performance, our proposed protocol has been implemented in $NS2$. The simulations are conducted with different number of nodes N, i.e., from 10 to 50, which are deployed in a $200m \times 200m$ area. All of the nodes can reach each other in one hop. The number of channels is $E = 4$. Each node discovers the neighbour nodes in scanning phase to form a sender-receiver pair. A node generates and transmits different number of packets, i.e., from 5 to 30, to its receiver. The number of beams is $B = 6$. The scanning round in the scanning phase is $A = 4$. The probability of becoming a master node is $p_s = 0.5$. The probability of reply of SREQ packet is $p_r = 0.5$. The slot number in the reservation phase is $C = 20$. The slot number in the data transmission phase is $D = 100$. Each simulation is conducted in a superframe duration and the simulation results are the average of 100 runs of different topologies.

4.2   Simulation Results

The aggregate transmitted packets with different number of channels, different number of nodes, and different number of packets are simulated, as shown in Fig. 2. There are two result groups. The first one is 10 packets per reservation, and the second one is 30 packets per reservation. That is to say once the reservation between neighbours success, 10 or 30 data slots will be reserved in the data transmission phase.

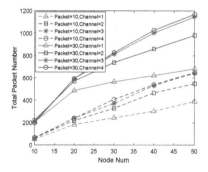

Fig. 2. Performance comparison of different reservation packets with multichannel

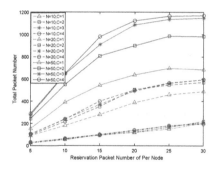

Fig. 3. Performance comparison of different node number with multichannel

From the simulation results shown in Fig. 2, the following conclusion can be drown.

– In general, the performance of the *packet=30* group is better than the *packet=10* one. This is because there are more data slots the *packet=30* group reserves.
– As shown in Fig. 2, the aggregate transmitted packets number increases as the number of nodes increases. This is because the number of concurrent transmission links increase in one data slot.

– In each group, the aggregate transmitted packets increase with different number of channels in the same group, which shows the collision scattering gain with the employing the multichannel. It also can be found that the collision scattering gain decreases as the number of employed multichannel increases. That is to say the gap between the curves *channel=1* and *channel=2* is larger than that between the curves *channel=2* and *channel=3*, and that is larger than the gap between the curves *channel=3* and *channel=4*. This discloses that to scattering the collisions between the concurrent transmission links, not so many channels should be employed.

Similar conclusion can also be drown from the simulation results shown in Fig. 3, where the number of packets is varied from 5 to 30. Figure 3 shows three groups results, i.e., *the nodes number* $N = 10, 20, 50$. In general, the aggregate transmitted packets number increases as the reservation packets number increases. The performance of the first group is almost no difference in the case of different channels, however, the gain of multiple channels is more and more obvious compared to the single channel with the increase in node number as showed in Fig. 3. When adding one channel and two channels, the performance is enhanced of about 30% and 35% as shown in the second group, respectively. Likewise, as the number of channels changes from 1 to 2 and 1 to 3, the resulting gain is 40% and 70% as shown in the third group, respectively. We can find out the gain by increasing channel number has great relevance with node numbers and the gain will become more and more obvious as the number of nodes increases. The reason for this result is that the collision of different node number can be scattered to be a low probability by a fixed channel number.

5   Conclusions and Future Work

In this paper, we propose a collision scattering based TDMA multichannel DMAC protocol for directional ad hoc networks. Our MAC exploit the multichannel reservation and multichannel data transmission to scatter the collisions between the concurrent transmission links. The preliminary simulation results show that our MAC can improve network performance in terms of aggregate packets number. The future work includes theoretical analysis of the collision scattering gain and the comparison with contention based multichannel DMACs.

Acknowledgments. This work was supported in part by the National Natural Science Foundations of CHINA (Grant No. 61771392, No. 61771390, No. 61501373, and No. 61271279), the Science and Technology on Communication Networks Laboratory Open Projects (Grant No. KX162600031, KX172600027), the National Science and Technology Major Project (Grant No. 2016ZX03001018-004), and the Fundamental Research Funds for the Central Universities (Grant No. 3102017ZY018).

References

1. Bazan, O., Jaseemuddin, M.: A survey on MAC protocols for wireless adhoc networks with beamforming antennas. IEEE Commun. Surv. Tutor. **14**(2), 216–239 (2012)
2. Wong, D.T.C., Chen, Q., Chin, F.: Directional medium access control (MAC) protocols in wireless ad hoc and sensor networks: a survey. J. Sens. Actuator Netw. **4**(2), 67–153 (2015)
3. Ren, B., Zhang, X., Gou, X.: System design of high speed ad hoc networking with directional antenna. In: 2016 12th International Conference on Mobile Ad-Hoc and Sensor Networks (MSN), Hefei, pp. 429–433 (2016)
4. Zhang, W., Peng, L., Xu, R., Zhang, L., Zhu, J.: Neighbor discovery in three-dimensional mobile ad hoc networks with directional antennas. In: 25th Wireless and Optical Communication Conference (WOCC), Chengdu, pp. 1–5 (2016)
5. Huang, Z., Shen, C.-C., Srisathapornphat, C., Jaikaeo, C.: A busy-tone based directional MAC protocol for ad hoc networks. In: MILCOM 2002 Proceedings, vol. 2, pp. 1233–1238 October 2002
6. Na, W., Park, L., Cho, S.: Deafness-aware MAC protocol for directional antennas in wireless ad hoc networks. Ad Hoc Netw. **24**, 121–134 (2014)
7. Tu, Y., Zhang, Y., Zhang, H.: A novel MAC protocol for wireless ad hoc networks with directional antennas. In: 2013 15th IEEE International Conference on Communication Technology, pp. 494–499, November 2013
8. Martignon, F.: Multi-channel power-controlled directional MAC for wireless mesh networks. Wirel. Commun. Mobile Comput. **11**(1), 90–107 (2011)
9. Dang, D.N.M., Le, H.T., Kang, H.S., Hong, C.S., Choe, J.: Multi-channel MAC protocol with directional antennas in wireless ad hoc networks. In: 2015 International Conference on Information Networking (ICOIN), pp. 81–86, January 2015
10. Singh, H., Singh, S.: A MAC protocol based on adaptive beamforming for ad hoc networks. In: IEEE 2003 International Symposium on Personal, Indoor and Mobile Radio Communications, vol. 2, pp. 1346–1350 (2003)
11. Chang, J.J., Liao, W., Hou, T.C.: Reservation-based directional medium access control (RDMAC) protocol for multi-hop wireless networks with directional antennas. In: IEEE International Conference on Communications, pp. 1–5 (2009)
12. Zhang, Z.: DTRA: directional transmission and reception algorithms in wlans with directional antennas for QoS support. IEEE Network **19**(3), 27–32 (2005)

A Classified Slot Re-allocation Algorithm for Synchronous Directional Ad Hoc Networks

Zhicheng Bai[1,2], Bo Li[1], Zhongjiang Yan[1(✉)], Mao Yang[1], Xiaofei Jiang[2], and Hang Zhang[1,2]

[1] School of Electronics and Information, Northwestern Polytechnical University, Xi'an 710072, China
baizhicheng@mail.nwpu.edu.cn, {libo,zhjyan,yangmao}@nwpu.edu.cn
[2] Science and Technology on Communication Networks Laboratory, Shijiazhuang 053200, China

Abstract. Several typical synchronous directional media access control (DMAC) protocols are proposed for directional ad hoc networks (DAHN), e.g., directional transmission and reception algorithms (DTRA) [4]. One of the slot allocation problems of these DMACs is the unfairness between links, or link starvation, which is caused by the distributed feature of DAHN. That is the earlier discovered link reserve much more slots which results in the later discovered links have few slots to reserve. To address the unfairness problem, in this paper a classified slot re-allocation algorithm (CSRA) is proposed. The basic idea is to classify the data slots into four types according to their status in the data transmission phase, and then when the unfairness problem is found different types of slots are re-allocated. The re-allocation order of these four types of these slots are free slots, sending slots, neighbour transmitting slots, and receiving slot. Extensive simulation are carried out to evaluate the performance of the proposed CSRA. The simulation results show that the Jain's fairness index is improved with little loss of the network throughput.

Keywords: Directional ad hoc networks · Classified slot
Re-allocation · Medium access control

1 Introduction

Directional ad hoc network (DAHN) is composed of wireless nodes equipped with directional antennas. Directional antennas have many advantages over the omnidirectional antennas, such as longer transmission distance, larger transmission/reception antenna gains, less interference from the neighbouring transmission links and large spatial reuse gains [1–3]. Several directional media access control (DMAC) protocols are designed to exploit the gains of the directional antennas [5,6]. These works show that the synchronous DMACs may outperform the contention based ones, and directional transmission and reception algorithms (DTRA) [4] is one of the classical synchronous protocols for the DAHN. However, one of the typical slot allocation problems of these synchronous DMACs is the unfairness between links, or link starvation.

Extensive synchronous DMACs are proposed in the literature. In [4,7], the author firstly proposes a wireless MAC protocol based on time division multiple access (TDMA) called DTRA. In the transmission and reception process, pure directional antennas are applied. In DTRA, a frame structure is divided into three phases, the neighbour discovery phase, the reservation phase and the data transmission phase. Each phase is divided into a plurality of slots, and each slot is divided into several mini-slots. In the neighbour discovery phase, the node finds its neighbours and selects a time slot for the reservation phase. In the reservation phase, the nodes confirm the neighbours, and choose slots for the data transmission phase. Reference [8] proposes a DMAC named SDVCS (Slotted Directional Virtual Carrier Sensing), which is different from DTRA in the slot allocation phase, i.e., the reservation phase. SDVCS dynamically allocate slots upon demand of each node, and tries to reduce the interference between the concurrent transmitting links when allocating slots for transmission. Reference [9] proposed a Reservation Directional MAC (RDMAC) for multi-hop wireless networks with directional antennas. The RDMAC protocol is divided into a reservation period and a transmission period. Reservations are done in the reservation period and data is transmitted in transmission period.

Note that DAHN is a distributed network. Though synchronous DMACs are designed to avoid some shortcomings of omnidirectional protocols successfully, the slot reservation based resource allocations also has some problems. One of them is the unfairness of the slot allocation between links, which is caused by the distributed nature of DAHN. That is the earlier discovered link reserves much more slots which results in the later discovered links have few slots to reserve. Take DTRA as an example, we illustrate the reasons of the unfairness problem.

– Although each node discovers its neighbours in the scanning phase and makes reservations with its neighbours. The data transmission requirements of its neighbours are unaware.
– In one super frame of DTRA, there may exist one scanning phase and several reservation phases and several data transmission phases, and the duration of each super frame may be about one seconds or much more longer. Such that, it is impossible to exchange the data transmission requirements between neighbours in the scanning phase, since some traffic may be delay sensitive and the data traffic of the nodes dynamically varies.
– When the traffic demand of the links increases, or the density of the network is large, if the earlier discovered neighbours reserve enough data slots, the later scanned node pairs could not get enough slots to transmit data, causing these links in starvation and resulting in the unfair problem.

Several related works are proposed to solve the unfairness problem. Reference [10] propose a frame based DMAC. To achieve the collision free data transmission, a graph coloring algorithm is proposed to optimally exploit the spatial reuse gain. The proposed algorithm runs on a central controlled node. To achieve a satisfactory trade-off between the utilization and fairness, Ref. [11] proposes a graph coloring algorithm to allocate data slots under singlebeam situation. However, the node needs to collects traffic information in the neighborhood periodically.

Note that these works either require the whole data transmission requirements or require the interference relationships between the concurrent transmission links, which are difficult to be obtained in DAHN since it is distributed. To address the unfairness problem in the slot allocation period, in this paper a Classified Slot Re-allocation Algorithm (CSRA) is proposed for the synchronous DAHN. The main contributions of this paper are concluded as follows.

- A data slot classified method is proposed to classify the data slots according to their transmission status. And the data slots are classified into four categories, i.e., the free data slots, the sending slots, the neighbour transmitting slots and the receiving slots.
- A Classified Slot Re-allocation Algorithm (CSRA) is proposed to re-allocate the data slots when the unfairness problem occurs. And the re-allocation order is given as the free data slots, the sending slots, the neighbour transmitting slots and the receiving slots.
- Extensive simulations are carried out to evaluate the performance of the proposed CSRA. The simulation results show that the Jain's fairness index is improved with litter loss of the network throughput.

The rest of this paper is organized as follows. In Sect. 2, we illustrate the system model of CSRA. In Sect. 3, the data slot classified method and the CSRA algorithm is presented. Performance evaluations based on CSRA are presented in Sect. 4. The conclusion and future work are given in Sect. 5.

2   System Model

In the directional ad hoc networks, M nodes are randomly deployed. Each node is equipped a switch-able directional antennas and a time synchronous device, e.g., GPS. The time line is slotted and in each time slot only one directional antenna can be activated. The number of directional antenna is denoted as β and the angle range of each directional antenna is set as ω, where $\omega = 2\pi/\beta$.

The DMAC protocol structure is shown in Fig. 1. The time line is divided into super frames, and each super frame is composed of the scanning, reservation and data transmission phases. Each phase consists of several slots. Let $\alpha \times \beta$, γ and δ denotes the number of slots of the scanning, reservation and data transmission phases, where α denotes the scanning round of the scanning phase. In the scanning phase, all of the nodes do the neighbour discovery and the beam aligning process, and the discovered neighbours reserve the slot in the reservation phase. In the reservation phase, the neighbours communicate with their data transmission requirements and reserve data slots for the data transmission phase. Each slot in the reservation phase is divided into 3 minislots, and the REQ-REP-ACK (REQuest, REPly, ACKnowledgement) packets exchanging procedure is

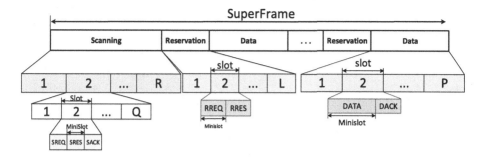

Fig. 1. DMAC protocol structure of CSRA.

carried out to make reservation of the data slots in the data transmission phase. In the data transmission phase, the neighbours transmit the traffic. Each slot in the data transmission phase is divided into 2 minislots, and the DATA-ACK packets exchanging procedure is carried out.

The proposed CSRA works in the reservation phase. To facilitate the illustration of the proposed CSRA, we define the data structures of the protocol as follows. After the scanning phase, each node discovers its neighbours and obtains the slot reservation status table in the reservation phase. Let $X = [x_i]_{1 \times \gamma}$ denote the slot reservation status table in the reservation phase, where $x_i = (s, r)$ denotes the sender s will transmit the REQ packet in the first minislot of the ith slot of the reservation phase. Similarly, let $Y = [y_i]_{1 \times \delta}$ denote the slot reservation status table in the data transmission phase, where $y_i = (s, r)$ denotes the sender s will transmit the REQ packet in the first minislot of the ith slot of the data transmission phase.

3   The Proposed Classified Slot Re-allocation Algorithm

In this section we illustrate the data slot classified method first, and then propose the classified slot re-allocation algorithm.

3.1   Data Slot Classified Method

We use Fig. 2 as an example to illustrate the basic idea of the proposed data slot classified method. In Fig. 2, suppose that in the reservation phase, node A has reserved the data slots with its neighbours B, C and D, and overhears that its neighbour link $\mathcal{L}_{E,F}$ will also transmit at some time slots. Specifically, we let $\delta = 5$ and let node A's slot reservation status table in the data transmission phase Y is given as

$$Y = [(A, B), (C, A), (D, A), (E, F), (-, -)].$$

Thus, according to the status of each slot in Y the data slots can be classified into four types. That is the free slot is $y_5 = (-, -)$, and the sending slot is

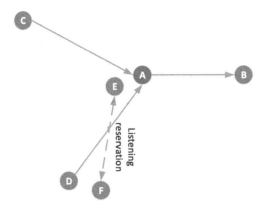

Fig. 2. Different types of data slots at node A.

$y_1 = (A, B)$, and the neighbour link transmitting slot is $y_4 = (E, F)$, and the receiving slots are $y_2 = (C, A)$ and $y_3 = (D, A)$.

To address the unfairness problem, some data slots may be needed to re-allocate to other nodes. Thus, we qualitatively analyse the properties of each type of the data slots in the follows.

– **Free slots:** There is no re-allocation problem for this type of data slots.
– **Sending slots:** If a sending slot is re-allocated to another node, two cases may occur. The first one is that this sending slot is also a sending slot, only with the receiving node of this data slot is changed. If this case happens there will exist no effect to the other nodes, or to the network. The second one is that this sending slot is changed to a receiving slot. If this case happens there will also exist no effect to the other nodes.
– **Neighbour link transmitting slots:** If a neighbour transmitting slot is re-allocated to another node, this may cause collisions between the concurrent transmission links.
– **Receiving slots:** If a receiving slot is re-allocated to another node, then the sending node of this slot may be not aware. And thus if the sending node will transmit data in this slot, and the new allocated node also transmit, these two data packets may collide at node A.

Therefore, if some data slots are needed to re-allocate to other nodes the priority order of the data slot types should be the free slots, the sending slots and the neighbour link transmitting slots. For different types of data slots, we have the following considerations.

– Firstly, when the data slots requirements of each link is very large, i.e., trending to infinity, no matter how to re-allocate the data slots, there may be no effect on the fairness.
– However, when the data slots requirements of each link is large, i.e., to be a large constant, if all of the data slots requirements are meet for the earlier

reserved links in the reservation phase only few of them can be satisfied, even though the data slots are re-allocated. Thus, a threshold for the satisfied data slots requirement is defined as F_r, $0 < F_r < 1$. The physical meaning of it is the average data slots requirement sanctification index. In other words, when the data slots requirements of a given link is obtained, only a fraction of F_r of them can be meet.

– We also note that for the sending slots and the neighbour link transmitting slots, there exists probability of collisions when they are re-allocated, and thus we can define the re-allocation proportion threshold. That is under which a given type data slot can be re-allocated, however if the re-allocated proportion is higher than the threshold that type of data slots should not be re-allocated. Let T_s and T_n denote the re-allocation proportion thresholds of the sending slots and the neighbour link transmitting slots.

– Furthermore, we would like to note that if a data slot is re-allocated it is better to re-allocate it again.

Finally, it can be found that the classification of the data slots do not consider the directions of the transmission links. It should have a higher gain if the direction of the transmission links is considered when classifying the data slots, which will be our future works.

3.2 The Proposed Classified Slot Re-allocation Algorithm

To facilitate the illustration of the proposed CSRA, the following variables are defined. Let $\mathcal{S}_f$, $\mathcal{S}_s$ and $\mathcal{S}_n$ denote the sets of the free slots, the sending slots and the neighbour link transmitting slots. Algorithm 1 presents the pseudo code of CSRA.

Algorithm 1 is called when the protocol runs into the reservation phase no matter for the first time or not. The inputs are the number of slots in the reservation phase γ, the number of slots in the data transmission phase δ, the slot reservation status table in the reservation phase after the completion of the scanning phase X, the average data slots requirement sanctification index F_r, the re-allocation threshold of the sending data slots T_s and the re-allocation threshold of the neighbouring link transmitting slots T_n. Note that only X will be obtained after the scanning phase, and the other parameters are the constant with a given protocol. The outputs is the slot reservation status table in the data transmission phase Y.

From line 1 to line 3, the temp variables are initialized, which includes setting the free slots set to be $\mathcal{S}_f = \{1, 2, \cdots, \delta\}$, setting the sending slots set and the neighbour link transmitting slots to be empty set, i.e., $\mathcal{S}_s = \emptyset$ and $\mathcal{S}_n = \emptyset$. And set the temp variable of the proportion of re-allocation sending slots $t_s = 0$, and the temp variable of the proportion of re-allocation neighbour link transmitting slots $t_n = 0$. Furthermore, the slot reservation status table in the data transmission phase Y is also initialized.

For each slot in the reservation phase, in line 5 after the data slots transmission requirements collection procedure is executed in the ith slot of the reservation phase, the decision is made that whether allocate/re-allocate data slots

Algorithm 1. Classified Slot Re-allocation Algorithm

Input: γ, δ, X, F_r, T_s, T_n.

Output: Y

1: $\mathcal{S}_f = \{1, 2, \cdots, \delta\}$, $\mathcal{S}_s = \emptyset$ and $\mathcal{S}_n = \emptyset$; $t_s = 0$, $t_n = 0$;

2: **for** $i = 0 : \delta$ **do**

3:     $y_i = (-, -)$

4: **for** $i = 0 : \gamma$ **do**

5:     executes data slots transmission requirements collection in the ith slot of the reservation phase, and let R_s, R_r denote the number of data slots requirements collected from neighbour m;

6:     **if** $R_s + R_r > 0$ **then**

7:         **if** $|\mathcal{S}_f| \geq F_r \times (R_s + R_r)$ **then**

8:             allocate $\mathcal{S}_f$ to neighbour m as $F_r \times (R_s + R_r)$, and update $\mathcal{S}_f$ and $\mathcal{S}_s$;

9:             break;

10:        **else**

11:            allocate $\mathcal{S}_f$ to neighbour m, and update $\mathcal{S}_f$ and $\mathcal{S}_s$; update R_s, R_r;

12:            **if** $(T_s - t_s) \times |\mathcal{S}_s| \geq F_r \times (R_s + R_r)$ **then**

13:                re-allocate $\mathcal{S}_s$ to neighbour m as $F_r \times (R_s + R_r)$, and update $\mathcal{S}_s$; update t_s;

14:                break;

15:            **else**

16:                re-allocate $\mathcal{S}_s$ to neighbour m, and update $\mathcal{S}_s$; update $t_s = T_s$; update R_s, R_r;

17:                **if** $(T_n - t_n) \times |\mathcal{S}_n| \geq F_r \times (R_s + R_r)$ **then**

18:                    re-allocate $\mathcal{S}_N$ to neighbour m as $F_r \times (R_s + R_r)$, and update $\mathcal{S}_s$ and $\mathcal{S}_n$; update t_n;

19:                **else**

20:                    re-allocate $\mathcal{S}_n$ to neighbour m, and update $\mathcal{S}_s$ and $\mathcal{S}_n$; update $t_n = T_n$; update R_s, R_r;

21:    **else**

22:        listen and receive the neighbour link transmitting slots, and update $\mathcal{S}_n$;

---

or update the neighbour link transmitting slots set $\mathcal{S}_n$. Let R_s, R_r denote the number of data slots requirements collected from neighbour m. If $R_s + R_r > 0$ then allocate/re-allocate data slots to neighbour m from line 7, else record the neighbour link transmitting slots and update the neighbour link transmitting slots set $\mathcal{S}_n$ in line 22.

To allocate/re-allocate data slots to neighbour m, the free data slots set is checked firstly in line 7. If the number of free data slots is larger than $F_r \times (R_s + R_r)$, then allocate $\mathcal{S}_f$ to neighbour m, and update $\mathcal{S}_f$ and $\mathcal{S}_s$ accordingly. Otherwise allocate all of the left free data slots in $\mathcal{S}_f$ first, and update $\mathcal{S}_f$ and $\mathcal{S}_s$ accordingly. When there are not enough free data slots, the sending data slots will be re-allocated from line 12.

Similarly, if the number of left sending slots is larger than $F_r \times (R_s + R_r)$, then allocate $\mathcal{S}_s$ to neighbour m, and update $\mathcal{S}_s$ accordingly. Otherwise allocate all of the left sending slots in $\mathcal{S}_s$ first, and update $\mathcal{S}_s$ accordingly. When there are not enough left sending data slots, the neighbour link transmitting slots will be re-allocated from line 17. The operation of re-allocation of the neighbour link transmitting slots is similar with that of sending slots, and is omitted due to space limitation.

4   Performance Evaluation

In this section, we evaluate the performance of the proposed CSRA and DTRA in two parts. In the first part, we keep the number of nodes unchanged, and investigate the performance of the Jain's fairness index and the sum throughput. In the second part, we verify the performance of these two protocols in terms of the Jain's fairness index under the condition that the number of nodes is constant.

The Jain's fairness index defined as follows.

Definition 1 (Jain's fairness index). *The Jain's fairness index indicates the relative fairness of the data transmission between different node pairs [12], and it can be expressed by*

$$FI = \frac{(\sum_{i=1}^{X} r_i)^2}{X * \sum_{i=1}^{X} r_i^2},$$

where r_i denotes the rate of the ith link, and X denotes the number of links for a given node.

4.1   Simulation Parameter Settings

M nodes are randomly deployed in a $200\,\text{m} \times 200\,\text{m}$ area. The simulation parameters are listed in Table 1.

Table 1. Simulation parameters

Parameters	Value in simulation
Number of nodes M	4−10
Number of beams β	4
Number of scanning rounds α	50
Reservation and data transmission's rounds	30
Slot number in reservation phase γ	10
Length of a data packet	2500 bytes
Length of per slot	500 μs

4.2   Evaluation on Throughput and the Jain's Fairness Index

Figures 3 and 4 show the total number of packets received and the Jain's fairness index of CSRA and DTRA varying with the number of the demanded traffic slots in the portion of total slots in data transmission phase, and the nodes number $M = 6$. For these two dotted lines, the sending slots' re-allocation threshold T_s are set as 0.3 and 0.6 separately, and the neighbour link transmitting slots' re-allocation threshold T_n is set as 0.9, and the average data slots requirement sanctification index is set as $F_r = 0.3$. From Fig. 3, it can be found that when the traffic demand is increased the proposed CSRA holds a much better performance in terms of Jain's fairness index. At the meantime, from Fig. 4 it can be found that there is a little reduction on throughput for CSRA with the given constant T_s. This implies that a varying T_s should be used with different traffic demand, which can be a future work.

Figures 5 and 6 show the performance of throughput and the Jain's fairness index varying with the node number while keeping the traffic demand as 0.3. For these two dotted lines, the master slots' re-allocation threshold T_s are set as 0.3 and 0.6 separately, and the neighbour link transmitting slots' re-allocation threshold T_n is set as 0.9, and the average data slots requirement sanctification index is set as $F_r = 0.3$. From Fig. 5, it can be found that when the node number M increases, the Jain's fairness index decreases for both these two protocols, but as a result of CSRA's re-allocation among multiple node pairs, the Jain's fairness

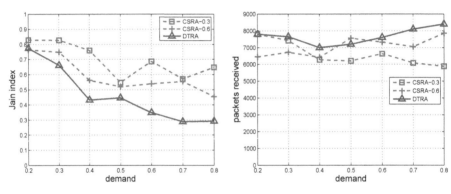

Fig. 3. Comparison of Jain's index varying with demand.

Fig. 4. Comparison of packets received varying with demand.

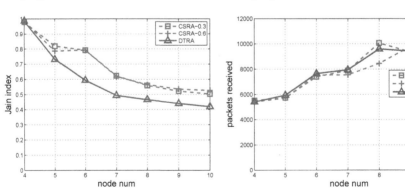

Fig. 5. Comparison of Jain's index varying with node number.

Fig. 6. Comparison of packets received varying with node number.

index of the proposed CSRA outperforms DTRA. From Fig. 6, it can be found that the throughput of these two protocol are close to each other.

5 Conclusion and Future Work

In order to solve the unfairness problem in DTRA, in this paper, we propose a Classified Slot Re-allocation Algorithm, shorted as CSRA. It classifies the data slots in data transmission phase according to the status of the slots into four types, and the re-allocation order is given as the free slots, the sending slots and the neighbour link transmitting slots. The simulation results show that CSRA can achieve an obvious advantage in term of fairness while keeping little performance loss in term of throughout. In the future, how to vary the re-allocation threshold of different types of slots will be studied.

Acknowledgments. This work was supported in part by the National Natural Science Foundations of CHINA (Grant No. 61771392, No. 61771390, No. 61501373, and No. 61271279), the Science and Technology on Communication Networks Laboratory Open Projects (Grant No. KX162600031, KX172600027), the National Science and Technology Major Project (Grant No. 2016ZX03001018-004), and the Fundamental Research Funds for the Central Universities (Grant No. 3102017ZY018).

References

1. Wang, Y., Motani, M., Garg, H.K., Chen, Q., Luo, T.: Cooperative multichannel directional medium access control for ad hoc networks. IEEE Syst. 11(4), 2675–2686 (2015)
2. Ren, B., Zhang, X., Gou, X.: System design of high speed ad hoc networking with directional antenna. In: 2016 12th International Conference on Mobile Ad-Hoc and Sensor Networks (MSN), Hefei, pp. 429–433 (2016)
3. Zhang, W., Peng, L., Xu, R., Zhang, L., Zhu, J.: Neighbor discovery in three-dimensional mobile ad hoc networks with directional antennas. In: 25th Wireless and Optical Communication Conference (WOCC), Chengdu, pp. 1–5 (2016)
4. Zhang, Z.: DTRA: directional transmission and reception algorithms in wlans with directional antennas for QoS support. IEEE Netw. 19(3), 27–32 (2005)
5. Bazan, O., Jaseemuddin, M.: A survey on MAC protocols for wireless adhoc networks with beamforming antennas. IEEE Commun. Surv. Tutor. 14(2), 216–239 (2012)
6. Wong, D.T.C., Chen, Q., Chin, F.: Directional medium access control (MAC) protocols in wireless ad hoc and sensor networks: a survey. J. Sens. Actuator Netw. 4(2), 67–153 (2015)
7. Zhang, Z.: Pure directional transmission and reception algorithms in wireless ad hoc networks with directional antennas. In: IEEE International Conference on Communications, ICC 2005, vol. 5, pp. 3386–3390, May 2005
8. Tu, Y., Zhang, Y., Zhang, H.: A novel MAC protocol for wireless ad hoc networks with directional antennas. In: 2013 15th IEEE International Conference on Communication Technology, pp. 494–499, November 2013

9. Chang, J.J., Liao, W., Hou, T.C.: Reservation-based directional medium access control (RDMAC) protocol for multi-hop wireless networks with directional antennas. In: IEEE International Conference on Communications, pp. 1–5 (2009)
10. Son, I.K., Mao, S., Gong, M.X., et al.: On frame-based scheduling for directional mmWave WPANs. In: IEEE INFOCOM, pp. 2149–2157. IEEE (2012)
11. Wang, J., Zhang, Y., Jiang, L.: A novel time-slot allocation scheme for ad hoc networks with single-beam directional antennas. In: IEEE International Conference on Communication Software and Networks, pp. 227–231. IEEE (2015)
12. Jain, R., Durresi, A., Babic, G.: Throughput fairness index: an explanation. Technical report, Department of CIS, The Ohio State University (1999)

Smart Applications

You Can Write Numbers Accurately
on Your Hand with Smart Acoustic Sensing

Mingshi Chen[1] , Panlong Yang[2(✉)], and Ping Li[1]

[1] College of Communications Engineering,
PLA Army Engineering University, Nanjing, China
cms603421@gmail.com, pingli0112@gmail.com
[2] School of Computer Science and Technology,
University of Science and Technology of China, Hefei, China
panlongyang@gmail.com

Abstract. Although smartwatch has drawn many attentions in recent years, small and inconvenient interaction mode limits the prevalence of smartwatches. Writing numbers with hands will naturally extend the input interface for smart watch. In this work, we design a passive acoustic sensing, where smart watches are collecting the ambient sound during writing. First of all, we use the wavelet transformation to mitigate the surrounding noise, and devise the time-frequency figures for AI enabled processing. After that, we apply the CNN(Convolutional Neural Network) model for number recognition, where three layers of convolution and three layers of max pool are incorporated. The number recognition accuracy rate could be above 95% when single person is well trained, and be around 92% when 7 to 9 persons are incorporated.

Keywords: Smartwatch · Wavelet transformation · CNN

1 Introduction

Smart devices have advanced to serve as an inseparable tool and aid for daily life. However, small touchscreen makes the basic selections cumbersome and fallible, and it's inconvenient when taking more complex actions such as typing a long list of phone numbers. For this concern, can we turn the hand-back into a virtual writing plane for interactions with the smart wearable device? Since skin has been applied for a natural extension for interaction [1–4], we can leverage it for operations beyond screen. For instance, we can treat our area of hand-back as a larger interaction surface for writing numbers keys. Such a system can be integrated into the smart wearable devices to enable more convenient operations. Existing work of skin computing and around device interaction either requires dedicated hardware [1–3, 5–8], or instruments the finger with a set of sensors [9–11], limiting their experience of interaction. It is worth nothing that, acoustic sensing is an innovative technology in extending the application scenarios of microphone. For acoustic sensing, it should include the following favorable properties:

© ICST Institute for Computer Sciences, Social Informatics and Telecommunications Engineering 2018
L. Wang et al. (Eds.): QShine 2017, LNICST 234, pp. 207–217, 2018.
https://doi.org/10.1007/978-3-319-78078-8_21

- High-accuracy: the traditional input mode is limited by the small screen, especially smart watch. For user-friendly experience and ease of input consideration, people need an input device with high accuracy.
- Adaptability: the input mode should be adaptive to different users and working environments. Especially when considering the personalized users, good performance should be provided in a consistent way.

Unfortunately, there are two intrinsic challenges need to be formally addressed before this inspiring vision could be achieved.

- First, the acoustic signal induced by writing numbers on hand-back is weak. Even worse, the background noise is usually strong, which will possibly lead to errors in number recognition.
- Second, the acoustic features are diverse across persons, even for same person at different time. A stable and sensitive design should be encouraged for ease of imputing when input behaviors are fully respected.

There are two major contributions in our work.

- We present a dual-threshold scheme to deal with the strong background noise for segmentation. The threshold values are carefully selected according to various tests and show satisfiable performance across those scenarios.
- We conduct extensive evaluations to validate our design. Evaluations are made across different volunteers in various scenarios. Specifically, we show effectiveness and accuracy of the number writing behaviors on hand-back. It paves the way for alphabet writing or drawing for future designs.

The rest parts of this paper are organized as follows: First of all, in Sect. 2, we outline the basic design idea and components with working flow illustrations, and then present a comprehensive introduction with technical details for system design and implementation in Sect. 3. Secondly, we demonstrate our design performance with experimental results and analysis in Sect. 4. Finally, we make a conclusion in Sect. 5.

2 System Design

As Fig. 1 shows, our system implementation consists of four primary parts, namely sampling, effective signal segmentation, feature extraction and input recognition.

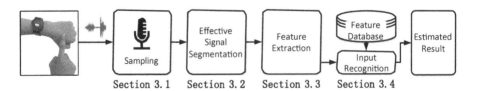

Fig. 1. Working flow

When user is writing on the hand-back, the acoustic signal, generated by the friction between the finger and the surface of hand-back, is captured by the built-in microphone sensor of smartwatches (Sect. 3.1). When it comes to input recognition through acoustic features, there are two points of feasibility:

First: hand-back is almost the closest input position to the smartwatch, except for the screen itself. Therefore, it is possible to capture the acoustic signal of input writing, in terms of the distance, which reduces the interference of ambient noise.

Second: as in the article [14], the acoustic characteristics generated by the desktop writing can identify user input. Similarly, the acoustic signal generated by users writing on the hand-back, even though weakness, it contains sufficient features to input recognition.

Then we segment the collected signal, and the effective writing signal fragments are extracted by analyzing the characteristics, such as short time energy and zero-crossing rate. In order to eliminate the impact of sudden noise, we take full advantage of the build-in gyro sensor in smart device to determine whether the user is in a writing state (Sect. 3.2). In the following, the effective acoustic fragments are subjected to spectral analysis and characteristics extraction. Since We use the convolution neural network (CNN) for classification training and recognition, we convert the features into picture for preservation (Sect. 3.3). Eventually, the characteristics and labels are imported into CNN, train in advance. In the actual writing recognition process, the user directly gets the results of CNN classification, which is done by off-line training and on-line identification (Sect. 3.4).

In our system implementation, the accuracy rate of 0–9 numbers recognition reaches more than 90%.

3 Implementation

3.1 Sampling Process

We use the built-in microphone on smartwatch, the position of which is closest from the hand-back of writing, to do a favourable collection of acoustic signals. In order to facilitate the subsequent segmentation and judgment of effective signal, we also collect gyro sensor data simultaneously. Through the vibration caused by finger sliding, we determine whether the user is in a state of writing. In the implementation, we used the Android smartwatch of HUAWEI WATCH 1, call the AudioTract API to collect the audio, AudioRecord API to record the audio and SensorManager API to collect the gyroscope data.

3.2 Effective Signal Segmentation

The main basis of signal segmentation is that, after filtering and denoising, the short-time energy of effective signal is higher than the ambient signal, so the position of the effective acoustic signal can be found by peak detection. Coupled with the gyro sensor peak detection as auxiliary confirmation, we can accurately split out the writing signal. This module is divided into three steps, respectively, preprocessing, peak detection, segmentation.

Preprocessing: built-in microphone sensor of smartwatch, whose default sampling rate is 44100, can fully collect the surrounding acoustic signal. First of all, we make a wavelet time-frequency analysis to acoustic signal, in favor of voice segmentation and feature extraction. As shown in the Fig. 2, the acoustic signal, in the intermediate frequency of which has a significant effective signal area, and the intensity is remarkable, there has almost no other interference signal in time domain of the entire frequency band. Since the acoustic signal is only used for location in this section, we do a 10 times down-sampling in the process of searching for the position, not only accurately locates the position of effective signal writing fragment, but also reduces the amount of data processing calculations.

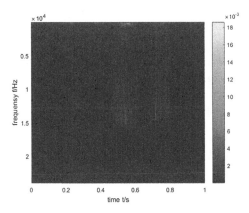

Fig. 2. Wavelet time-frequency figure

Peak detection: we denote amplitude data of the original signal, which has been down-sampled, as x(n). As for the acoustic signal, in the 10–30 ms short time, can be regarded as a quasi-steady state, we split it through short-term energy and zero-crossing rate (the formula is as following). These two features are often used for a voice signal detection, and segmenting effective voice. We set the two thresholds of short-term average energy and zero-crossing as 0.2 and 0.3, based on experiment and experience.

Short time energy formula:

$$E_n = \sum_{m=0}^{N-1} x_n^2(m) \tag{1}$$

Zero-crossing rate formula:

$$Z_n = \sum_{m=0}^{N-1} |sgn[x_n(m)] - sgn[x_n(m-1)]| \tag{2}$$

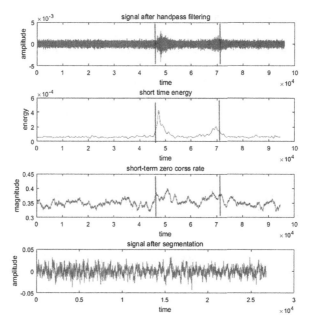

Fig. 3. Segmentation through short time energy and short-term zero cross rate

Where sgn[.] is a sign function, N is the size of window and n is the sequence number.

$$\text{sgn}[x] = \begin{cases} 1, & (x \geq 0) \\ -1, & (x < 0) \end{cases} \tag{3}$$

As we can see from Fig. 3, these two features ensure that we can split out effective signals, but there may be a sudden outbreak of environmental noise is partitioned into an effective fragment, which increases the false error rate. Thus, we introduce the gyro sensor data, and the gyroscope data x, y and z of the three directions are summed to obtain g. Calculating the short term energy of g, and then, we perform peak detection to find the peak position. If the peak position is within one second interval on the middle of the effective signal previously split, it determined the current fragment is an effective writing signal.

Segmentation: with the position of effective signal, we segment effective fragment on original signal, for the following operation.

3.3   Feature Extraction

As we know from the previous, the acoustic signal generated by writing on hand-back, whose frequency distribution is ranged from 5 k to 15 k, and has a time characteristic. After bandpass filtering, the main part is the writing signal, with less IF(intermediate frequency) noise. Since its own acoustic signal of hang-back writing is very weak, we need to find a efficient and complete descriptor, which can characterize it. After experimental comparison, as shown in the Fig. 4, we find that the sound spectrum has a optimum performance of the complete time-frequency characteristic. The other characteristic such as the MFCC(Mel-Frequency Cepstral Coefficients) [15], commonly used in the voice recognition, is not suitable for hand-written IF signal feature extraction. Because it mimics the human ear structure for feature extraction, is more sensitive to the low-frequency signal, in which the medium-high frequency feature information is damaged.

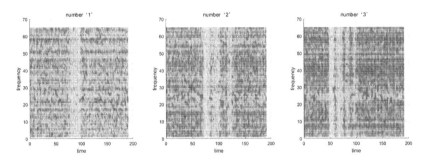

Fig. 4. Spectrograms of different numbers

Thus, we perform a sound spectrum analysis to the effective signal and save it as a spectrogram. We intercept the middle band 64 frames long, the eigenvalue of the whole time, converted to grayscale image for saving.

3.4   Feature Matching

In this paper, the structure of CNN is shown in Table 1. In addition to the input and output layers, the middle layer consists of three layers of convolution and three layers of the pool, the core sizes are 11 * 11, 5 * 5 and 3 * 3, respectively. Our framework was inspired by AlexNet [13], published in 2012, which obtained Imagenet best results in current year. AlexNet [13] is improvement of LeNet [12], which is the first neural network method of handwriting numeral recognition, emphasises more on the role of the whole connection layer. It adds the dropout layer, to prevent over-fitting, and reduce the number of weights. In the course of the experiment, we randomly divide the data into 8:2, the former is the training set, the latter is the test set, and calculate the final accuracy. Our recognition accuracy rate of single hand-back numbers writing reach 96% or more, even adopting multi-person data, the accuracy rate is more than 92%.

4   Performance Evaluation

In order to fully verify the performance of our proposed algorithm, we conduct a comprehensive experiment in real environment.

Table 1. Structure of CNN

Layer	Name	Configuration
1	Image input	64 × 64 × 3 images with 'zerocenter' normalization
2	Convolution	64 11 × 11 convolutions with stride [1 1] and padding [2 2]
3	ReLU	ReLU
4	Normalization	Cross channel normalization with 5 channels per element
5	Max pooling	3 × 3 max pooling with stride [2 2] and padding [0 0]
6	Convolution	128 5 × 5 convolutions with stride [1 1] and padding [2 2]
7	ReLU	ReLU
8	Normalization	Cross channel normalization with 5 channels per element
9	Max pooling	3 × 3 max pooling with stride [2 2] and padding [0 0]
10	Convolution	256 3 × 3 convolutions with stride [1 1] and padding [2 2]
11	ReLU	ReLU
12	Max pooling	3 × 3 max pooling with stride [2 2] and padding [0 0]
13	Dropout	50% dropout
14	Fully connected	256 fully connected layer
15	ReLU	ReLU
16	Fully connected	10 fully connected layer
17	Softmax	Softmax
18	Classification output	Cross-entropy

4.1 Experiment Setup

We set up the experiments in the lab, dormitory and canteen, where people often appear, and the noise level gradually increased. We implement our algorithm in the HUAWEI WATCH I with android 4.3 OS, by which we collect the user's acoustic signals of hand-back writing. The smartwatch collects the writing signal and transmits the effective signal to the server, while, the server sends the result back to the watch terminal after processing. We achieve off-line processing, on-line identification.

We invited 10 volunteers (7 males, 3 females, evenly distributed at different ages), each of whom writes 50 times of each number, with total 5000 acoustic samples.

4.2 Various Experiments

Average accuracy of each number recognition: We first evaluate the average recognition accuracy of different numbers. We let volunteers wear smart-watch in their comfortable environment for hand-back writing. For purpose of marking labels, we require the volunteers write each number repeatedly at least 50 times. Then, we put collected signals into the algorithm, and statistics recognition accuracy of each number, the results shown in Fig. 5. As we can see that the overall accuracy rate is 90%, and the accuracy rates of some numbers, such as 4, reach 98%. It is 6 and 9, of which the lowest accuracy rates are only 88%. For a more deeply analysis of the differences in accuracy among numbers, we calculate the confusion matrices about recognition accuracy. As shown in the Fig. 6, the number 6 is easily mistaken for 1.

Recognition Accuracy
0 0.1 0.2 0.3 0.4 0.5 0.6 0.7 0.8 0.9 1
0.96 0.92 0.90 0.93 0.98 0.92 0.88 0.93 0.92 0.88
average
0.9275
0 1 2 3 4 5 6 7 8 9

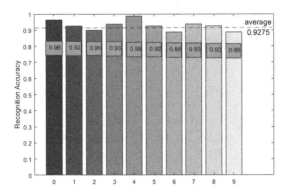

Fig. 5. Average accuracy of each number recognition

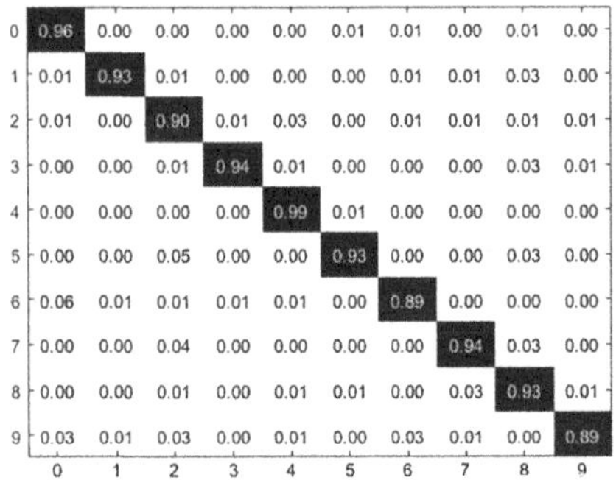

0 0.96 0.00 0.00 0.00 0.00 0.01 0.01 0.00 0.01 0.00
1 0.01 0.93 0.01 0.00 0.00 0.00 0.01 0.01 0.03 0.00
2 0.01 0.00 0.90 0.01 0.03 0.00 0.01 0.01 0.01 0.01
3 0.00 0.00 0.01 0.94 0.01 0.00 0.00 0.00 0.03 0.01
4 0.00 0.00 0.00 0.00 0.99 0.01 0.00 0.00 0.00 0.00
5 0.00 0.00 0.05 0.00 0.00 0.93 0.00 0.00 0.03 0.00
6 0.06 0.01 0.01 0.01 0.01 0.00 0.89 0.00 0.00 0.00
7 0.00 0.00 0.04 0.00 0.00 0.00 0.00 0.94 0.03 0.00
8 0.00 0.00 0.01 0.00 0.01 0.01 0.00 0.03 0.93 0.01
9 0.03 0.01 0.03 0.00 0.01 0.00 0.03 0.01 0.00 0.89
0 1 2 3 4 5 6 7 8 9

Fig. 6. Confusion matrix among different digits

Average accuracy in different scenarios: To prove the strong environmental adaptability of our algorithm, we perform it in lab, dormitory and canteen, with the increasing noise level of environment, which were 45, 60 and 80 respectively. Similarly, each scenario, where we repeat 0–9 each for 100 times. From the Fig. 7, even in

Recognition Accuracy
0 0.1 0.2 0.3 0.4 0.5 0.6 0.7 0.8 0.9 1
0.94456
0.90553
0.85476
Lab(43dB)
Dormitory(65dB)
Canteen(81dB)

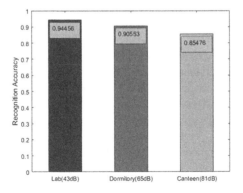

Fig. 7. Average accuracy in different scenarios

the most noisy place, canteen, our recognition accuracy rate still reaches 85%, that shows the excellent performance of our algorithm.

Average accuracy with different users: To evaluate the robustness of our algorithm to different users with write differences. We invite 10 volunteers, in the laboratory, repeatedly writing 50 times of each number. After that, the average writing accuracy of each person is calculated, of which the results are shown in Fig. 8. It can be seen that our algorithm performs well among different users although the accuracy of different users varies in the average accuracy rate of 95% fluctuation.

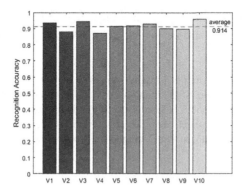

Fig. 8. Average accuracy with different users

The impact of training instances on recognition accuracy: The accuracy of CNN recognition depends on the effect of training, which definitively lies on the instances of training. So we put the acoustic samples into CNN, record statistics accuracy of recognition at different training times. As shown in the Fig. 9, as the increasing of training times, the recognition accuracy grows positively. But after 16 with reaching the peak of 94.5%, there has been a slight decrease in the rate of accuracy. Therefore, we set the number of training as 16 in the subsequent experiment process.

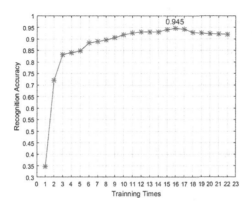

Fig. 9. Recognition accuracy with different training instances

5 Conclusion and Future Work

In this paper, we innovate the way we used for gestures recognition, which is directly based on the one-dimensional acoustic feature. Acoustic characteristics of two-dimensional information, time domain and frequency domain, is completely extracted and converted into images, combined with CNN, which has excellent performance in image classification, achieving fantastic results. In the identification of 0–9 numbers, we achieved an average accuracy of 92%, in a quiet environment, it even reached a 96% accuracy rate. Thus, not only the ability to identify numbers is demonstrated, but the possibility of discerning alphabets is also verified.

In the future work, we will add the experiment and verification of 26 alphabets. Let hand-back written changes people's input experience, and achieves innovation of wearable equipment.

Acknowledgement. This research is partially supported by 2017YFB0801702, National key research and development plan, NSFC with No. 61772546, 61632010, 61232018, 61371118, 61402009, 61672038, 61520106007, China National Funds for Distinguished Young Scientists with No.61625205, Key Research Program of Frontier Sciences, CAS, No. QYZDY-SSW-JSC002, and NSF OF Jiangsu For Distinguished Young Scientist: BK20150030.

References

1. Harrison, C., Tan, D., Dan, M.: Skinput: appropriating the body as an input surface. In: Sigchi Conference on Human Factors in Computing Systems, pp. 453–462 (2010)
2. Weigel, M., Lu, T., Bailly, G., Oulasvirta, A., Majidi, C.: iSkin: flexible, stretchable and visually customizable on-body touch sensors for mobile computing. In: ACM Conference on Human Factors in Computing Systems, pp. 2991–3000 (2015)
3. Huang, D.Y., Chan, L., Yang, S., Wang, F., Liang, R.H., Yang, D.N., Hung, Y.P., Chen, B.Y.: Digitspace: designing thumb-to-fingers touch interfaces for one-handed and eyes-free interactions. In: CHI Conference on Human Factors in Computing Systems, pp. 1526–1537 (2016)
4. Zhang, Y., Zhou, J., Laput, G., Harrison, C.: Skintrack: using the body as an electrical waveguide for continuous finger tracking on the skin. In: CHI Conference on Human Factors in Computing Systems, pp. 1491–1503 (2016)
5. Kratz, S., Rohs, M.: Hoverflow: exploring around-device interaction with ir distance sensors. In: International Conference on Human-Computer Interaction with Mobile Devices and Services, p. 42 (2009)
6. Hansen, J.P., Biermann, F., Jonassen, M., Lund, H., Agustin, J.S., Sztuk, S.: A gaze interactive textual smartwatch interface. In: ACM International Joint Conference, pp. 839–847 (2015)
7. Xiao, R., Laput, G., Harrison, C.: Expanding the input expressivity of smart-watches with mechanical pan, twist, tilt and click, pp. 193–196 (2014)
8. Perrault, S.T., Lecolinet, E., Eagan, J., Guiard, Y.: Watchit: simple gestures and eyes-free interaction for wristwatches and bracelets. In: SIGCHI Conference on Human Factors in Computing Systems, pp. 1451–1460 (2013)
9. Chen, K.Y., Lyons, K., White, S., Patel, S.: uTrack: 3D input using two magnetic sensors. Springer (2015)

10. Chan, L., Liang, R.H., Tsai, M.C., Cheng, K.Y., Su, C.H., Chen, M.Y., Cheng, W.H., Chen, B.Y.: FingerPad: private and subtle interaction using fingertips. In: ACM User Interface Software and Technology Symposium, pp. 255–260 (2013)
11. Chen, K.Y., Patel, S., Keller, S.: Finexus: tracking precise motions of multiple fingertips using magnetic sensing. In: CHI Conference on Human Factors in Computing Systems, pp. 1504–1514 (2016)
12. Lecun, Y., Bottou, L., Bengio, Y., Haffner, P.: Gradient-based learning applied to document recognition. Proc. IEEE **86**(11), 2278–2324 (1998)
13. Krizhevsky, A., Sutskever, I., Hinton, G.E.: Imagenet classification with deep convolutional neural networks. In: International Conference on Neural Information Processing Systems, pp. 1097–1105 (2012)
14. Zhang, M., Yang, P., Tian, C., Shi, L., Tang, S., Xiao, F.: Soundwrite. In: The International Workshop, pp. 13–17 (2015)
15. https://en.wikipedia.org/wiki/Mel-frequency_cepstrum

On the Use of Smart Wearable Technology for Gynecology and Obstetrics Care

Shang-Yun Sun[1(✉)], Chung-Chin Lin[2,3], and Jie Wang[4]

[1] Department of Innovation Center, Y-FA Technology Co., Ltd.,
Taoyuan, Taiwan (R.O.C.)
sunshangyun@yfa.com.tw
[2] Department of Computer Science and Information Engineering,
Chang Gung University, Taoyuan, Taiwan (R.O.C.)
cclin@mail.cgu.edu.tw
[3] Department of Neurology, Chang Gung Memorial Hospital Linkou Medical
Center and College of Medicine, Taoyuan, Taiwan (R.O.C.)
[4] School of Software Technology, Dalian University of Technology,
Dalian 116620, China
wangjie1003@163.com

Abstract. This paper applies Smart Wearable Technology (SWT) to Gynecology and Obstetrics Care, to protect new born babies from being stolen. We designed a wearable infant bracelet based on Bluetooth Low Energy (BLE) technology which can monitor posture of baby, and built BLE Gateway (BLEG) network to collect broadcast data from the former; at the same time, we developed Infant Management Software System (IMSS) for indoor positioning and events classification. We also designed three experiments: Experiment A is to build RSSI-Distance Model of infant bracelet and the results show that the RSSI will attenuate with distance increasing within ten meters; Experiment B is to test the reliability of BLEG and the results show that two BLEGs cooperation can reduce the missing rate compared with only one BLEG; Experiment C is to evaluate three BLEG Threshold Configure Methods (BTCM) including Static, Half-Dynamic and Dynamic used in indoor positioning and the results show that Dynamic is the best method of three Methods by miss rate of 3.66%. The product of this paper has been applied to the fourth hospital of Shijiazhuang City.

Keywords: Wearable Technology · Bluetooth Low Energy · Infant bracelet
BLE Gateway · Infant Management Software System · RSSI-Distance Model
BLEG Threshold Configure Method

1 Introduction

Since October 2015, China has implemented a comprehensive two-child policy. The number of newborns has increased year by year, and the phenomenon of adding extra beds in maternity hospitals has become even more serious which brings much confusing to gynecology and obstetrics. Moreover, most of hospitals are lack of objective management methods other than security guard. As a result, the baby's safety cannot be guaranteed.

© ICST Institute for Computer Sciences, Social Informatics and Telecommunications Engineering 2018
L. Wang et al. (Eds.): QShine 2017, LNICST 234, pp. 218–227, 2018.
https://doi.org/10.1007/978-3-319-78078-8_22

Automatic Identification System (AIS) such as Bar codes and Radio Frequency Identification (RFID) are applied to logistics [1], transportation [2], medical [3], access control [4]. According to the survey, wearing double RFID tags still has a probability of 3% cannot be identified, wearing only one RFID tag just has correct recognition rate of 78% [5, 6]. In addition, RFID signal is of direction and easy to be blocked [7]. Taking these into account, Apple Inc. proposed a new technology called iBeacon [8] based on Bluetooth Low Energy [9] in 2013, which is widely used in indoor positioning [10, 11] and Identification. Smart phones are frequently carried by peoples, and there is a lot of research on the use of mobile phone APP for health monitoring [12, 13]. Bluetooth is an effective way to send data from wearable device to smartphone compared to RFID. In this work, we want to develop a product based on SWT and BLE for Gynecology and Obstetrics Care which should include wearable infant bracelet, monitoring network, algorithm, safety design, software. In addition, we also need to verify this product through experiments.

2   Methods

2.1   Infant Bracelet Design

The hardware of infant bracelet is made up of three main modules, it reads data from three-axis accelerometer module to collect the baby's moving signal, and uses the master module to measure the battery voltage and potential difference between two wrist strap contacts, then broadcasts data together out via the BLE module. The accelerometer adopts the MC3410 manufactured by the mCube which communicates with the master module via the IIC. The master module uses the nRF51822 manufactured by Nordic Semiconductor with a BLE module included. The hardware structure of infant bracelet shows in Fig. 1.

As shown in Fig. 2, the components of infant bracelet consist of PCBA, battery, shell and conductive wrist strap. The button battery CR1620 of standard voltage of 3 V, is assembled on one PCBA side; The conductive wrist strap can be adjusted to

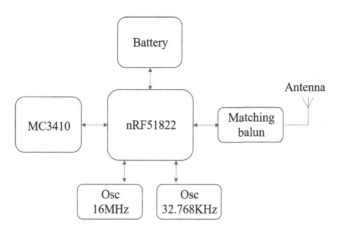

Fig. 1. Hardware structure diagram

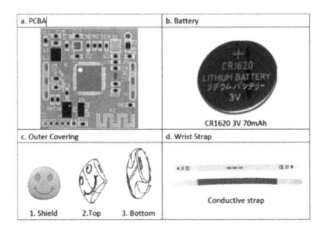

Fig. 2. Components of infant braceletHeadings.

match the baby wrist, and its conductive characteristics is designed to contact PCBA as a circuit to prevent malicious removal.

2.2   BLEG Network

The BLEG used in this study is xbeacon_cloud produced by Lan-ke-Xun-Tong Technology Inc. as shown in Fig. 3, which is powered by POE. It transmits the collected data broadcasted from infant bracelet to the server through Ethernet with TCP/IP protocol. The system network is shown in Fig. 4.

Fig. 3. xbeacon_cloud

2.3   Algorithm Design

Indoor Positioning Algorithm. In this study, an algorithm based on RSSI is proposed. The algorithm is divided into three steps: (1) Ten-Point Window Processing, remove the maximum and minimum value of RSSI in ten points before the current point, then calculate the average RSSI value of remaining eight points as the current point value; (2) Threshold Comparison, position the bracelet in the BLEG coverage area if the current time RSSI value is greater than the BLEG Threshold; (3) Intersection BLEG RSSI Comparison, the infant bracelet's signal may be monitored by multiple BLEGs, in this case, the location of the BLEG of greater RSSI will be current position unless the bracelet is detected by a senior BLEG arranged at the exit.

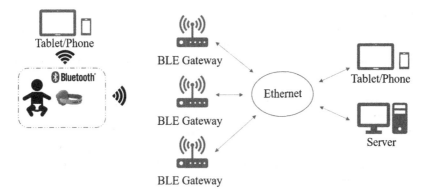

Fig. 4. System network

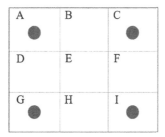

Fig. 5. 3 * 3 range

BTCM. This study uses Dynamic BTCM for each BLEG. In the case of Fig. 5, the space is divided into 3 * 3 range, BLEG is arranged at position E, and the reference transmitter (infant bracelet label) is arranged in the region A, C, G and I. Threshold of BLEG is updated with the minimum RSSI value of four reference transmitters every hour.

2.4 Safety Design

BLEG Filter. There are many other BLE devices in the actual field, which increase the pressure of the BLEG and affect the system performance. Therefore, this study adds a filter function in the BLEG to distinguish infant bracelet from other devices by Bluetooth name.

BLEG Layout of Dangerous Area. The dangerous area is set as the boundary of the monitoring range. This study requires accurate and timely detection of infants through this area. In order to reduce the detection miss rate, two complementary BLEGs are arranged.

BLEG Grade. In this study, BLEG is divided into three grades: Safety BLEG is arranged in ward and corridor, which has the most number and monitors infant gesture, position and bracelet status; Nurse Station BLEG is used for pairing infant bracelet and baby data; Dangerous Area BLEG of the highest grade is to monitor whether there are babies cross its coverage.

Events Classification. This study classifies events which may occur on bracelet and baby into five: Crossing Dangerous Area (CDA), Wrist Strap Cut (WSC), Bracelet Undetected (BU), Low Power (LP), Moving Posture (MP). The responses of the different events including Dangerous Area Alarm (DAA), Nurse Station Alarm (NSA), Nurse Station APP Notification (NSAN) and Nurse/Mom APP Notification (N/MAN) are shown in Table 1.

Table 1. Events response classification

Events	Notification platform			
	DAA	NSA	NSAN	N/MAN
CDA	✓	✓	✓	✓
WSC		✓	✓	✓
BC		✓	✓	✓
LP			✓	✓
MP			✓	✓

2.5   Software Design

This study designed IMSS such as Nurses Station Management System (NSMS) on Windows platform and Nurse/Mom APP on Android platform, as shown in Fig. 6. NSMS software has features including baby status monitoring, go out application, bracelet pairing, BLEG setting, event history and so on. Nurse APP can monitor all baby's statuses. Mother can use APP to look after their babies.

Infant Bracelet Pairing. In this research an innovation pairing method is proposed as can be seen in Fig. 7: type baby's information in NSMS; wake up bracelet by using conductive wrist strap to connect it; click on the pairing button on the software interface and shake the bracelet; write MAC of bracelet into database and complete pairing.

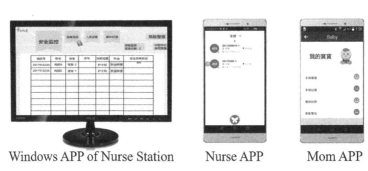

Windows APP of Nurse Station   Nurse APP   Mom APP

Fig. 6. APP of multi platforms

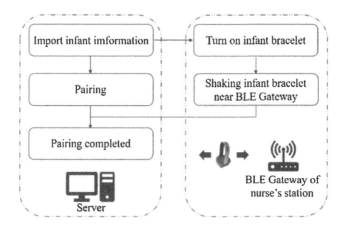

Fig. 7. Bracelet pairing flow diagram

Nurse/Mom Phone Registering. This study uses UUID read by Nurse/Mom APP to distinguish between different mobile devices. Type the work id of nurse or the case id of mother into their APP to register (see Fig. 8).

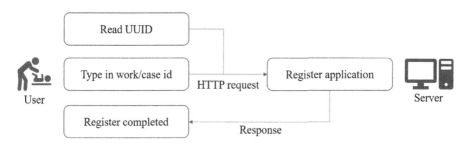

Fig. 8. Flow diagram of phone registering

3   Experiments

3.1   RSSI-Distance Model

Experiment Description. The purpose of this experiment is to establish a RSSI-Distance Model of infant bracelet using an indoor square of twenty meters long and ten meters wide for the test field. A BLEG is placed in the square center with eighty centimeters height position. The fifteen infant bracelets are placed two, five, eight and ten meters away from the BLEG with 100 RSSI data recorded each time. At last, we calculates the mean value of RSSI to establish the RSSI-Distance Model.

Results. Results show that RSSI value is linearly related to distance between infant bracelet and BLEG in the range of ten meters (see Table 2), and the signal is too weak for more than ten meters.

Table 2. RSSI-distance model

Distance	RSSI
<2	>−88
2–5	−93–−88
5–8	−95–−93
8–10	−110–−95
>10	Very wake

3.2   BLEG Reliability Test

Experiment Description. This test is conducted to test the reliability of the BLEG in the dangerous area by changing the number of infant bracelets (one, five, ten and thirteen) and the speed of crossing the region (walk, jog and sprint). The average speed of walk is about 0.99 m/s, jog about 2.61 m/s, sprint about 4.97 m/s. Test area is a corridor of twenty meters long and 2.5 meters wide, as shown in Fig. 9. BLEGs are arranged in the middle of the corridor on both sides with a radius of five meters range. The tester carries infant bracelets through the corridor from the left side to the right side ten times under the same condition and records the miss rate by Eq. 1.

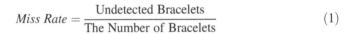

$$Miss\ Rate = \frac{Undetected\ Bracelets}{The\ Number\ of\ Bracelets} \tag{1}$$

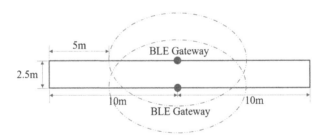

Fig. 9. Testing area

Results. The test results of single and two BLEG under different test pressures are shown in Table 3. Increasing in the number of bracelets and the speed will make the miss rate rise, and the cooperation of two BLEGs can reduce the miss rate.

3.3   BTCM Evaluating

Experiment Description. The purpose of this experiment is to analyze the effect of different BTCM on positioning accuracy. BTCM are divided into Static, Half-Dynamic and Dynamic. The Static uses the minimum RSSI value of the bracelet as the threshold for the first time; The Dynamic takes the minimum RSSI value of four reference

Table 3. Miss rate (%) of detecting

BLEG	Bracelet numbers	Crossing speed		
		Walk	Jog	Sprint
BLEG A	1	0	0	20
	5	0	2	4
	10	0	2	9
	13	0	1.53	14.61
BLEG B	1	0	0	0
	5	0	0	6
	10	0	1	13
	13	0.77	1.53	18.46
BLEG A&B	1	0	0	0
	5	0	0	0
	10	0	0	3.03
	13	0	0	4.61

bracelets as a threshold every hour; The Half-Dynamic updates the threshold with the mean of the previous day's Dynamic threshold. Position area is a square of seven meters long side with wall thickness of fifteen centimeters, as shown in Fig. 10 A–I. Reference bracelets are place at A, C, G and I. The BLEG is placed at position E. The eleven test infant bracelet are placed in the A–D, F–L area. Three minutes of data is recorded each time.

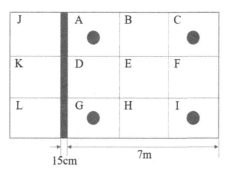

Fig. 10. Position area

Results. The positioning error rate calculated by Eq. 2 corresponding to the three BTCMs is shown in Table 4. The average error rate of Static is 5.19%; The Half-Dynamic is 3.92%; The Dynamic is 3.77%. The results show that the Dynamic method can improve the positioning accuracy.

Table 4. Error rate (%) of position

Area	Threshold config methods		
	Static	Half-dynamic	Dynamic
A	0	0	0
B	4.75	4.75	2.97
C	0.24	0.24	0.24
D	0.74	0.98	0.49
F	6.52	4.83	5.56
G	10.86	8.84	5.56
H	6.37	4.66	5.15
I	20.2	11.22	14.46
J	0	0	0
K	0	0	0
L	5.82	6.58	5.82
Average	5.04	3.82	3.66

$$Error\ Rate = \frac{\text{The Number of Error Positioning Bracelets}}{\text{The Number of Bracelets}} \qquad (2)$$

4   Conclusion

In this study, we have designed an infant bracelet device, established monitoring network and developed IMSS.

Furthermore, We have designed three experiments to verify our system: First, we designed RSSI-Distance Model experiment to verify the relationship between RSSI and distance, and results showed that the RSSI will attenuate with distance increasing within ten meters; Second, we designed BLEG Reliability Test with pressure of different number of infant bracelets and speed of crossing, and results showed that the cooperation of two BLEGs can reduce the miss rate of 4.61% compared with 14.61% and 18.46% of only one BLEG; Last, we designed an experiment to evaluate three BTCMs, and results showed that the average error rate of Static is 5.04%, the Half-Dynamic is 3.82%, and the Dynamic is 3.66% which is the best.

The product of this paper has been applied to the fourth hospital in Shijiazhuang City.

The shortcomings of this study are as follows: (1) The accuracy of positioning algorithm should to be improved due to indoor positioning is easily impacted by environment. but this is limited by the bottleneck of Bluetooth technology. (2) This study only takes into account CDA, WSC, BU, LP, and MP five events, but the actual case will be more complex.

References

1. Yan, Q.: Research on fresh produce food cold chain logistics tracking system based on RFID. Adv. J. Food Sci. Technol. **7**(3), 191–194 (2015)
2. Al-Lawati, A., Al-Jahdhami, S., Al-Belushi, A., et al.: RFID-based system for school children transportation safety enhancement. In: GCC Conference and Exhibition, pp. 1–6. IEEE (2015)
3. Li, X., Yao, D., Pan, X., et al.: Activity recognition for medical teamwork based on passive RFID. In: IEEE International Conference on RFID. IEEE (2016)
4. Woo-Garcia, R.M., Lomeli-Dorantes, U.H., López-Huerta, F., et al.: Design and implementation of a system access control by RFID. In: Engineering Summit, II Cumbre Internacional De Las Ingenierias, pp. 1–4. IEEE (2016)
5. Lo, N.W., Weh, K.H.: Anonymous coexistence proofs for RFID tags. J. Inf. Sci. Eng. **26**(4), 1213–1230 (2010)
6. Jarvis, M., Tarlow, B.: Wi-Fi position fix. European Patent Application EP 2 574 954 A1, March 2013
7. Stamatescu, G., Sgarciu, V.: Evaluation of wireless sensor network monitoring for indoor spaces. In: 2012 International Symposium on Instrumentation and Measurement, Sensor Network and Automation (IMSNA), vol. 1, pp. 107–111 (2012)
8. Newman, N.: Apple iBeacon technology briefing. J. Direct Data Digit. Mark. Pract. **15**(3), 222–225 (2014)
9. Bluetooth SIG Core Specification v4.1 (2013)
10. Fard, H.K., Chen, Y., Son, K.K.: Indoor positioning of mobile devices with agile iBeacon deployment. In: Electrical and Computer Engineering, pp. 275–279. IEEE (2015)
11. Rida, M.E., Liu, F., Jadi, Y., et al.: Indoor location position based on bluetooth signal strength. In: International Conference on Information Science and Control Engineering, pp. 769–773. IEEE (2015)
12. Higgins, J.P.: Smartphone applications for patients' health and fitness. Am. J. Med. **129**(1), 11–19 (2016)
13. Wang, J., Wang, Y., Wei, C., et al.: Smartphone interventions for long-term health management of chronic diseases: an integrative review. Telemed. J. E Health **20**(6), 570–583 (2014)

TALENTED: An Advanced Guarantee Public Order Tool for Urban Inspectors

Mingchu Li[(✉)], Gang Tian, and Kun Lu

School of Software Technology, Dalian University of Technology, Dalian, China
mingchul@dlut.edu.cn

Abstract. In the streets of Chinese cities, we often see that illegal pedlars sell some fake and inferior products such as outdated food and inferior household goods to people who do not know about this, which may cause serious health problem. Besides, pedlars often cause people to gather and so may lead to traffic accidents. Thus, there are great requirements how to control illegal pedlars, and how to analyze, model and predict illegal pedlars activities. Such research will help urban inspectors decide better strategies to guarantee public order. Thus, in this paper, we explore this problem, and propose a model called TALENTED (Target Attributes LEarNing model with TEmporal Dependence) to deal with the problem. TALENTED provides three main contributions. First, a new learning model is proposed to predict the probability of each target being attacked, and our model consists of three aspects: (i) This model considers a richer set of domain features; (ii) Adversaries' previous behaviors affect their new actions; (iii) Each target has different attributes and the adversaries weight them differently. Second, we adopt a game-theoretic algorithm to compute the defender's optimal strategy. Finally, simulation results illustrate the reasonability and validity of our new model.

Keywords: Learning model · Public order
Stackelberg Security Game

1 Introduction

In the cities of China, illegal pedlars often sell fake and inferior products (household goods and outdated food) to people who do not know about these products in relatively prosperous places with the large flow of people, which may cause serious health problem. Besides, pedlars often cause people to gather and so may contribute to traffic accidents (as shown in Fig. 1(a)). We call the pedlars illegal sale problem as public order problem. To address the problem, the governments have to send urban inspectors to patrol the street and to catch the illegal pedlars (as shown in Fig. 1(b)) to maintain public order. Thus how to assign limited resources of urban inspectors to monitor these illegal actions is a very important issue problem for Chinese governments. In this paper, we model

© ICST Institute for Computer Sciences, Social Informatics and Telecommunications Engineering 2018
L. Wang et al. (Eds.): QShine 2017, LNICST 234, pp. 228–237, 2018.
https://doi.org/10.1007/978-3-319-78078-8_23

this problem using Stackelberg game, and propose a model called TALENTED (Target Attributes LEarNing model with TEmporal Dependence). Our TAL-ENTED is to help urban inspectors improve patrol efficiency such that illegal pedlars are deterred from selling in the streets of the city. In addition, different patrol strategies are generated for urban inspectors according to the distribution of illegal pedlars. However, illegal pedlars, in turn, can continually conduct surveillance on the urban inspectors' patrol strategy and then change the places of selling accordingly. Thus urban inspectors and pedlars form a game. As the urban inspectors, their primary objectives are to stop illegal sale, and their main method of doing so is to patrol the streets of city. During a patrol, urban inspectors will catch illegal pedlars who sell in the streets, confiscate any fake and inferior products, and a corresponding fine is imposed on the illegal pedlars. Therefore, it is important to help the urban inspectors to identify and predict the most likely spots/locations of illegal pedlars and to generate patrolling strategies so that public order problem is solved.

Defender-attacker Stackelberg Security Game (SSG) has been successfully applied to infrastructure security problems and wildlife protection [1–4]. In SSGs, In SSGs, the defender attempts to allocate her limited resources to protect a set of targets against the adversary who plans to attack one of the targets. Several models have been proposed to protect against perfectly rational and bounded rational adversaries [5–7]. In fact, previous work which (such as SSG-based anti-poaching tool called PAWS [3]) has been successfully applied in the wildlife protection domain. However, PAWS still has some limitations. First, PAWS is based on an existing adversary behavior model named as Subjective Utility Quantal Response (SUQR) [3], which has several limitations: (i) This model just relies on three domain attributes which can not provide a detailed description of the impact of environmental and topographic features on the poachers' behaviors; (ii) Poachers' activities are independent between time periods; (iii) The parameter which measures the weight of each factor in the decision making process for adversary is a single parameter vector. Second, in PAWS, the utility of players at each target is fixed. Actually, the utilities of players at each target vary with the migration of animals in real world.

Motivated by the success of defender-attacker (SSG) applications, we model the pedlars' illegal deal problem as a SSG, in which the urban inspectors play as the defenders and the illegal pedlars are the attackers. The regions where illegal pedlars often appear represents a target. In essence, TALENTED (Target Attributes LEarNing model with TEmporal Dependence) attempts to address all aforementioned limitations in PAWS while providing the following two key contributions. First, TALENTED attempts to address SUQR's limitations in modeling adversary behavior. More specifically, TALENTED introduces a new behavioral model based on softmax [8] to predict illegal pedlars' actions, and consists of three aspects: (i) This model considers a richer set of domain features in addition to the three features used in SUQR in analyzing the probability of each target being attacked; (ii) We incorporate the dependence of the illegal pedlars' behavior on their activities in the past into the component for predicting the probability of each target being attacked; (iii) In our new learning model, each target has different attributes and the adversaries weight them differently. Second, TALENTED presents the dynamic rewards and penalties of defenders functions according to the number of illegal pedlars. In detail, the number of illegal pedlars corresponds to the number of rewards and penalties of the urban inspectors, and defenders generate patrol strategies according to the distribution of adversaries. At the same time, the patrol strategies of defenders also affect adversaries' decisions. Therefore, the rewards or penalties of the defenders vary at each target in different period.

(a) Illegal pedlars sell on the street   (b) Urban inspectors catch illegal pedlar

Fig. 1. Illegal pedlars and urban inspectors

The rest of the paper is structured as follows. In Sect. 2, we give the domain description. In Sect. 3, we introduce our new learning model. In Sect. 4, we give the game-theoretic algorithm of computing the defender's optimal strategy. In Sect. 5, the results of simulation and performance analysis are presented. In Sect. 6, our conclusions are presented.

2   Domain

In China, we often see that illegal pedlars sell some fake and inferior products (household goods and outdated food) in the streets of the city, and often cause people to gather and so may lead to traffic accidents. To deal with the problem, the urban inspectors have to patrol the streets and catch the illegal pedlars. In addition to their normal patrol duties, urban inspectors also collect and analyze data on illegal pedlars' activities. These data will be used to obtain best patrol strategies for urban inspectors.

In the public order domain, the urban inspectors plays as the leaders and the illegal pedlars are the followers. City area is divided into grids, where each cell represents an attack target and contains potential customers for illegal pedlars. Note that each cell represents $1 \, km^2$ (maybe less or more according to different city's requirement). An attack is that illegal pedlars sell items in the cell. If illegal pedlars attack a target which is uncovered by urban inspector, they receive a reward which is related to the number of potential customers in the target. Otherwise, they receive a penalty which corresponds to the fine being caught. At the same time, if urban inspectors patrol a target, they receive a dynamic reward which corresponds to the total fine received from the captured illegal pedlars. Otherwise, they receive a dynamic penalty. The dynamic rewards and penalties of defenders would vary with the number of adversaries in each target distribution. The purpose of the illegal pedlars is to sell as many goods as possible and not to be caught. Therefore, the flow of people, the flourishing degree of target and the urban inspectors' patrol strategies have an impact on illegal pedlars' decisions. Moreover, for a long-term benefit, illegal pedlars may tend to come back to the areas where they have attacked before. Our work will focus on incorporating all these factors into our model. Because of limited resources, urban inspectors can not patrol all potential targets. Thus, we propose a model called TALENTED to aid patrol managers and determine an optimal strategy so that urban inspectors can effectively cover these numerous places with their limited resources.

3   Behavioral Learning

As we know, in order to guarantee public order, we need to study a model to analyze and predict the probability of each target being attacked so that urban inspectors can effectively decide their strategies to solve public order problem. This paper introduces a new behavioral model to predict the probability of each target being attacked for urban inspectors in the public order domain.

In the public order domain, there are many illegal pedlars in the urban streets of China that affect urban transportation, city sanitation and public health. The public order domain is different from wildlife protection or illegal fishing [3,5,9,10]. We choose to represent the regions as targets, where illegal pedlars often appear. Therefore, we assume that all targets must be attacked. Specially, the new learning model is proposed to predict the probability of each target being attacked, and learn the different weights for each factor different target. This new model helps urban inspectors to find the attacked targets which is most likely attacked, and to generate their patrol strategies.

3.1   Proposed Model

We use K to denote the set of locations that can be targeted by the illegal pedlars, where $i \in K$ represents the ith target. We denote by M the number of resources, N the number of adversaries, L the number of domain features, and T the number of time periods. Overall, each target has a set of feature values $t_i = \{t_i^l\}$, where $l = 1, \ldots, L$ and t_i^l is the value of the lth feature at target i. In our model, we adopt five domain features: road number, number of residential areas, visitors flow rate, market distance, and station distance which impact illegal pedlars' decisions. In addition, $x_{t,i}$ is defined as the coverage probability of the resources in time period t on target i. Moreover, at each time step t, N^t is defined as the total number of illegal pedlars at all targets, N_i^t is defined as the number of illegal pedlars at target i, at time period t. In other words, we have $N^t = \sum_{i \in K} N_i^t$, and $N_i^t > 0$ for all time step t.

Our new model considers poachers' behavior to be dependent between different time steps, we incorporate the dependence of the illegal pedlars behavior into their activities in the past, as illegal pedlars may tend to come back to the areas where they have attacked before. Therefore, we define the exponential update function to describe the degree of target i being attacked at the past time period $(p'_{t-1,i})$. We evaluate the impact of illegal pedlars' activities in the previous period and prior behavior in the past period. Furthermore, the exponential update function of target i before time period t is shown as Eq. (1):

$$p'_{t-1,i} = \begin{cases} \alpha p'_{t-2,i} + (1-\alpha)\frac{N_i^{t-1}}{N^{t-1}} & \text{if } t > 2 \\ \frac{N_i^{t-1}}{N^{t-1}} & \text{if } t = 2 \end{cases}, \tag{1}$$

where α is the weight factor, and $0 \leq \alpha \leq 1$. Moreover, $\frac{N_i^{t-1}}{N^{t-1}}$ indicates illegal pedlars' activities in the previous period at each target. In other words, $\frac{N_i^{t-1}}{N^{t-1}}$ is the ratio of target i being attacked at time period $t-1$; $p'_{t-2,i}$ indicates the exponential update function of target i at time step $t-2$. N_i^{t-1} and N^{t-1} are the data which is collected in the past time period.

To predict the probability of each target being attacked, we adopt the softmax regression model which takes int account the several factors above. Thus, given the urban inspectors' coverage probability of target i at time period t: $x_{t,i}$, the exponential update function of target i in the past time step: $p'_{t-1,i}$, and the domain features: $t_i = \{t_i^l\}$, we aim at predicting the probability of target i being attacked at time period t as Eq. (2):

$$p(k = i | 1, x_{t,i}, p'_{t-1,i}, t_i) = \frac{e^{\theta_i^T [1, x_{t,i}, p'_{t-1,i}, t_i]}}{\sum_j e^{\theta_j^T [1, x_{t,j}, p'_{t-1,j}, t_j]}}, \tag{2}$$

where $k \in K$, and $\theta_i = \{\theta_{ij}\}$ is the $(L+3) \times 1$ parameter vector of target i which measures the importance of all factors with the target i being attacked and L are the number of domain features. θ_{ij} is the jth parameter in θ_i. θ_{i1} is the free parameter and θ_i^T is the transpose vector of θ_i. $\theta = \{\theta_1^T, \ldots, \theta_K^T\}^T$ is the parameter matrix of all targets. In essence, our new model learns all targets' weights for target attributes in predicting the probability of each target being attacked at the same time.

3.2   Parameter Estimation

We employ Maximum Likelihood Estimation (MLE) to learn the parameters matrix $\theta = \{\theta_1^T, \ldots, \theta_K^T\}^T$ for each target [11]. First we formulate the log-likelihood of softmax, given the defender strategy $\mathbf{x} = \{x_{t,i}\}$, and a set of samples of the adversaries choices as Eq. (3):

$$\log L(\theta) = \sum_n \log \prod (p(y^{(n)} = i|\theta))^{1 \cdot \{y^{(n)} = i\}}, \tag{3}$$

where $y^{(n)}$ is the nth sample, i is the chosen target in that sample, and $p(y^{(n)} = i|\theta)$ presents the probability that the target i is chosen in Eq. (2), $1 \cdot \{y^{(n)} = i\}$ is indicative function, if $y^{(n)} = i$ is true, $1 \cdot \{y^{(n)} = i\} = 1$, otherwise, $1 \cdot \{y^{(n)} = i\} = 0$. Then we have:

$$\log L(\theta) = \sum_n \sum_i 1 \cdot \{y^{(n)} = i\} \log\left(\frac{e^{\theta_i^{\mathrm{T}}[1,x_{t,i},p'_{t-1,i},t_i]}}{\sum_j e^{\theta_j^{\mathrm{T}}[1,x_{t,j},p'_{t-1,j},t_j]}}\right) \qquad (4)$$

Essentially, we can see that $\log L(\theta)$ in Eq. (4) is a concave function, this function has an unique local maximum point, since the Hessian matrix is negative semi-definite. Thus, we can compute the optimal weights matrix $\theta = \{\theta_1^{\mathrm{T}}, \ldots, \theta_K^{\mathrm{T}}\}^{\mathrm{T}}$ as follow.

$$\theta = arg \max_\theta \log L(\theta) \qquad (5)$$

4   Patrol Planning

Once the model parameter vector of each target $\theta_i = \{\theta_{ij}\}$ is learned, we can compute the optimal strategies for the urban inspectors in the next time period with the new learning model, given the urban inspectors patrol strategies and domain features.

In our model, the number of illegal pedlars corresponds to the number of rewards and penalties of the urban inspectors. Defenders generate patrol strategies according to the distribution of adversaries. At the same time, the patrol strategies of defenders also affect adversaries' decisions. Therefore, the rewards or penalties of the defenders vary at each target in different period. We call the rewards or penalties as dynamic rewards or penalties for urban inspectors.

At each time period, if urban inspectors patrol target i, they receive a dynamic reward $R_{t,i}^d$, otherwise they receive a dynamic penalty $P_{t,i}^d$. At the same time, if illegal pedlars attack target i which is covered by urban inspector, they receive a penalty P_i^a, otherwise, they receive a reward R_i^a. The dynamic rewards and penalties of defenders will vary with the number of adversaries in each target distribution at different time steps. Therefore, given the probability of each target being attack, if urban inspectors patrol target i at time period t, they receive a dynamic reward $R_{t,i}^d$. Their dynamic rewards are computed as Eq. (6):

$$R_{t,i}^d = p_{t,i} N_i^t, \qquad (6)$$

where $p_{t,i}$ is the abbreviations of the probability that target i is attacked at time period t in Eq. (2). Similarly, urban inspectors' dynamic penalty: $P_{t,i}^d = -R_{t,i}^d$.

In this paper, we consider a long-term benefit for the players. Suppose that N^t and N_i^t are known for the players, where $t = 1, \ldots, T$ and $i = 1, \ldots, K$. Similar to standard SSGs. We assume that if the urban inspectors patrol, they obtain a dynamic reward $R_{t,i}^d$, otherwise, they receive a dynamic penalty $P_{t,i}^d$. Therefore, at each time period, the urban inspectors' expected utility at target i is computed as Eq. (7):

$$U_{t,i}^d = x_{t,i} R_{t,i}^d + (1 - x_{t,i}) P_{t,i}^d \tag{7}$$

The purpose of the urban inspectors is to obtain the maximum expected utility. Thus, given the urban inspectors' patrol history data N^t and N_i^t, and the model parameters matrix θ, the problem of computing the optimal strategies $x_{t+1,i}$ for urban inspectors at the next time period $t + 1$ can be formulated as follows:

$$\max_{x_{t+1,i}} \sum_i U_{t+1,i}^d \tag{8}$$

$$s.t. \quad 0 \le x_{t+1,i} \le 1; \quad i \in K \tag{9}$$

$$\sum_i x_{t+1,i} \le M; \quad i \in K \tag{10}$$

where M is the total number of resources and $U_{t+1,i}^d$ is the urban inspectors' expected utility in Eq. (7), and K is the set of locations that can be targeted by the illegal pedlars.

Therefore, we can piecewise linearly approximate $U_{t+1,i}^d$ and represent (8–10) as a Mixed Integer Program which can be solved by CPLEX. The details of piecewise linear approximation can be found in [12]. Essentially, the piecewise linear approximation method provides an $O(\frac{1}{P})$-optimal solution for (8–10) where P is the number of piecewise segments [12].

5   Experiments

In this section, we aim to evaluate the solution quality and runtime of the TALENTED planning for generating patrols. The results are obtained using CPLEX to solve the MILP for TALENTED. All experiments are conducted on a standard 2.00 GHz machine with 4 GB main memory. In the following, we provide a brief description of experiment settings to our new model.

In the first time period, we randomly generate a defender strategy, then we simulate the target choices made by illegal pedlars according to the strategy. We call this process as a round of games. At next time period, we change the defender strategy according to the adversary's behavior. At each time period, we conduct 10 rounds game, after each period, we count up the number of illegal pedlars choosing each target i, N_i^t. We assume that these date are known by players. Then, we learn the parameter vector $\theta_i = \{\theta_{ij}\}$ for each target and compute the average expected utility of defenders and constantly update the parameter vector $\theta_i = \{\theta_{ij}\}$.

In both Fig. 2(a) and (b), the y-axis displays the average EU (Expected Utility) of the urban inspectors after each time period, and the x-axis displays the number of time period. In Fig. 2(a), we compare the average EU of TALENTED with stochastic strategy at different periods. In Fig. 2(b), we compare two different approaches: SUQR, and maximin strategy. In both Fig. 2(a) and (b), we set the number of adversaries to 200, the number of targets to 20, the number of resources to 5, and $\alpha = 0.25$ in Eq. (1). The parameter vector $\theta_i = \{\theta_{ij}\}$ are learned by our new model in Sect. 3.2. As shown in the figure, taking into account the dependence of the illegal pedlars behavior on their activities in the past is critical for urban inspectors to predict the probability of each target being attacked. TALENTED outperforms stochastic strategy, SUQR that just consider single parameter vector and independent adversaries activities between time periods and maximin strategy.

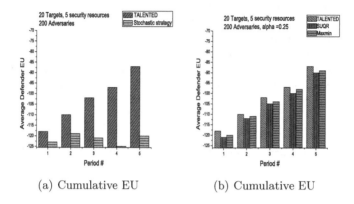

(a) Cumulative EU   (b) Cumulative EU

Fig. 2. Simulation results over period

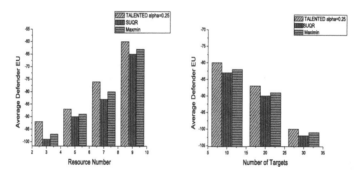

(a) 20 Targets, 200 Adversaries (b) 5 security resources, 200 Adversaries

Fig. 3. Comparing cumulative EU at period 5

Then, we compare the average EU achieved by the three different methods under different number of targets and different amount of resources. In both Fig. 3(a) and (b), the y-axis displays the average EU of the urban inspectors after 5 time periods. In both figures, we also simulate 200 illegal pedlars. In Fig. 3(a), we vary the number of resources on the x-axis while fixing the number of targets to 20. It shows that the average EU increases as more resources are added. In addition, TALENTED outperforms the other two approaches regardless of resource quantity. Similarly, we vary the number of targets on the x-axis in Fig. 3(b) while fixing the amount of resources to 5. The better performance of TALENTED over the other two methods can be seen from the figure regardless of the number of targets.

Furthermore, we give the runtime of our model. We present the runtime results in Fig. 4(a) and (b). In all two figures, the y-axis display the runtime, the x-axis displays the variables which we vary to measure their impact on the runtime of the algorithms. In both Fig. 4(a) and (b), M is the number of resources, N is the number of adversaries, and K is the set of targets. α is the weight factor in Eq. (1). We compare the runtime when $P = 5$, $P = 10$, and $P = 20$, where P is the number of piecewise segments in [12]. According to the two figures, we find that TALENTED can deal with large-scale problems and get better results.

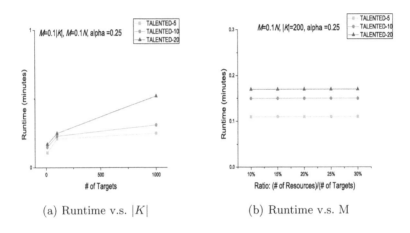

(a) Runtime v.s. $|K|$ (b) Runtime v.s. M

Fig. 4. Evaluate the runtime

6   Conclusions

As we know, pedlars' illegal deal problems seriously affect urban transportation and public health in China and may lead heavily transportation accidents. In this paper, we propose a new method called TALENTED to deal with the problem in public order domain, and will be applied in the Kaifa district of Dalian, China. TALENTED adopts a novel learning model which considers a richer set of domain features and incorporates the dependence of the illegal pedlars behavior into their activities in the past. Our new learning model can effectively predict the probability of each target being attacked in the public order domains. Moreover, we adopt a game-theoretic algorithm to compute the defender's optimal strategy. Finally, we have a large number of simulation experiments to testify the reasonability and validity of our new model. The experimental results demonstrate the superiority of our model compared to other existing models.

Acknowledgments. This paper is supported by Nature Science Foundation of China under grant No. 61572095.

References

1. Basilico, N., Gatti, N., Amigoni, F.: Leader-follower strategies for robotic patrolling in environments with arbitrary topologies. In: AAMAS (2009)
2. Ford, B., Brown, M., Yadav, A., Singh, A., Sinha, A., Srivastava, B., Kiekintveld, C., Tambe, M.: Protecting the NECTAR of the Ganga River through game-theoretic factory inspections. In: Demazeau, Y., Ito, T., Bajo, J., Escalona, M.J. (eds.) PAAMS 2016. LNCS (LNAI), vol. 9662, pp. 97–108. Springer, Cham (2016). https://doi.org/10.1007/978-3-319-39324-7_9
3. Yang, R., Ford, B., Tambe, M.: Adaptive resource allocation for wildlife protection against illegal poachers. In: Proceedings of the 2014 International Conference on Autonomous Agents and Multi-agent Systems, pp. 453–460. AAMAS (2014)
4. Nguyen, T.H., Sinha, A., Gholami, S.: CAPTURE: a new predictive anti-poaching tool for wildlife protection. In: Proceedings of the 2016 International Conference on Autonomous Agents and Multiagent Systems, pp. 767–775. AAMAS (2016)
5. Kar, D., Fang, F., Delle, F.F.: A game of thrones: when human behavior models compete in repeated Stackelberg security games. In: Proceedings of the 2015 International Conference on Autonomous Agents and Multiagent Systems, pp. 1381–1390. AAMAS (2015)
6. Kiekintveld, C., Jain, M., Tsai, J.: Computing optimal randomized resource allocations for massive security games. In: Proceedings of The 8th International Conference on Autonomous Agents and Multiagent Systems, pp. 689–696. AAMAS (2009)
7. Carthy, S., Marie, M., Tambe, M.: Preventing illegal logging: simultaneous optimization of resource teams and tactics for security. In: AAAI Conference on Artificial Intelligence (2016)
8. Duan, K., Keerthi, S.S., Chu, W., Shevade, S.K., Poo, A.N.: Multi-category classification by Soft-Max combination of binary classifiers. In: Windeatt, T., Roli, F. (eds.) MCS 2003. LNCS, vol. 2709, pp. 125–134. Springer, Heidelberg (2003). https://doi.org/10.1007/3-540-44938-8_13
9. Gholami, S., Wilder, B., Brown, M., Sinha, A.: A game theoretic approach on addressing collusion among human adversaries. In: Proceedings of the 2016 International Conference on Autonomous Agents and Multiagent Systems (2016)
10. Haskell, W.B., Kar, D., Fang, F.: Robust protection of fisheries with compass. In: AAAI, pp. 2978–2983 (2014)
11. Hastie, T., Tibshirani, R., Friedman, J.: The Elements of Statistical Learning. Springer Series in Statistics. Springer, Berlin (2001)
12. Yang, R., Ordonez, F., Tambe, M.: Computing optimal strategy against quantal response in security games. In: Proceedings of the 11th International Conference on Autonomous Agents and Multiagent Systems, pp. 847–854. AAMAS (2012)

Classification-Based Reputation Mechanism
for Master-Worker Computing System

Kun Lu$^{(\boxtimes)}$, Jingchao Yang, Haoran Gong, and Mingchu Li

School of Software Technology, Dalian University of Technology,
Dalian 116620, China
lukun@dlut.edu.cn

Abstract. Master-worker computing is a parallel computing scheme, which makes master and worker collaborate. Due to its high reliability availability and serviceability, it is widely used in scientific computing fields. However, lack of cooperation and malicious attack in Master-worker computing can greatly reduce the efficiency of parallel computing. In this paper, we consider a reputation system based on individual classification to inducing worker nodes returning true answer and separate malicious worker nodes. By introducing reinforcement learning, rational workers are induced to behave cooperatively and auditing rate of the master decreases. Our model is based on evolutionary game theory. Simulation results show that our reputation system can not only effectively guarantee eventual correctness, separate malicious worker nodes, but also save the master node's auditing cost.

Keywords: Node classification · Reinforcement learning · Reputation system

1 Introduction

The high-performance computing is needed in scientific field over past decades. Many internet-based systems are proposed over years, such as SETI [1], Turk [2], etc. Master-worker model (MW-model) [3] is a widely used high-performance computing model. In MW-model, there is one master node and several worker nodes. In each computing task, the master node first sends the task to all worker nodes; then worker nodes return a computing result; finally, master then evaluates each worker's results. Each worker node that helps computer the task may get a reward.

However, computing a task cost a lot of resources of each worker node, such as CPU and memory. Due to the rational nature, the worker nodes tend to re- turn random results without actual computation. Thus, incentivizing rational workers to perform cooperatively in distributed systems is a critical issue [4, 5].

Reward and punishment mechanisms [6–8] are most widely used mechanisms in promoting cooperation in MW-model. Generally, in MW-model, those cooperative worker nodes that return correct results are given extra rewards and those worker nodes

This paper is supported by the Liaoning Provincial National Science Foundation of China under grant No. 2017540158.

© ICST Institute for Computer Sciences, Social Informatics and Telecommunications Engineering 2018
L. Wang et al. (Eds.): QShine 2017, LNICST 234, pp. 238–247, 2018.
https://doi.org/10.1007/978-3-319-78078-8_24

return false results may be sanctioned a penalty. As mentioned before, worker nodes are treated as rational and strategic workers, game theory is an appropriate tool to model the nodes and interactions among them [9].

Preventing malicious attacks is a critical issue in MW-model. As worker nodes are rational, they tend to return false results. To solve this problem, Kondo et al. [15] proposed a classical solution to consider all workers are altruistic and proposed a malicious-tolerant protocol. However, malicious nodes intentionally send false results with complex behavior modes. A most common attack is persistent attack that a malicious node keeps sending false results to master node. One of the most dangerous attack is on-off attack, where malicious nodes send good and dangerous services in turn to keep reputation to a certain level. Only be tolerant to malicious attacks is not enough to guarantee system robustness. Reputation management systems are proved to be most effective to resist attacks. Generally, a reputation system relies on users' feedbacks: a worker node that provides a positive feedback. A worker node with a high reputation has a higher probability to be chosen as a correct result and to be rewarded. However, the effectiveness of getting accurate reputation is critical.

In this paper, we propose a classification based reputation system for master-worker computing scheme. Workers are divided into two types: type A and type B. Type A workers are those can be fully trusted and the master node takes their returned results as correct results in priority. And type B workers are those worker nodes with reputation less than 1. Type B workers can be promoted to Type A only if they continuously send correct results. Vice versa, Type A worker can be degrade to Type B if they send false results. Both worker and master nodes use enforcement learning to adapt cheating rate and audit rate. Simulation results show that, with our proposed mechanism, the system can quickly evolve to system eventual correctness and save master node's cost on auditing.

The rest of this paper is organized as follows. In Sect. 2, we introduce our system model in details. In Sect. 3, we present system evaluation results and analysis. In Sect. 4, we conclude this paper.

2   System Model

2.1   System Overview

In this paper, we consider a static internet-based master-worker system, where no worker nodes join and leave the system after initialization.

Consider that one master node distributes tasks to a set of W with n worker nodes. A subset Wc of workers return correct answer and a subset W_f of workers return false answer, where $W_c \subseteq W$ and $W_f = W \backslash W_c$. The computation of a task consists of multiple rounds. In each round, the master node sends a subtask to all worker nodes and the worker nodes return the result. Then, the master node evaluates the result, and reward worker nodes with correct answer and punish those with false answer.

The basic assumptions are as followings: (1) each subtask has one unique right answer and all false answers are same; (2) each worker node finishes a task individually;

(3) the goal of the master node is to get eventual correctness; (4) both the master node and worker nodes are rational, they participate in the system to maximize their own payoffs.

2.2   Game-Based Transaction Model

In our model, both master and worker nodes are rational and selfish, they are trying to maximize their benefits. Thus, Game theory is a suitable tool to model these nodes and interactions among them.

Computing is costly to the worker nodes. Thus, for each computing task, the cooperative worker node bears a WC_t (see Table 1) cost if it really does the computing. To incentive rational worker compute the tasks, the master node implements auditing, reward and punishment mechanism.

Table 1. Definition of notations

Notation	Definition
WB_y	reward of workers returning correct answer
WC_t	cost of a worker computing a task
WP_c	punishment of workers cheating
asp	worker's expect payoff
payoff$_i$	payoff of worker i
pA	master's specified probability of audition
a_m	the rate of master's reinforcement learning
a_w	workers' rate of reinforcement learning

Auditing mechanism refers to that the master node validates each worker node's returned result. Master node chooses a correct answer and rewards those worker nodes who return correct results by WB_y. However, validating process is costly. Thus, master node audits with a probability $p_A(t)$ at time t. However, to keep the system always robust, the master node remains a minimum auditing rate $p_A^{\min} > 0$.

Each time the master node audits, it recognizes worker nodes who returns right answer. Thus, to encourage computing, the master node gives each defective worker who returns false results a punishment WP_c in auditing rounds. Thus, payoff of a worker node i, payoff$_i$, is the total reward minus cost (or punishment) in auditing and non-auditing rounds as shown in Eq. 1.

$$
\text{payoff}_i =
\begin{cases}
-WC_t, & \text{if honest, not selected and not audit} \\
WB_y - WC_t, & \text{if honest, selected and not audit} \\
WB_y, & \text{if cheating, selected and not audit} \\
0, & \text{if cheating, not selected and not audit} \\
WB_y - WC_t, & \text{if honest, audit} \\
-WP_c, & \text{if cheating and audit}
\end{cases}
\tag{1}
$$

2.3   Reputation Mechanism

Reputation Usage. Reputation is measured by the master node, and the main usage of reputation in our proposed model is to select a correct answer. After collecting all received answers, the master node uses a "voting" method to select a right answer when no auditing mechanism is used.

In this voting mechanism, the master node chooses a correct answer with highest average reputation. For instance, suppose that there are 4 worker nodes with reputation 0.6 return answer "1" and 5 worker nodes with reputation 0.5 return answer "2", then the master node assumes "1" is the correct answer as the average reputation of those 4 worker nodes is higher. When there is a tie, the master node selects the correct answer randomly.

Comparison of Existing Reputation Algorithms. In this paper, we consider three different existing reputation algorithms. In the following sections, reputation of worker i at time t is denoted by $rep_i(t)$.

   Type 1 algorithm is a widely used simple reputation algorithm [13]. As shown in Eq. 2

$$rep_i(t) = \frac{v_i(t) + 1}{aud(t) + 2} \tag{2}$$

Type 2 algorithm is propose by Christoforou [12]. As shown in Eq. 3

$$rep_i(t) = \epsilon^{aud(t) - v_i(t)}, \epsilon \in (0, 1) \tag{3}$$

Type 3 is a reputation algorithm inspire by BONIC [14]. As shown in Algorithm 1

Algorithm 1. Type 3 Algorithm

Require: Transaction of each node i;
Ensure: Reputation of each node i
 1: **Step 1:**
 2: $\beta_i(t) = 0.1$
 3: **if** worker returns correct answer **then**
 4:     $\beta_i(t) = \beta_i(t) * 0.95$
 5: **else**
 6:     $\beta_i(t) = \beta_i(t) + 0.1$
 7: **end if**
 8: **Step 2:**
 9: **if** $\beta_i(t) > A$ **then**
10:     $rep_i(t) = 0.001$
11: **else**
12:     $rep_i(t) = 1 - \sqrt{\frac{\beta_i(t)}{A}}$
13: **end if**

Classification-Based Reputation Mechanism. In order to avoid aforementioned weakness in Type 1–3 reputation mechanisms, we propose a classification- based reputation mechanism, which is referred as **Type 4** in following parts.

In our proposed reputation mechanism, worker nodes are classified into two categories: WorkerA and WorkerB. WorkerA nodes are those node that can be fully trusted (for each WorkerA i, $rep_i = 1$) and WorkerB nodes are those with reputation $0 < rep_i < 1$.

Algorithm 2. Type 4 Algorithm

Require: Returning result of each node, S_i;
　　Number of each worker's accumulated returning correct answer, CT_i.
Ensure: Reputation and category of each node i
 1: // **Step 1:** Find WorkerA
 2: **for all** worker node i **do**
 3:　　Mark all of the WorkerA nodes
 4: **end for**
 5: //**Step 2:** Choose correct answer
 6: **if** There exists WorkerA nodes **then**
 7:　　**if** all workerA nodes have the same answer **then**
 8:　　　　Choose WorkerA's answer as a correct answer.
 9:　　**else**
10:　　　　Audit to find correct answer.
11:　　**end if**
12: **else**
13:　　Vote for a correct answer
14:　　Audit to find correct answer with probability p_A
15:　　GOTO **Step 3**
16: **end if**
17: //**Step 3:** Reputation Update
18: **for all** worker node i **do**
19:　　**if** worker node i returns correct answer **then**
20:　　　　**if** worker node i is of WorkerB **then**
21:　　　　　　**if** $CT_i >= M$ **then**
22:　　　　　　　　Node$_i$ promoted as WorkerA node
23:　　　　　　**end if**
24:　　　　**end if**
25:　　**else**
26:　　　　Set Node$_i$'s reputation to 0
27:　　**end if**
28: **end for**

As shown in Algorithm 2, classification-based reputation mechanism consists of three steps: (1) find WorkerA nodes (Lines 2–4); (2) choose correct answer (Lines 6–16); (3) reputation update (Lines 18–28).

2.4 Reinforcement Learning

As mentioned above, both master and worker nodes are rational. Thus to maximize correct rate for master node and payoff for worker nodes, reinforcement learning mechanism is introduced.

For master node in MW-model, it adjusts auditing rate according to all worker nodes' reputation. As shown in Eqs. 4 and 5. We use k to find whether the system is safe or not. If the system is considered to be safe, the auditing rate decreases. To ensure the system robustness, the master node maintains a minimum auditing rate p_A^{min}. Learning rate α_m indicates the speed of adjusting auditing rate: if α_m is large, then master node adjusts its auditing rate dramatically; if $\alpha_m = 0$, master node never adjusts auditing rate.

$$p_A(t+1) = \min\{1, \ \max\{p_A(t) - \alpha_m(k - T), \ p_A^{min}\}\} \tag{4}$$

$$k = \frac{\sum\limits_{i \in W_c} rep_i(t)}{\sum\limits_{j \in W} rep_j(t)} \tag{5}$$

For a worker node, it wants to maximize its payoff. This payoff depends on its own calculating computing task and master node's auditing actions (see Table 1). After receiving its payoff, each worker i adjusts its cheating rate pC_i by using Eq. 6. If its payoff is higher than its aspiration a_i, then it more prefers this action in the following rounds. S_i indicates the action of worker node i in this round, where $S_i = 1$ means i sends correct result in this round and $S_i = -1$ means it cheats. We assume each worker has the same learning rate α_w.

$$pC_i(t) = \max\{0, \ \min\{1, pC_i(t - 1) - \alpha_w(payof f_i - a_i)S_i\}\} \tag{6}$$

3 Simulation and Analysis

In this paper, we perform a simulation in a master-worker network with one master node and nine worker nodes. In each round of task, the worker node first distributes a task, then each worker node i returns a correct answer with the probability $1 - pC_i$ and a false answer with the probability pC_i. After worker nodes returning results, the master node performs auditing mechanism with the probability p_A. If master node audits, it updates each worker's reputation by different reputation mechanism (see Sect. 2, Type 1–4) and its own auditing rate using Eq. 4. After selecting correct answer, all worker nodes update payoff and cheating rate.

To validate the effectiveness of our proposed mechanism, we perform simulations in the following aspects: (1) fairness of evaluating reputation; (2) robustness under stochastic attacks; (3) cost of defending attacks. Without special emphasis, we use the parameters in Table 2 for following simulations. We mainly compare our results with

Table 2. Simulation parameters

Parameter	Value	Parameter	Value
WB_y	1	WC_t	0.1
WP_c	0	a_i in Eq. 6	0.1
$p_A(0)$	0.5	p_A^{min}	0.01
$p_C(0)$	0.5	a_m	0.1
a_w	1	ϵ (in Type 2)	0.01
τ (in Eq. 4)	0.5	M (in Type 4)	30

three types of reputation mechanisms mentioned in Sect. 2.3, and "Type 4" refers to our proposed reputation mechanism.

3.1 Effectiveness on Calculating Reputation

First of all, we capture the reputation dynamics of four different reputation algorithms. Figure 1 presents reputation dynamics of nine rational worker nodes.

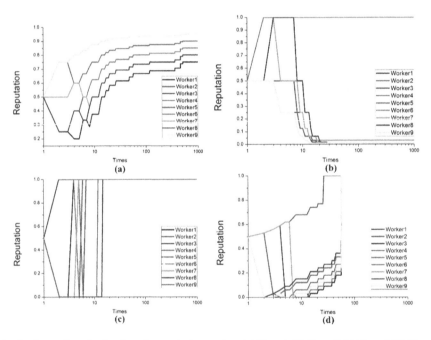

Fig. 1. Dynamics of rational worker nodes' repuation. (a) Type 1 (b) Type 2 (c) Type 3 (d) Type 4

In Type 1, 3 and 4 algorithms, finally, all rational worker nodes get a high reputation as they constantly return correct results. Type 1 and 4 algorithm has a stable reputation, however, type 3 algorithm has a dramatically dynamics due to its restrict punishment. In type 2 algorithm, due to the feature of function Eq. 3, once a worker node cheats, it can never raise its reputation again. In our proposed algorithm, there exists a mutation that a rational worker node may raise its reputation to 1 directly. That is due to its great performance by sending correct results constantly over 30 times. Thus, our proposed reputation mechanism can ensure that rational worker nodes who never cheat can have a very high reputation, so that the fairness of reputation algorithm can be guaranteed.

From the master node perspective, we capture the dynamics of audit times. As shown in Fig. 2, the speed of auditing times increasing decrease along with times. Due to reinforcement learning algorithm, the master node audits less in future rounds. Type 1, 3 and 4 algorithms perform better than type 2 as the total audit times of type 2 are much more than the other 3 algorithms.

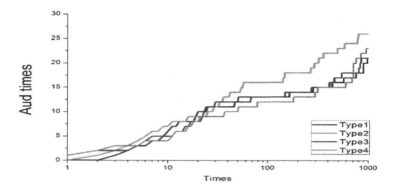

Fig. 2. Dynamics of master node's audit times.

Generally, our proposed type 4 algorithm has similar results to other three algorithms on guarantee reputation calculation fairness.

3.2 Effectiveness on Defending Attacks

In this section, we mainly discuss the robustness of reputation algorithms under stochastic attack.

A randomly chosen worker node performs as a malicious node, randomly selects 10 computing rounds to perform cheating action in the selected round and 9 rounds following this, total 100 rounds of cheating actions are performed by this chosen worker node.

As shown in Fig. 3, the three existing reputation algorithm have similar results shown in Fig. 1, which means these three algorithms are not sensitive to stochastic attacks. Thus, the malicious worker node that performs this stochastic attack cannot be found.

However, as shown in Fig. 4, our proposed algorithm successfully finds out that worker node 7 is a malicious node. In node 7's cheating rounds, this node's reputation is set to 0. So that a malicious worker is separated. Thus, our proposed model is very sensitive to stochastic attack and more effective on defending stochastic attack compared to other three algorithms.

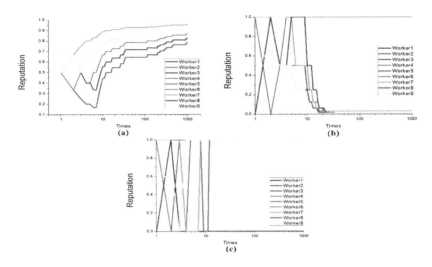

Fig. 3. Dynamics of reputation under stochastic attack. (a) Type 1 (b) Type 2 (c) Type 3

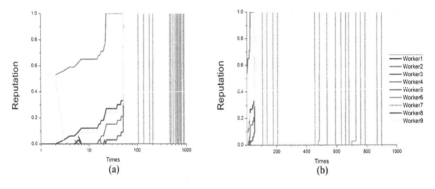

Fig. 4. Dynamics of reputation under stochastic attack with type 4 algorithm. (a) Normal version (b) Zoomin version

4   Conclusion and Future Work

In this paper, we propose a classification-based reputation mechanism. In our proposed mechanism, worker nodes are classified into two categories, which helps reduce master node's auditing cost. Simulation results show that our mechanism can more effectively induce rational worker nodes return correct answers and malicious nodes can be separated quickly.

Nevertheless, malicious attacks are complex in real systems. For further research, we will consider more realistic scenarios that worker nodes can collaborate to forge results and gain advantages from the master node. Thus, the prevention of more complex attack model is future research direction.

References

1. Korpela, E.J., et al.: SETI@home-massively distributed computing for SETI. Comput. Sci. Eng. **3**(1), 78–83 (2001)
2. Amazonas Mechanical Turk. https://www.mturk.com
3. Goux, J.P., et al.: An enabling framework for master-worker applications on the computational grid, vol. 4(1), pp. 43–50 (2000)
4. Anta, A.F., Georgiou, C., Mosteiro, M.A., Pareja, D.: Multi-round master-worker computing: a repeated game approach. In: 2016 IEEE 35th Symposium on Reliable Distributed Systems (SRDS), pp. 31–40. IEEE, September 2016
5. Christoforou, E., Anta, A.F., Georgiou, C., Mosteiro, M.A.: Algorithmic mechanisms for reliable master-worker internet-based computing. IEEE Trans. Comput. **63**(1), 179–195 (2014)
6. Nguyen, T.T.H., Brun, O., Prabhu, B.J.: Performance of a fixed reward incentive scheme for two-hop DTNs with competing relays: short talk. ACM SIGMETRICS Perform. Eval. Rev. **44**(3), 39 (2017)
7. Seregina, T., Brun, O., El-Azouzi, R., Prabhu, B.J.: On the design of a reward-based incentive mechanism for delay tolerant networks. IEEE Trans. Mob. Comput. **16**(2), 453–465 (2017)
8. Lu, K., Wang, S., Xie, L., Wang, Z., Li, M.: A dynamic reward-based incentive mechanism: reducing the cost of P2P systems. Knowl. Based Syst. **112**, 105–113 (2016)
9. Gupta, R., Somani, A.K.: Game theory as a tool to strategize as well as predict nodes' behavior in peer-to-peer networks. In: International Conference on Parallel and Distributed Systems (2005)
10. Orset, J.M., Ana, C.: Security in ad hoc networks. In: Ad Hoc Networking Towards Seamless Communications. Springer Netherlands, pp. 756–775 (2002)
11. Ciccarelli, G., Cigno, R.L.: Collusion in peer-to-peer systems. Comput. Netw. **55**(15), 3517–3532 (2011)
12. Christoforou, E., Anta, A.F., Georgiou, C., Mosteiro, Miguel A., Sánchez, A.: Reputation-based mechanisms for evolutionary master-worker computing. In: Baldoni, R., Nisse, N., van Steen, M. (eds.) OPODIS 2013. LNCS, vol. 8304, pp. 98–113. Springer, Cham (2013). https://doi.org/10.1007/978-3-319-03850-6_8
13. Sonnek, J., Chandra, A., Weissman, J.: Adaptive reputation- based scheduling on unreliable distributed infrastructures. IEEE Trans. Parallel Distrib. Syst. **18**(11), 1551–1564 (2007)
14. BONIC reputation platform. http://bonic.berkeley.edu/trac/wiki/
15. Kondo, D., et al.: Characterizing result errors in internet desktop grids. In: European Conference on Parallel Processing, pp. 361–371 (2007)

HFA-MD: An Efficient Hybrid Features Analysis Based Android Malware Detection Method

Yang Zhao, Guangquan Xu$^{(\boxtimes)}$, and Yao Zhang

Tianjin Key Laboratory of Advanced Networking (TANK),
School of Computer Science and Technology,
Tianjin University, Tianjin 300350, China
{zhaoyang6621,losin,zzyy}@tju.edu.cn

Abstract. Lack of supervision and management of many Android third-party application markets has led to a growing number of malware on android platforms. This causes a serious privacy threat to the user's sensitive information. To solve this problem, in this paper, a new hybrid features analysis method aiming at Android malware detection is proposed, which obtains a hybrid feature vector by extracting the information of permission requests, API calls and runtime behaviors. The characteristic of this work is the use of machine learning classification algorithms to detect malicious software. In addition, the feature selection algorithm is used to further optimize the extracted information to remove some useless features. Our experiments are based on real-world Apps, and use five different classification algorithms to detect the malware. The experiment results show that our proposed hybrid feature extraction method can improve the accuracy rate of Android malware detection compared with using static methods alone.

Keywords: Android malware detection · Machine learning · Static analysis
Dynamic analysis · Feature selection

1 Introduction

With Internet-centric mobile applications becoming more and more popular, the varieties and quantities of mobile applications have been increasing rapidly. Due to the open-source nature and openness of the Android system and the fact that many Android third-party application markets do not have a rigorous application review mechanism, resulting in hackers and malware developer are more inclined to Android operating system as the preferred target of attack [1]. Reports from Symantec show that the number of malicious apps increased by 152% in 2015 and increased by 105% in 2016 [2]. The user's mobile phone privacy data has become an ideal target for malicious software to steal. Besides the threat to user privacy, malware may severely threat the underlying infrastructure since it may open a gate to the legal access if the core network is vulnerable in for example fog/edge computing or mobile edge computing. Mobile-edge Computing provides IT and cloud-computing capabilities within the

© ICST Institute for Computer Sciences, Social Informatics and Telecommunications Engineering 2018
L. Wang et al. (Eds.): QShine 2017, LNICST 234, pp. 248–257, 2018.
https://doi.org/10.1007/978-3-319-78078-8_25

Radio Access Network (RAN) in close proximity to mobile subscribers, which are mostly mobile phones for users.

In recent years, some researchers have begun to introduce data mining and machine learning methods into Android malware detection [3]. The Machine learning-based detection method of extracting features for each Android APP is divided into static analysis or dynamic analysis. The static analysis method [4] has the advantages of fast detection and high efficiency. However, in some cases, the static analysis method may cause false positives, which reduce the overall accuracy of static detection. Moreover, utilizing code obfuscation techniques can bypass the use of static analysis method of detection. Therefore, it can be combined with dynamic analysis to improve the accuracy rate. To some extent, the dynamic analysis method [5] can bypass code obfuscation and other code protection mechanism, but the speed of detection is relatively slow.

In order to improve the shortcomings of the existing research methods, we propose a hybrid analysis method for the detection of the Android malware that integrates the advantages of static and dynamic analysis methods. In this study, the hybrid features vector is extracted using a hybrid feature analysis method. We train the five different machine learning classifiers with vectors, respectively, in order to find a more efficient detection method to deal with Android malware threats. Experimental results show that compared with single analysis method, the feature set extracted by hybrid analysis method is more efficient in training classifier.

The rest of this paper is organized as follows. Related works are discussed in Sect. 2. Section 3 briefly describes the Android malware detection model for we proposed approach and analysis the various feature extraction. Our research methodology is introduced in Sect. 3.4 including feature selection algorithms and machine learning classifier. Section 4 presents the experimental results. Finally, in Sect. 5, we conclude our work and proposal for future work.

2 Related Work

In recent years, there have been a lot of related research works applying machine learning methods in Android malware detection field. In the static analysis method, Chan et al. [6] proposed a static Android malware detection method that extracts the permissions and API calls characteristics of each APP as the feature vector set for classifier training. Drebin [7] makes a static analysis of the Android APK file, mainly from the manifest file to extract the permissions of the application request, the contained components and other information, while also analyzing the application of the sensitive API calls and some network addresses from the Dex file. Wu et al. [8] proposed a method of malicious behavior analysis based on static behavior characteristics. In the dynamic analysis method, Amos et al. [9] proposed STREAM, a feature vector collection framework, which accelerated the large-scale verification of machine learning classification of Android malware. STREAM is a distributed mobile malware detection framework that can automatically train and evaluate malware classifiers. Dash et al. [10] proposed DroidScribe, a method of automatic classification of Android malware based on dynamic runtime behavior analysis. Rieck et al. [11] proposed a framework for automatically analysing the malware behavior using machine learning methods that perform behavioral analysis in an incremental manner, avoiding the run-time and memory overhead of previous methods.

3   The Proposed Detection Method

3.1   Architecture of the Proposed Approach

An overview of the methods we presented is shown in Fig. 1. The methods of using machine learning to detect malware are mainly divided into the following parts: data collection, feature extraction, feature data preprocessing, classifier model training and classification results. The entire malware detection process can be divided into two phases: the training phase and the testing phase. In the training phase, firstly, we extract feature vectors from benign software and malicious software respectively; secondly, the feature vectors are selected to remove the feature which have no effect on the classification results, and the optimized feature vectors are obtained; finally, a hybrid feature vector is formed as input of the classifier model, and then different classifier models are selected to train, and the classifier models are obtained through continuous training. In the detection phase, the unknown samples are detected by the obtained classifier model. Since the classifier models are obtained by means of training the hybrid feature vectors, the classifier models will output the detection results when the unknown samples are inputted into the classifier models in the detection.

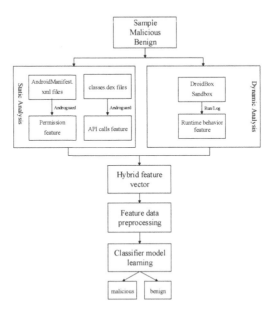

Fig. 1. Architecture of the proposed detection method

3.2   Feature Extraction

3.2.1   Static Analysis and Static Features

(1) Permission Extraction. Some applications that want to make malicious behavior must request appropriate sensitive permissions. The differences on these permissions information provide the theoretical feasibility of the permissions as a feature of the Android malware detection. In this paper, we use the open source tool Androguard [12] to extract the permission features from AndroidManifest. xml file in the APK package. We use the androlyze.py tools to extract sensitive permission features from normal samples and malicious samples respectively. By analyzing the results extracted from a large number of application samples, those applications that have malicious behavior often requires many sensitive permissions, such as malicious fee-absorbing applications often frequently apply for SMS-related permissions. In this case, excluding individual permissions that rarely appear, we counted the top 10 permissions that occurred most frequently, the permissions and their functions as shown in Table 1. In this step, we optimized the initial extracted permission feature sets and got 45 the highest relevance permissions as features. Each APP can be represented by a 45-dimensional vector $[Per]_{1\times45}$, and each dimension corresponds to a permission. If an APP's AndroidManifest.xml file contains this permission, the value is 1, otherwise it is 0.

Table 1. Permissions and their functions

Permission	Functional description
INTERNET	Allow accessing to network connections
READ_PHONE_STATE	Allow reading only access to phone state
ACCESS_NETWORK_STATE	Allow accessing to network information
WRITE_EXTERNAL_STORAGE	Allow writing to external storage
READ_SMS	Allow reading of SMS messages
RECEIVE_BOOT_COMPLETED	Allow applications to boot up
RECEIVE_SMS	Allow to receive SMS messages
SEND_SMS	Allow to send SMS messages
CHANGE_WIFI_STATE	Allow to change Wi-Fi connectivity state
READ_CONTACTS	Allow accessing to user's contact information

(2) API Calls Extraction. The APIs studied in this paper refers to the function provided by the Android system itself. It may also trigger high-risk behaviors such as secretly connecting the network and sending SMS message for malicious deducting expenses. These APIs, which are related to sensitive data and high-risk behaviors, are referred to as sensitive APIs in this paper. As with the permissions information, there are significant differences in the use of these sensitive APIs due to the difference between benign software and malicious software. The malicious application of the number of calls to sensitive APIs is far more than the benign application, which can reflect the real behavior characteristics of an application to

some extent, and therefore can be used as a feature of the application to identify malicious behavior. We use the open source tools baksmali [13] and Androguard to reverse the analysis of classes.dex files, from which to extract the relevant sensitive APIs. In this step, we extracted the API calls features from a large number of sample sets, and then we used the filter feature selection algorithm Relief [14] to optimize it, and we count the number of times each API is called as the initial value of the relevant statistic vector component. After the feature selection process, we obtain an optimal set of features with 22 API calls, each of which can be represented by a 22-dimensional vector $[API]_{1 \times 22}$, with each dimension corresponding to an API. Table 2 shows the 22 selected API calls.

Table 2. Sensitive API calls

API calls	
getDeviceID()	sendTextMessage()
getCellLocation()	sendDataMessage()
getLinelNumber()	getConnectionInfo()
getNetworkOperator()	getWifiState()
getSimSerialNumber()	setWifiEnabled()
getOutputStream()	getSubscriberId()
getInputStream()	addCopletedDownload()
getNetworkInfo()	AudioRecord.read()
startService()	AudioRecord.getRecordingState()
getLatitude()	MediaRecorder.setCamera()
getLogitude()	MediaRecorder.setOutputFile()

3.2.2 Dynamic Analysis and Dynamic Features

In the dynamic analysis phase, the main work of dynamic behavior acquisition is to collect the runtime behavior features of each application. In order to collect the runtime behavior features of the unknown sample as much as possible in the behavioral detection of the application, when the application installed in the simulator is running, we use the automated test tool monkey [15] to simulate the event flow to run all the components of the application. It can automatically test unknown samples and trigger the relevant malicious code, so that the monitoring program can record its malicious behavior.

We used the open source tools DroidBox [16] to monitor the runtime behavior of the application. We install and run each APP on DroidBox, and then use automated test techniques to monitor whether each APP has malicious behavior such as automatic connection to the network, sending malicious SMS messages, and obtaining privacy information and so on. In this step, we count the number of occurrences of each runtime behavior feature as the initial value of the relevant statistic vector component. After the feature selection process, we collect a total of 20 features (i.e., runtime behavior features) for each monitored APP from a large variety of aspects such as the battery, binder, network, user activity. Among them, behavior_sentSMS represents the behavior of sending SMS messages, behavior_openingKeyboard is the behavior that opens keyboard input, and behavior_packetsWiFi represents the behavior of sending packets over a WiFi. As a result, we obtain a set of features containing 20 runtime behaviors. Each APP can be represented by a 20-dimensional vector $[Runbehavior]_{1 \times 20}$, and each dimension corresponds to a runtime behavior.

3.2.3   The Integrated Feature

After the feature extraction of the above 2 sections, three feature vectors of three kinds of features are formed, each APP can obtain a set of permission feature vector $[Per]_{1 \times 45}$, a set of API calls feature vector $[API]_{1 \times 22}$, a set of runtime behaviors feature vector $[Runbehavior]_{1 \times 20}$. Combining these three feature vectors sets, each APP can be represented by an 87-dimensional hybrid feature vector $[Pre, API, Runbehavior]_{1 \times 87}$. Each feature in the hybrid feature vectors is binary, indicating that if an APP contains this feature, the value of the feature is 1, and if not, the value is 0. The combination of the hybrid feature vectors can better representation the characteristics of the application to distinguish between malware and benign software, and further improve the detection accuracy.

3.3   Feature Selection

Feature selection is an important process of data preprocessing. In the feature extraction of this paper, a greater number of features are extracted, but some of which have no effect on the results of classification. In order to improve the efficiency and accuracy of the classifier, it is necessary to remove the features which have no effect on the classification. At the same time, too many irrelevant features have an influence on the effect of classification. This paper assumes that the initial feature set contains all the important information.

In this paper, we use the filter feature selection algorithm to select the data sets firstly, and then training the classifier. The feature selection process is independent of the subsequent classifier. Kira et al. [14] proposed Relief is a highly efficient filter feature selection algorithm, which designs a "relevant statistic vector" to measure the importance of features. The algorithm is mainly aimed at solving two classification problems. The key of the Relief is how to determine the value of the "relevant statistic vector". Assume that the training set D is $\{(x_1, y_1), (x_2, y_2), \ldots, (x_m, y_m)\}$, for each sample x_i, its feature j corresponds to the relevant statistic vector is as follows:

$$\delta^j = \sum_i -diff(x_i^j, x_{i,nh}^j)^2 + diff(x_i^j, x_{i,nm}^j)^2 \tag{1}$$

Where the greater the value of the formula (1) is, the stronger the classification ability of the feature is. From the formula (1), the evaluation value of each feature is obtained, and the relevant statistic vector component of the feature is obtained by averaging the evaluation value of all the samples to the same feature, the greater the vector component value, the stronger the classification ability.

3.4   The Machine Learning Classifier

Android malware detection belongs to the two-classification problems, and we choose use different classifier algorithms to detect malicious software. In this paper, the following five classifier algorithms are used include Support Vector Machine (SVM) [17], k-Nearest Neighbor [18], Naive Bayes [19], Decision Tree (J48) [20] and Random Forest [21]. Among them, the J48 decision tree algorithm we used in our experiment is the implementation of C4.5 algorithm in WEKA [22]. Selecting different classifier algorithms brings different detection effects, so it is very important to select the appropriate classifier algorithm. The comparison and analysis of different classifier algorithms is a key point in this paper.

4   Experiments and Result

In this section, we use the machine learning tool WEKA [22] to train the classification model for the features obtained from the experimental samples. All experiments were carried out on a computer with a CPU of 3.20 GHz Intel (R) Core (TM) i5 and 8 GB of memory. We collected a total of 359 malicious apps and 500 benign apps as experimental samples. The malicious samples were derived from third-party sample collection platform VirusShare [23]. The Benign samples used in this paper are mainly downloaded from the Google Play store to ensure the availability of the experimental data. In this experiment, we randomly selected 150 malicious apps and 150 benign apps from the experimental samples, and then mixed them together as a training set. Similarly, we get a test set in the same way. The following experiments are carried out on these two data sets.

4.1   Performance Metrics

The following three performance measures that calculate and evaluate the performance of a classification algorithm.

$$True\ positive\ rate = Recall = \frac{TP}{TP + FN} \tag{2}$$

$$False\ positive\ rate = \frac{FP}{TN + FP} \tag{3}$$

$$Accuracy = \frac{TP + TN}{TP + TN + FP + FN} \tag{4}$$

where True positive rate (TPR), or Recall rate, is the proportion of malware being correctly predicted by the classifier. False positive rate (FPR), is the proportion of malware being incorrectly predicted by the classifier as benign software. Accuracy is the proportion of all samples being correctly classified to all samples, which is used to measure system errors, and the larger the value, the smaller the system error. The higher the value of Accuracy and TPR, the lower the value of FPR, the better the classification effect.

4.2   Experiment Results

In Table 3, we firstly list the classification results for five different classifiers when using only static methods to extract features (i.e., Permission, API calls). The results show that the Random Forest algorithm has the highest accuracy rate and the accuracy rate reaches 92.07%, and its classification effect is the best. In contrast, Table 3 also shows the classification results of five different classifier algorithms when the feature extraction uses the hybrid analysis method (i.e., Permission, API calls, Runtime behavior). As we can see from Table 3, the performance of the Random Forest algorithm is still the best, with an accuracy rate of 94.89% and 2.81% higher accuracy rate than using only static methods. The classification accuracy of SVM algorithm is improved by nearly 2.4%, which achieves 91.27%.

Figure 2 shows more visual and intuitive the classification effects of different classifier algorithms in Android malware detection. We can clearly see that the Random Forest algorithm has the best classification effect, followed by the SVM algorithm. All in all, the experimental results show that the feature extraction method of hybrid

Table 3. Classification results from only static methods, and hybrid methods

Classifier model	Measure metrics (%)					
	Only static methods			Static & dynamic methods		
	TPR	FPR	Accuracy	TPR	FPR	Accuracy
SVM	92.47	9.74	91.27	95.17	7.74	93.66
J48	91.97	14.72	88.19	93.38	14.02	89.34
Naive Bayes	93.49	19.77	85.74	89.39	19.05	84.52
KNN	90.01	19.41	84.56	92.31	17.65	86.71
Random Forest	92.57	8.55	92.07	95.30	5.30	94.89

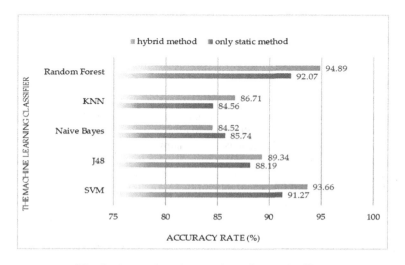

Fig. 2. Accuracy analysis: Using different classifiers

analysis can improve the accuracy of classification results in Android malware detection. At the same time, through the comparison of the performance of five different classifiers, we can know that the Random Forest algorithm has the best detection effect.

5 Conclusions and Future Works

In this paper, we propose a hybrid features analysis method for detection of Android malwares by extracting permissions, API calls and runtime behavior as feature set. We validate the method proposed in this paper through simulation experiments. The experimental results show that this method can effectively detect and classify Android malware, and obtain higher detection rate. Generally speaking, due to the diversity of malicious behavior in malicious applications, the features extracted by the hybrid analysis method can more comprehensively and effectively show the characteristics of Android applications. We demonstrate that the hybrid analysis method combined with static and dynamic methods can improve the accuracy of Android malware detection compared to single static feature extraction methods. Additionally, after reducing the dimension of the extracted hybrid feature vectors, some useless features are removed, which makes the classification accuracy become higher and achieves better detection effect. Finally, we choose the different classification algorithm to bring the classification effect is different, and we find through the analysis that the Random Forest algorithm and SVM algorithm are higher accuracy rate.

For future work, we consider the approach of semantics learning into feature extraction to analyze the behavior of malware. In this way, we can further mine the association rules between features select better feature selection algorithms to reduce the redundancy of features, and further improve the efficiency of classification.

Acknowledgments. This work has partially been sponsored by the National Science Foundation of China (No. 61572355) and Tianjin Research Program of Application Foundation and Advanced Technology under grant No. 15JCYBJC15700, and Fundamental Research of Xinjiang Corps under grant No. 2016AC015.

References

1. Malhotra, A., Bajaj, K.: A survey on various malware detection techniques on mobile platform. Int. J. Comput. Appl. **139**(5), 15–20 (2016)
2. Symantec: Internet Security Threat Report 2017. https://www.symantec.com/security-center/threat-report
3. Tan, D.J., Chua, T.W., Thing, V.L.: Securing Android: a survey, taxonomy, and challenges. ACM Comput. Surv. (CSUR) **47**(4), 58 (2015)
4. Shabtai, A., Moskovitch, R., Elovici, Y.: Detection of malicious code by applying machine learning classifiers on static features: a state-of-the-art survey. Inf. Secur. Tech. Rep. **14**(1), 16–29 (2009)
5. Tam, K., Khan, S.J., Fattori, A.: CopperDroid: automatic reconstruction of Android malware behaviors. In: NDSS (2015)

6. Chan, P.P., Song, W.K.: Static detection of Android malware by using permissions and API calls. In: 2014 International Conference on Machine Learning and Cybernetics (ICMLC), vol. 1, pp. 82–87. IEEE (2014)

7. Arp, D., Spreitzenbarth, M., Hubner, M.: DREBIN: effective and explainable detection of Android malware in your pocket. In: NDSS (2014)

8. Wu, D.J., Mao, C.H., Wei, T.E.: Droidmat: Android malware detection through manifest and API calls tracing. In: 2012 Seventh Asia Joint Conference on Information Security (Asia JCIS), pp. 62–69. IEEE (2012)

9. Amos, B., Turner, H., White, J.: Applying machine learning classifiers to dynamic Android malware detection at scale. In: 2013 9th International Wireless Communications and Mobile Computing Conference (IWCMC), pp. 1666–1671. IEEE (2013)

10. Dash, S.K., Suarez-Tangil, G., Khan, S.: Droidscribe: classifying Android malware based on runtime behavior. In: 2016 IEEE Security and Privacy Workshops (SPW), pp. 252–261. IEEE (2016)

11. Rieck, K., Trinius, P., Willems, C.: Automatic analysis of malware behavior using machine learning. J. Comput. Secur. 19(4), 639–668 (2011)

12. Androguard. https://code.google.com/archive/p/androguard

13. Baksmali. https://github.com/JesusFreke/smali

14. Chandrashekar, G., Sahin, F.: A survey on feature selection methods. Comput. Electr. Eng. 40(1), 16–28 (2014)

15. Monkey. https://developer.android.com/studio/test/monkey.html

16. DroidBox: An Android Application Sandbox for Dynamic Analysis. http://code.google.com/p/droidbox

17. Gu, B., Sheng, V.S., Wang, Z.: Incremental learning for v-support vector regression. Neural Netw. 67, 140–150 (2015)

18. Liao, Y., Vemuri, V.R.: Use of k-nearest neighbor classifier for intrusion detection. Comput. Secur. 21(5), 439–448 (2002)

19. Buntine, W.: Learning classification rules using Bayes. In: Proceedings of the Sixth International Workshop on Machine Learning, pp. 94–98 (2016)

20. Bhargava, N., Sharma, G., Bhargava, R.: Decision tree analysis on J48 algorithm for data mining. Proc. Int. J. Adv. Res. Comput. Sci. Softw. Eng. 3(6) (2013)

21. Chutia, D., Bhattacharyya, D.K., Sarma, J.: An effective ensemble classification framework using random forests and a correlation based feature selection technique. Trans. GIS 21(6), 1165–1178 (2017)

22. Hall, M., Frank, E., Holmes, G.: The WEKA data mining software: an update. ACM SIGKDD Explor. Newsl. 11(1), 10–18 (2009)

23. VirusShare Malware dataset. https://virusshare.com

Author Index

Printed in the United States
By Bookmasters